Dr. Johnson

PREFACE TO SHAKESPEARE

Dr. Johnson

PREFACE TO SHAKESPEARE

[Edited with Complete Introduction, Biography, Author's Background, Complete Text, Select Criticism and Bibliography]

Anshu Mallika Sawhney
M.A. English, Delhi University
M. Phil., Himachal Pradesh University

ANMOL PUBLICATIONS PVT. LTD.
NEW DELHI - 110 002 (INDIA)

ANMOL PUBLICATIONS PVT. LTD.

H.O.: 4374/4B, Ansari Road, Darya Ganj,
New Delhi-110 002 (India)
Ph.: 23278000, 23261597

B.O.: No. 1015, Ist Main Road, BSK IIIrd Stage
IIIrd Phase, IIIrd Block
Bangalore - 560 085 (India)
Visit us at: www.anmolpublications.com

Preface to Shakespeare

First Published, 2009

PRINTED IN INDIA

Printed at Mehra Offset Press, Delhi.

Contents

Preface *vii*

1. Introduction 1
2. Samuel Johnson the Man and His Masterpiece 5
3. Samuel Johnson Biography 12
4. Samuel Johnson and Politics: An Introduction 18
5. Samuel Johnson Works 24
6. Time Line 25
7. The Restoration Period and the 18th Century 35
8. Introduction: Shakespeare 46
9. Shakespeare as Actor and Play Wright 59
10. William Shakespeare Timeline 67
11. William Shakespeare- List of Works 69
12. Important Aspects of Elizabethan Drama 71
13. The History of the Globe Theater 75
14. William Shakespeare and Existentialism 84
15. Preface to Shakespeare: Text 88
16. Selected Notes from Some of the Plays 134
17. Johnson's Preface to Shakespeare: Then and Now 150
18. Critical Essays 159

Bibliography 252

Preface

Samuel Johnson was born on September 18 1709 and died on 13 December 1784. His father was a poor book seller, Michael Johnson. He was born in Lichfield and enrolled in Lichfield Grammar School. In the year 1728, he got enrolled as a fellow commoner in Pembroke College, Oxford. He was nineteen only. He left Oxford without completing his degree to Lichfield.

One of his most renowned works, A Dictionary of the English Language had been written between 1745 to 1755. A few popular works of 1747 Plan for a Dictionary of the English Language, 1750-1752. The Rambler, 1753-1754 The Adventurer, 1755 Preface to a Dictionary of the English Language, 1758-1760 The Idler (1758-1760), 1765 Preface to the Plays of William Shakespeare, 1770 The False Alarm, 1771 Thoughts on the Late Transactions Respecting Falkland's Islands, 1774 The Patriot , 1775 Taxation No Tyranny etc.

Author

Chapter 1

Introduction

Perhaps because his works are little read today, we tend to see Samuel Johnson (through the medium of Boswell's great biography) primarily as a personality, as a conversationalist, as a great and eccentric character. He was, however, first and foremost a man of letters. He was a superb poet, a great moralist and critic, a remarkable lexicographer, a novelist, a journalist, a biographer, a playwright, an essayist, a satirist, a bibliographer, an autobiographer, a diarist, a journalist, a book reviewer, an editor, a scholar, a translator, a sermon writer, and a writer on travel and politics. He wrote his philosophical poems, essays, and classical tragedies, his satires in the classical tradition, his fiction and his criticism in a style, which was at once polished, witty, urbane, heavy, Latinate, and ponderous. He was the literary dictator of his era, and he remains the central figure of what is still called the Age of Johnson — the period between 1750 and 1798 when a still-dominant Neoclassicism was slowly giving way before the incipient Romantic Movement.

After a long period of obscurity, of poverty, of hardship and disappointment, he emerged in his later years as a famous and beloved personality, loved as much for his eccentricities, for his mythic qualities. He was an enormous, uncouth, shambling man, with, all his life, a provincial accent, his face scarred by smallpox and by scrofula, full of quirks and quarrels and convulsive starts and tremors, slovenly in appearance, indolent, generous, melancholy, peevish, and arrogant, a great drinker of tea, a great admirer of ladies, a great monopolizer of conversation—as for his remarkable intellectual brilliance.

He presided over and dominated the famous Literary Club, formed in 1764, which created or influenced contemporary literary tastes and styles: its members included Edmund Burke, Oliver Goldsmith, Bishop Percy, David Garrick, Edward Gibbon, Adam Smith, and James Boswell, all-important figures in them.

After his death his conservatism, his stylistic mannerisms, his didacticism, and his rationalism all went out of fashion. With a few notable exceptions among literary artists and critics during the nineteenth century—it has been only in recent years that the real quality and depth of his thought—which had become obscured in his endearing Boswellian persona—have once again begun to be appreciated. He has only one real theme, but it is a noble one, one of the great themes of literature, as it was the theme of his own life. He writes about man's unceasing search for happiness, about the inevitable hopelessness of that search, and about his refusal, in spite of his awareness of the fact that he is doomed to fail, to give up his quest.

Johnson's Religion

Johnson was deeply but not necessarily conventionally religious: he struggled within himself most of his life to sustain his belief in God in the face of enormous pressures, disappointments, and psychological calamities. On the surface, and in much of his work, he appeared to be an orthodox, conventional, conservative adherent of revealed religion, of the Church of England. But the conventional Anglican explanations for the existence of evil in the world failed to satisfy him, and in any case his characteristic reluctance to believe without evidence, his fear of credulity, his dislike of mysteries, continually undermined his attempts to accept conventional beliefs.

He was remarkable, privately, for his tolerance; maintaining that the differences between Christian sects (Protestants and Roman Catholics, for example) were trivial, and due primarily to political rather than religious differences.

His religious difficulties began at a very early age. His

mother, when he was only three, told him of "a fine place filled with happiness called Heaven" and "a sad place, called Hell." Many years later he recalled that (as one might expect) this account did not impress him very deeply: it is significant, however, that he remembered it at all. After the age of nine, and through his adolescence, he stopped going to church. One part of him remained a skeptic for the rest of his life, and, as his private journals show, even after he had regained his faith he struggled continually (and privately) with fears, guilt, and disbelief. In The Vanity of Human Wishes, written when he was forty, he returns to a traditional religious theme as well as a personal preoccupation and insists that we cannot find genuine or permanent happiness in this world, and that we must therefore turn to religious belief and a faith in the existence of a better world after death if we are to endure our existence here. It was a belief; however, which he himself had difficulty maintaining.

The happiness derived from such belief was in any case a limited one, but the only alternative to religious faith, as Johnson saw it, was a dull apathy, a stoical disengagement from life. He was troubled, too—a better word would be tormented—by a fear of death and by a deeper fear that he might in spite of his best efforts be so guilty, so sinful, that he merited damnation. And beneath that fear was another, even deeper—the fear that God might not exist at all, that death might bring annihilation, mere nothingness, the loss of personal identity. He struggled all his life—in the end, successfully—not so much to overcome these fears as to coexist with them. In public, he was much more conventional, much more characteristically paternalistic. He maintained in print, for example, that religion was a valuable asset to society and to mankind and that Anglicanism, as the English state religion, ought therefore to be carefully protected. "Permitting men to preach any opinion contrary to the doctrine of the established church," he wrote, "tends, in a certain degree, to lessen the authority of the church, and, consequently, to lessen the influence of religion." In private, though, his religious beliefs were much less doctrinaire, and much more complicated.

Samuel Johnson and Philosophy

Johnson's works are the productions of a mind, which was profoundly pessimistic and innately melancholy: he was desperately conservative in religion and politics because he believed that only the maintenance of order-protected individuals and whole human societies from despair; and that authority and tradition were not ends in themselves but rather means of upholding and sustaining order.

He despised the French philosophies, remarking, of Voltaire and Rousseau, that "It is too difficult to settle the proportion of iniquity between them." When his reason conflicted with his fear of disorder, that fear often won out, and manifested itself in an outburst of temper or a refusal to pursue the subject further. When Boswell suggested that it was impossible to refute Bishop Berkeley's assertion that matter did not exist, Johnson reacted in characteristic fashion: "I shall never forget," wrote Boswell, "the alacrity with which Johnson answered, striking his foot with mighty force against a large stone, till he rebounded from it, 'I refute it thus.'"

A friend wrote that "His religion... made his extraordinary talents of Mind continually at War with each other," but when he came upon scientific evidence, which suggested that the biblical account of the creation of the earth could not be taken literally, he rejected it out of hand. Overall, Johnson had a conservative belief in the necessity of order, and in the dangers of disorder.

Chapter 2

Samuel Johnson the Man and His Masterpiece

As an English Language major, it was to learn more about Samuel Johnson the lexicographer, as well as his Dictionary of the English Language, that I initially decided on taking the individual author course, which bears his name (as well as that of his now-famous biographer). However, as the course progressed and I found the Dictionary to have maintained its place of prominence in my admiration for this great man, I nevertheless perceived the task of writing about it as something more than daunting. Like the mountain climber who possesses neither rope nor piton, I was ill equipped to take on a meaningful examination of that monolithic work. It was not until learning of Frederick Pottle's three-point formula of literary criticism that I realized I had at my disposal the perfect method with which to confront and examine Johnson's Dictionary. Therefore, I shall proceed in this brief monograph to examine the questions of just what Samuel Johnson was trying to achieve with his Dictionary, how well he achieved it, and, finally, whether it was worth it.

Before going into Johnson's intentions, however, it is important to give a little background first, in order to place Johnson's achievement in its proper historical perspective. The first work designed specifically for the use of English-speaking people to find listings and definitions of English words was Robert Cawdrey's A Table Alphabetical (1604). This work was formulated for the purpose of defining only difficult words in the language and was by no means intended to be comprehensive. Others were to follow, including Bullokar's An English Expositour (1616), Cockerams's English Dictionarie (1623), Blount's Glossographia (1656), Phillip's New World of English Words (1658), Cocker's English Dictionary (1704), and, finally, Nathan Bailey's two offerings, the Universal Etymological English Dictionary (1721) and the Dictionarium Britannicum (1730). The latter, containing some 48,000 entries, was to be Johnson's basis for his own dictionary. (While Johnson's Dictionary contains only 40,000 words, one might well wonder what became of the other 8,000 contained in Bailey; Johnson addresses these omissions in the preface to the Dictionary, going to great lengths to enumerate the various types of words he considered inappropriate, including technical terms, foreign words, and, the bane of his linguistic existence, "cant words.")

It is significant to note that by continental standards, mid-eighteenth century England was far behind the times, linguistically speaking. The Tuscan dictionary of the Accademia della Crusca, the standing Italian dictionary, had appeared in 1612, and the dictionary of the Academie Francaise was out as of 1694. It is even more amazing to consider that one man set out to do the work that had taken whole national think tanks decades to achieve. (Johnson's well-know quip about the ratio of Englishmen to Frenchmen would prove to be more than mere boast, as generations of Englishmen were soon to find out. Indeed, upon completion, David Garrick was quoted as exclaiming that Johnson had "beat forty Frenchmen and will beat forty more!")

In addressing the question of Johnson's intentions regarding his Dictionary, we must first debunk one of many popular misconceptions held by the general public, as well as linguistic and literary scholars who should know better, namely that Johnson was trying to "fix" the English language. Indeed, while his original Plan of an English Dictionary of 1747 is full of prescriptive sentiment, indicating that he was determined to set English in stone once and for all, in fact, through the very process of writing the mighty tome, Johnson became far more modern in his awareness of language. While it was, no doubt, his personal dream to have his fellow Englishmen speak and write correctly, the lesson of his own dictionary taught him the difference between stability and stagnation, as well as imparting a deeper understanding of the living, fluid quality of his native tongue.

He declared as much in the preface to the Dictionary when he wrote, "Those who have been persuaded to think well of my design will require that I should fix our language, and put a stop to those alterations which time and chance have hitherto been suffered to make in it without opposition. With this consequence I will confess that I flattered myself for a while; but now begin to fear that I have indulged expectation which neither reason nor experience can justify." This is not to say that he had thrown up his hands and fallen in with what in modern parlance would be termed the "descriptive school." He remained extremely conservative in his views on language, as he stated in the very same preface that, "Much less ought our written language to comply with the corruptions of oral utterance, or copy that which every variation of time or place makes different from itself, and imitate those changes which will again be changed, while imitation is employed in observing them."

As we have seen, Johnson's intention in writing his Dictionary was an evolving one, changing over the course of the writing itself. The final version of it can be seen in the preface to the abridged edition, published in 1756, wherein he states, "I lately published a Dictionary like those compiled by the academies of Italy and France, for the use of such as aspire to exactness of criticism, or elegance of style." It is this two-fold intention, the creation of a dictionary to serve the pursuits of criticism and style that has, as I shall endeavor to prove in the summation of this paper, been gloriously and effectively realized.

At this point, I think it important to look in on Johnson's garret at Number 17 Gough Square to get an idea of just how the Dictionary took shape. One might assume that Johnson simply grabbed his copy of Bailey's Dictionarium Britannicum and started revising. In fact, the initial preparation was quite different and, not to be too redundant, classically Johnsonian: He read. Johnson pored over all the works of the great English authors; Shakespeare, Milton, Watts, Spenser, Baker, Pope, Hooker, Boyle, Dryden, Addison, Bacon, Swift, Locke, and many more, men of science as well as men of letters, and wherever he found a passage that seemed to illustrate a particular word, he marked it, citing the word's first letter in the margin, and passed the book to one of his six amanuenses. (A facsimile of a page so marked is attached to the end of this paper.) The amanuensis would then copy the quotations onto slips of paper, cross off the letter from the margin of the marked page, and paste the quotation slip onto a larger sheet of paper allotted to the word in question.

The idea was to have a barrage of quotations for each word with which to supplement a given definition. In this way, the reader would be provided with a specific definition (or, as was often the case, a list of definitions), as well as having the opportunity of seeing the word used in context; not only that, but the reader could enjoy the luxury of seeing how a given word had been utilized by one of the great writers of the sixteenth and seventeenth centuries. This was Johnson's unique contribution to lexicography: the addition of illustrative quotations, some 114,000 in all. (It should be noted that the modern use of quotations, such as in the Oxford English Dictionary, has become more a method of showing the historical evolution of a given word, while Johnson's intention was more that of displaying an exactness and excellence of usage.) Once the bulk of quotations had been compiled, the making of master word lists was taken up, consulting Bailey as well as others. Definitions were composed, etymologies appended and additional quotes added.

The enormity of the task is beyond belief, and one might think that spending nine years with six amanuenses, five of whom were Scots, would have been too much for the supposedly Scot-hating Johnson. Here again we find the truth underlying the myth, in this case the erroneous conception of a prejudiced Samuel Johnson. The amanuenses Johnson employed were Shiels, the two Macbean brothers, Stewart,

Maitland, and Peyton, the latter being the single Englishman. Over time, Johnson came to look on these men as not just mere employees, but as dependents, supporting Stewart, who died during the process, Shiels, who died shortly afterward, as well as literally burying Peyton.

The much-quoted joke definition for "oats" was designed more as a good-natured jibe toward the Scots on his team than some arrogant slap at Scotland in general. This is not to imply that Johnson and his assistants enjoyed a non-stop, rosy joviality; there was plenty of backbiting, gossiping, time-wasting and trips to the pub when the boss was away. But the fact remains that Johnson treated these men, Scots though they were, with the same kindness he reserved for all common people.

Much criticism has been leveled at Johnson for the supposed inferiority of his etymologies, and, here again; it is my intention to correct the record. Amongst his early detractors was William Smellie, the first editor of the Encyclopaedia Britannica, who expressed his own misgivings in the entry for "dictionary" in the original 1768 edition.

Then, in 1775, John Whitaker, himself a decidedly bad etymologist, attacked Johnson's etymologies of Celtic derivatives. 1786 saw Horne Tooke, in The Diversions of Purley, taking aim at Johnson for violating his (Tooke's) own bizarre theory that there should be only one meaning per word.(This torch was picked up and carried as late as 1836 by Tooke's literary disciple, Charles Richardson, in his A New Dictionary of the English Language.) In 1807, for reasons of his own, Noah Webster climbed on the Johnson-bashing bandwagon. Macaulay called him a "wretched etymologist." Even the supreme acolyte, James Boswell, stated, "The etymologies, though they exhibit learning and judgement, are not, I think, entitled to the first praise amongst the various parts of this immense work." Wherefore this veritable plethora of condemnation?

Before answering this question, we must look into the mind of Samuel Johnson, for, as he had for everything else, he had formulated his own philosophy regarding etymology. For one thing, since Latin was still much in use, he saw little need to fill in every variation between a Latin derivative and its English counterpart. Secondly, his brevity in etymological entries stemmed from a combination of his own staunch nationalism and an empirical, Occam's Razor-type approach which precluded undue concern for the various continental forms of the Latin derivatives.

It is important to note that much of the earlier criticism came from direct comparisons of Johnson's Dictionary and Bailey's Dictionarium Britannicum. However, the latter's so-called "etymologies" were in fact no more, in most cases, than wholesale listings of every possible form of a given word from all of the various continental languages, with little concern for what Johnson would have termed "concatenation." (Even the use of the term "etymological" in the title of Bailey's earlier work was more a selling point and an excuse to publish a new dictionary than a genuine innovation in the science of lexicography.) In addition, whenever Johnson felt that such concatenations were significant, his usual brevity was breached and a more complete etymology was provided. Finally, it must be realized that Johnson's Dictionary was, in fact, written some 250 years ago, and it is inappropriate to judge it by modern standards of language study; taken in context, it remains the outstanding work of its century.

Having looked at a bit of lexicographical history, Johnson's evolving intentions for his Dictionary, his methods of execution, his innovative use of quotations, his working relationship with his crew of amanuenses, and his theory of etymology, as well as clearing up a few popular misconceptions, it remains for us to ask the final question: Was it worth it? The answer is a resounding and unequivocal YES. Samuel Johnson's Dictionary remained the authoritative work in its field for a century after its publication and set the standard by which subsequent dictionaries would be judged. Its importance cannot be understated. To the dilettante, the occasional, much-quoted joke definitions found sprinkled throughout the work, together with the more eccentric characterizations provided by Boswell, might make the

Dictionary, as well as its author, seem silly and inconsequential; it is only through depth of examination that we begin to see the real merit of such a phenomenal achievement, and appreciate Johnson for the intellectual giant that he was.

Samuel Johnson was a man of his age. As John Wain puts it, "The eighteenth-century aim was a language which would not seem obsolete in two generations, and this aim was brilliantly achieved." Today we can read Johnson with complete comprehension, and it is this fact, which says more for his achievement than any other. Further, this continuity of language carries a greater significance: the continuity of culture. The Dictionary provided for the critic and the stylist of Johnson's day a greatly improved instrument with which to pursue their literary and, as a consequence, cultural goals, a tool to serve the pursuit and ultimate mastery of the English language. It is for this reason that we revere him, respect him, and will not forget him.

Chapter 3

Samuel Johnson Biography

Samuel Johnson was born on September 18, 1709 (N.S.) in the country town of Lichfield in Staffordshire, the son of Michael Johnson, aged 50, a bookseller and stationer, and his wife Sara, aged 37. The elder Johnson was prone, as his son would be, to bouts of melancholy, but he was a man of some local repute—at the time of Johnson's birth, he was Sheriff of the city. Johnson, a sickly child, was not expected to live: in 1711, at the age of two, he was taken, nearly blind, partially deaf, suffering from scrofula and a tubercular infection, to be touched for the "King's Evil" by Queen Anne, the last of the Stuarts to rule England. No miraculous cure, however, took place.

In 1716 Johnson, sensitive, clumsy, and precocious, entered the Lichfield Grammar School which was headed by the scholarly but brutal John Hunter, who beat his students, as he said, "to save them from the gallows." Later in life Johnson would insist that had he not been beaten he would have done nothing, but under Hunter's tutelage he learned Latin and Greek and began to write poetry. In 1725 at the age of sixteen, a very provincial Johnson came for a six-month visit with his cousin, Cornelius Ford, a sophisticated and somewhat rakish former Cambridge don, and became aware for the first time of the existence of the larger intellectual and literary world represented by Cambridge and London.

In 1726, Johnson left school and went to work in his father's bookshop, which was failing: he spent the next two years were unhappy ones, but during this time he continued—avidly if unsystematically—to study English and classical literature. In 1728, with a small legacy of forty pounds left to his mother upon the death of a relative, he was—very unexpectedly—able to enter Pembroke College at Oxford. At Oxford, however, he was unable to keep himself adequately supplied with food or clothing—a problem which he would have for many years—and though he occasionally displayed considerable erudition symptoms of the melancholia which would haunt him for the remainder of his life were already beginning to manifest themselves. He paid, in consequence, little attention to his studies, and in 1789, extremely depressed and too poor to continue, he left Oxford without taking a degree.

Johnson's Latin translation of Pope's "Messiah," written at Oxford, was published in 1731, but by that time Johnson, poor, in debt, depressed, partially blind, partially deaf, scarred by scrofula and smallpox, found himself (understandably enough) fearing for his sanity. In December of that year his father died, a virtual bankrupt.

In 1732, Johnson found employment as an usher at Market Bosworth Grammar School. On a visit to Birmingham, he made the acquaintance of Henry Porter and his wife Elizabeth. The following year, lying in bed during another lengthy visit to a friend in Birmingham, Johnson dictated an abridged English version of a French translation of a travel book—A Voyage to Abyssinia—which had been written by a seventeenth-century Portuguese Jesuit. It became his first published book, and he earned five guineas by it.

In 1735, aged twenty-five, Johnson married his "Tetty," the by-now-widowed Elizabeth Porter, aged forty-six. With his wife's dowry of £700, Johnson established, in the following year, an ill-fated private academy at Edial, near Lichfield: boarding pupils included David Garrick, who would become the most famous actor of his day, and one of Johnson's closest friends. By 1737, the academy had proved a failure, and Johnson, determined to make his fortune by writing, left for London, accompanied by Garrick.

In 1738, living in London in extreme poverty, Johnson began to write for Edward Cave's The Gentleman's Magazine, and published his "London," an imitation of Juvenal's satire on the decadence of ancient Rome, for which he receives ten guineas. He also made the acquaintance of Richard Savage, another impoverished poet of dubious reputation. A year later, Samuel Johnson, who had never met Johnson but who had admired his "London," attempted to get him an M. A. degree from Trinity College in Dublin so that he could become headmaster at a school: the attempt, however, failed, and Johnson was forced to continue his life of poverty and literary drudgery in (metaphorically speaking) Grub Street.

Between 1740 and 1743, he edited parliamentary debates for the Gentleman's Magazine: when, years later, he was complimented for his impartial approach to his task, he stated, characteristically, that though he "saved appearances tolerably well," he nevertheless "took care that the WHIG DOGS should not have the best of it."

In 1744, Richard Savage ended a miserable existence in a Bristol jail. Johnson was moved to write a Life of Savage—remarkable for its honest portrayal of the strenghs and weaknesses of his friend's character—which became the first of Johnson's prose works to attract the attention of the reading public. 1745 saw the publication of Johnson's "Miscellaneous Observations on the Tragedy of Macbeth." The following year he signed a contract with a group of publishers and (alotting himself, intially, three years) undertook the enormous task of compiling an English dictionary which would be analogous to that which had been produced, in French, by the forty members of the French Academy. He addressed his "Plan of a Dictionary" to the Earl of Chesterfield, who would prove to be a most unsatisfactory patron.

In 1748, with six assistants, Johnson moved into a large house in Fleet Street and began work upon his dictionary. In 1749 his great but melancholy "The Vanity of Human Wishes" appeared, and Garrick produced Johnson's tragedy Irene at Drury Lane: though Johnson made a small profit, the play proved unsuccessful.

Between 1750 and 1752, writing two a week, he produced the more than two hundred Rambler essays. In 1752, his wife Tetty died. Two years later Johnson returned to Oxford, where he became acquainted with Thomas Warton, the future Poet Laureate. The following year, with Warton's help, Johnson received an M. A. degree from Oxford. In the same year his great Dictionary of the English Language was finally completed and published, and, though he was still very poor, his literary reputation was finally established. During this period he made new friends of the much younger Joshua Reynolds, Bennet "Lanky" Langton, and Topham Beauclerk.

In 1756, Johnson produced his "Proposals for a New Edition of Shakespeare," which would not, however, appear until 1765, and continued his activities as a journalist, editing, writing prefaces, and contributing articles to journals. Briefly arrested for debt, he was bailed out by Samuel Richardson. Between 1758 and 1760, he wrote another series of essays, The Idler, for a weekly periodical. In 1759 his mother Sarah died, and, in a somber mood, he wrote the moral fable Rasselas to pay, as he said, for her funeral.

In 1762, upon the succession to the throne of George III, Johnson was provided (much to his satisfaction, but much, also, to his embarrassment, for he was an unrepentant old Tory, and, with Whig abuses in mind, had defined "pension" in his dictionary as "pay given to a state hireling for treason to his country") with a pension of £300 per year. For the first time in his life he was not forced to scrape for money, and though his personal appearance was still remarkably and unavoidably uncouth he became one of the most prominent literary lions in polite society. When several young ladies, encountering him at a literary soiree, surrounded him "with more wonder than politeness," and contemplated his odd figure "as if he had been some monster from the deserts of Africa," Johnson is said to have remarked "Ladies, I am tame; you may stroke me."

In 1763 he met James Boswell (aged twenty-two) for the first time, and after he got over the fact that Boswell was Scottish (Johnson abhorred the Scots—hence his famous definition, in his dictionary, of "oats": "A grain, which in England is generally given to horses, but in Scotland supports the people") the two got on very well together. 1764 brought the formation of the Literary Club, whose members included Johnson, Reynolds, and Edmund Burke, as well as (eventually) David Garrick and Boswell.

In 1765, Johnson's edition of Shakespeare's Plays, with its splendid and perceptive preface, was finally published, and he received an honorary LL.D. from Trinity College in Dublin. He also met the wealthy Henry and Hester Thrale, with whom he would spend much of his time during the next sixteen years, talking brilliantly but writing little‹"No one but a blockhead," he once remarked, "writes but for money." In 1769 Boswell, by now an Edinburgh lawyer, married, and remained in Scotland until 1772. Between 1770 and 1775 Johnson produced a series of fiercely but characteristically opinionated political pamphlets. In August of 1773, though he had always despised Scotland, Johnson undertook his memorable trip to the Hebrides with Boswell. In July of 1774, Johnson went to Wales with the Thrales. During that same year Oliver Goldsmith, one of the few contemporaries whom Johnson genuinely admired, died, and Johnson felt a tremendous sense of loss.

In 1775, Johnson published his A Journey to the Western Islands of Scotland. During the same year he received an honorary LL.D. from Oxford, and visited to France (which he finds worse than Scotland) with the Thrales. He reacted furiously to the American Revolution, characterizing the rebellious colonists as "a race of convicts." In 1776 he travelled with Boswell to Oxford, Ashbourne, and Lichfield, where he stood bareheaded in the rain in the market-place before the stall which had housed his father's bookshop, in order to atone for a "breach of filial piety" committed fifty years before.

In 1778 he made the acquaintance of Fanny Burney, aged twenty-four, and soon to be the successful authoress of Evelina. In the following year David Garrick, Johnson's old pupil and close friend, died, and he was again shaken. In 1781, after Johnson's The Lives of the English Poets had been published, Henry Thrale died. Johnson consoled his widow and, though he ought perhaps to have known better, contemplated marrying her.

In 1783, however, his health began to fail, and he suffered

a stroke. The following year, partially recovered, he broke with Mrs. Thrale when she announced her intention of marrying Gabriele Piozzi. Johnson, frail and troubled by gout, asthma, dropsy, and a tumour, found that his his life-long fear of death had begun to preoccupy him, but he faced it bravely, as he had faced all adversities. On December 13 he died, aged seventy-five: he was buried in Westminster Abbey, with appropriate ceremony, on December 20.

Chapter 4

Samuel Johnson and Politics: An Introduction

Politically, Johnson was a conservative and a Tory, though the eighteenth-century Tory was not necessarily the frequently caricatured and insistently conservative member of the political establishment (and alter ego of the liberal Whig) whom we would encounter in England in the nineteenth or even the twentieth century. Johnson's own political statements, made over the course of his life, are frequently mutually contradictory. In part because his views altered with time and events (he was always a rebel, always a supporter of the underdog), in part because he always sought to be truthful even if it meant being inconsistent, and in part (though this may seem paradoxical) because he loved to argue, and frequently argued both sides of a question (though on different occasions) with equal dexterity and with (apparently) equal sincerity.

W. Jackson Bate identifies a common principle in all of Johnson's political thought, and calls it "protective subordination," or "subordination for the sake of protection"—a principle which we can also detect in his religious thought. Johnson believed that mankind, though capable of good, is also inherently sinful, and that a state of nature—in which mankind would be deprived, that is, of a paternalistic government which could benevolently impose order and regulation, and in so doing protect the weak and the poor from the exploitation of the strong and the wealthy—would be a state of savagery. In what sense is this neoclassical sentiment? Johnson was therefore, on occasion, fiercely protective of the prerogatives of government—he violently condemned, for example, the American Revolution and its underlying principles. On the other hand, when he saw government as tyrannical rather than paternal, he could be equally fierce—as he was in his "London"—in his condemnation of its betrayal of its responsibilities.

During the 1730's and 1740's he wrote pamphlets denouncing what he saw as a tyrannical and corrupt government. In the 1750's he denounced the hidden imperialist and economic factors which lay behind Britain's entry into the Seven Year's War; in the 1770's his concern with political morality led him to denounce, in various works, political jingoism, false patriotism, American complaints about British "oppression." Always he sought the truth, and party labels always meant a great deal less to him than an individual's sense of charity, of responsibility for the spiritual and material well-being of his fellow man. To his mind wisdom, not political rhetoric was the key: in important matters, Johnson said, "a wise Tory and a wise Whig, I believe, will agree." What they could or should agree upon, Johnson believed, were the sentiments he expressed in "The Vanity of Human Wishes" and in Rasselas.

Johnson Literary Career

"No man but a blockhead," said Johnson, "ever wrote except for money." The doctrine is, of course, perfectly outrageous, and specially calculated to shock people who like to keep it for their private use, instead of proclaiming it in public. But it is a good expression of that huge con-tempt, for the foppery of high-flown sentiment which, as is not uncommon with Johnson, passes into something which would be cynical if it were not half humorous. In this case, it implies also the contempt of the professional for the amateur. Johnson despised gentlemen who dabbled in his craft, as a man whose life is devoted to music or painting despises the ladies and gentlemen who treat those arts as fashionable accomplish-ments. An author was, according to him, a man who turned out books as a brick-layer turns out houses or a tailor coats. So long as he supplied a good article and got a fair price, he was a fool to grumble, and a humbug to affect loftier motives.

Johnson was not the first professional author, in this sense, but perhaps the first man who made the profession respectable. The principal habitat of authors, in his age, was Grub Street — a region which, in later years, has ceased to be ashamed of it, and has adopted the more pretentious name Bohemia. The original Grub Street, it is said, first

became associated. with authorship during the increase of pamphlet literature, produced. by the civil wars. Fox, the martyrologist, was one of its original inhabitants. Another of its heroes was a certain Mr. Welby, of whomthe sole record is, that he "lived there forty years without being seen of any." In fact, it was a region of holes and corners, calculated. to illustrate that great advantage of London life, which a friend of Boswell's described by say- ing, that a man could there be always "close to his bur- row." The "burrow" which received the luckless wight, was indeed no pleasant refuge. Since poor Green, in the earliest generation of dramatists, bought his "groat's worth of wit with a million of repentance," too many of his brethren had trodden the path which led to hopeless misery or death in a tavern brawl.

The history of men, who had to support themselves by their pens, is a record of almost universal gloom. The names of Spenser, of Butler, and of Otway, are enough to remind us that even warm contemporary recognition was not enough to raise an author above the fear of dying in want of necessaries. The two great dictators of literature, Ben Johnson in the earlier and Dryden in the later part of the century, only kept their heads above water by help of the laureate's pittance, though reckless imprudence, encouraged by the precarious life, was the cause of much of their sufferings. Patronage gave but a fitful resource, and the author could hope at most but an occasional crust, flung to him from better provided tables.

In the happy days of Queen Anne, it is true; there had been a gleam of prosperity. Many authors, Addison, Congreve, Swift, and others of less name, had won by their pens not only temporary profits but permanent places. The class which came into power at the Revolution was willing for a time, to share some of the public patronage with men distinguished for intellectual eminence. Patronage was liberal when the funds came out of other men's pockets. But, as the system of party government developed, it soon became evident that this involved a waste of power.

There were enough political partisans to absorb all the comfortable sinecures to be had; and such money as was still spent upon literature, was given in return for services equally degrading to giver and receiver. Nor did the patronage of literature reach the poor inhabitants of Grub Street. Addison's poetical power might suggest or justify the gift of a place from his elegant friends; but a man like De Foe, who really looked to his pen for great part of his daily subsistence, was below the region of such prizes, and was obliged in later years not only to write inferior books for money, but to sell himself and act as a spy upon his fellows.

One great man, it is true, made an independence by literature. Pope received some 8000 for his translation of Homer, by the then popular mode of subscription — a kind of compromise between the systems of patronage and public support. But his success caused little pleasure in Grub Street. No love was lost between the poet and the dwellers in this dismal region. Pope was its deadliest enemy, and carried on an internecine warfare with its inmates, which has enriched our language with a great satire, but which wasted his powers upon low objects, and tempted him into disgraceful artifices. The life of the unfortunate victims, pilloried in the Dunciad and accused of the unpardonable sins of poverty and dependence, was too often one, which might have extorted sympathy even from a thin-skinned poet and critic.

Samuel Johnson, His Influence and Reputation

Both the scope of Johnson's reading and the tenacity of his memory were prodigious. It would be difficult to name a major author, either what his contemporaries called an Ancient or a Modern, with whose works he was not familiar, though he was perhaps most influenced by Shakespeare, Donne, Dryden, and Pope. He was a fine classical scholar, and he was, perhaps, the best-read man, so far as modern literature was concerned, of his day. He did not dabble in literature, but wallowed in it, ponderously; and yet he was able to bring all of his learning, all of his accumulated knowledge, aptly and appropriately to bear upon whatever subject he had in hand, whether he was writing an original work or an imitation of a work by a classical author. He was the central figure of the literary period still referred to as the Age of Johnson, and yet because he was essentially a miscellaneous writer (though all of his important works in various genres share certain themes and concerns) he received a great deal of criticism during his lifetime, and even more criticism after it. During his lifetime, he did not mind it much: "It is advantageous to an author," he wrote, "that his book should be attacked as well as praised. Fame is a shuttlecock. If it were struck only at one end of the room, it will soon fall to the ground. To keep it up, it must be struck at both ends."

Johnson's shuttlecock, of course, has been kept in the air ever since. Succeeding generations, familiar with him less from their acquaintance with his own work than through Boswell's great Biography, read him "through Boswell's spectacles," and reacted according to their own tastes and predelictions: Jane Austen would continue to admire both Johnson and his works, while Carlyle would profess admiration for the one, transforming Johnson into a Carlylean Hero, and disdain for the other. The Romantics rejected all of what they believed to be Johnson's most important assumptions concerning man, nature, and human existence: Blake, Coleridge, Hazlitt, and De Quincey all attacked him.

Coleridge derided "The Vanity of Human Wishes" (text) as "bombast and tautology." Jeremy Bentham referred to him as "that pompous preacher of melancholic moralities." Lytton Strachey, as late as 1906, could write with smug equanimity, of Johnson's Lives of the Poets, that "as serious criticism, they can hardly appear to the modern reader to be very far removed from the futile. Johnson's aesthetic judgements are almost invariably subtle, or solid, or bold; they have always some good quality to recommend them — except one: they are never right." With a few significant exceptions, it was not until the twentieth century and the explosion of scholarly criticism that his works were read seriously again: it was T. S. Eliot, in 1930, who wrote that "London" and "The Vanity of Human Wishes" were "amongst the greatest verse satires of the English or any other language."

Chapter 5

Samuel Johnson Works

- The Idler
- "London"
- "The Vanity of Human Wishes"
- The Rambler
- 172. The effect of sudden riches upon the manners
- 180. The study of life not to be neglected for the sake of books
- 182. The history of Leviculus, the fortune-hunter
- 183. Envy
- 184. The subject of essays often suggested by chance
- 196. Human opinions mutable. The hopes of youth fallacious.
- Rasselas
- The Adventurer
- 50. On Lying.
- 84. Folly of false pretences to importance. A journey in a stage coach.
- 108. On the uncertainty of human things.
- Lives of the Poets
- Dictionary

Chapter 6

Time Line

Year	Age	Major/Well Known Writings	Events
1709	°	°	Samuel Johnson born (September 18 —the tercen-tenary is coming) in Lichfield, England, to Michael Johnson (bookseller, age 52), and Sarah Johnson *nee* Ford (age 40). He is their first child, and they are proud parents. It is Michael's pre-appointed duty, as Sheriff of Lichfield, to lead the citizens of the town around the town's borders a couple days later, and he is generous to all in doing so. Johnson is put out to a wetnurse whose milk was tubercular. Bate correctly describes the results as "disastrous." J's eyes are infected, and he contracts scrofula; he is almost blind in his left eye, and his right eye is also affected. He is deaf in one ear. His face is also scarred.
1712	2	°	Brother Nathaniel born (October).

1725	15	°	Johnson spends time living with his older 1st cousin, the Rev. Cornelius Ford. Ford had a huge influence on Johnson. In the words of Pat Rogers *(The Samuel Johnson Encyclo-pedia)*, "the worldly Ford first opened the young man's eyes to a world of sophistication which he had never seen as a boy in Lichfield. It is probable that SJ acquired his first knowledge of the London literary scene from his cousin during a prolonged stay in 1725-26."
1726 -28	16 -18	°	Johnson returns home, and reads a lot. A Lot. Discovers Petrarch and The Classics.
1728	18	°	Johnson enters Oxford University (Pembroke College).
1729	19	°	Johnson experiences deep depression, described by Boswell as "overwhelmed with an horrible hypochondria... dejection, gloom, and despair." Johnson leaves Oxford without a degree; exit is due to a lack of funds.
1731	21	°	J's father Michael dies in December.
1732	22	°	Works as usher in a school at Market-Bosworth.
1733	23	°	Spends time living in Birmingham, with Edmund

			Hector (a schoolfellow and lifelong friend). He contributes a few essays to a local publisher, and meets a number of people, including Elizabeth Porter, whom he will eventually marry. He works on his translation of Lobo, with a lot of assistance from Hector.
1734	24	°	J returns to Lichfield. Writes a letter (November) to Edward Cave, London magazine publisher (*Gentleman's Magazine*), offering the services of someone he knows well, uh, er, probably J himself, now that you mention it, who would make sundry contributions to his publi-cation.
1735	25	J's translation of Lobo'sVoyage to Abyssinia published.	J marries Elizabeth "Tetty" Porter, age 46, in July. She is the widow of a mercer he met in Birmingham in 1733. J tries his hand as a schoolmaster in Edial. The effort is unsuccessful. David Garrick is one of his students. "From Mr. Garrick's account he did not appear to have been profoundly reverenced by his pupils," says Boswell. "His oddities of manner, and uncouth gesticulations, could not but be the subject of merriment to them."

1736 -37	26 -27	°	While working as a schoolmaster, J works on his play *Irene.*
1737	27	°	Brother Nathaniel dies, perhaps a suicide. J goes to London with Garrick, seeking fame and fortune (the education industry providing neither), and leaving his wife in Lichfield for the time being. J makes further proposals to Cave. In the summer he returns to Lichfield and Tetty, and to finish *Irene.* Later this year they both move to London.
1738	28	*London;Life Of Sarpi.*	J gets work as a hack writer for Cave's *Gentleman's Magazine.* J gets ten guineas from publisher Robert Dodsley for *London.* On rea-ding *London,* Alexander Pope is impressed.
1739	29	*Complete Vindication of the Licensers of the Stage; Marmor Norfolciense;* Life of Boerhaave.	°
1740	30	Start of the Parliamentary Debates; *Life of Admiral Drake; Life of Admiral Blake; Life of Barretier.*	
1744	34	Life Of Savage	°
1745	35	Miscellaneous	°

		Observations on the Tragedy of Macbeth, part of a planned edition of Shakespeare's plays. The project was aborted after a publisher of another edition threatened to sue for copyright infringement.	
1746	36	o	J is approached by a consortium of booksellers, and begins work on the *Dictionary*.
1747	37	Plan for a Dictionary of the English Language	o
1748	38	Vision of Theodore the Hermit	o
1749	39	The Vanity of Human Wishes; *Irene* opens.	Founds the Ivy Lane Club (not to be confused with The Club, founded in 1764).
1750	40	Start of *The Rambler* essays.	o
1751	41	*Life of Cheynel*	o
1752	42	End of *The Rambler* essays.	Wife Tetty dies. (They had no children, but she had a daughter from her previous marriage.)
1753	43	Contributes essays to *The Adventurer* series.	Considers remarrying. Bate and others have concluded that the object of his affection was a woman named Claire

			Hill Boothby (1708-56). However, "any thought of marriage was quickly dropped," says Bate.
1754	44	*Life of Edward Cave*	
1755	45	The famous Letter to Lord Chesterfield; *A Dictionary of the English Language,* 1st edition.	Johnson receives an Oxford University (an M.A.), which will appear on the title page of his *Dictionary.*
1756	46	2nd edition of the *Dictionary.*	In March, Johnson is arrested for debt, and released with the help of Richardson.
1758	48	Start of *The Idler* essays; *On the Bravery of the Common English Soldier.*	Money continues to be a problem, and Johnson avoids being arrested for debt again with another loan from a friend.
1759	49	Rasselas, Prince of Abyssinia	J's mother Sarah dies.
1760	50	End of *The Idler* essays.	°
1762	52	°	J receives an annual pension from the crown. He greeted the offer with apprehension — he had earlier characterized pensioners in his *Dictionary* as state hirelings and traitors to the country. However, he is assured that the pension is for his *past* efforts, not work to be done in the future.
1763	53	The Life Of Ascham Account of the Imposture	On May 16, J meets Boswell (age 23), in Thomas Davies bookshop,London.

		of the Cock Lane Ghost.	Biography will not be the same.
1764	54	°	The Club is formed, with J as a charter member. The list of eventual members is impressive: among them are Joseph Banks, Boswell, Edmund Burke, Charles Burney, Charles James Fox, Garrick, Edward Gibbon, Richard Brinsley Sheridan, Adam Smith, and William Windham.
1765	55	Johnson's edition of Shakespeare's plays.	J meets Hester (1741-1821) and Henry (1728?29?-1781) Thrale. J is very depressed when they meet him, and they take him in. J's visits with them, exposure to their family life in Streatham, and their friendship mean a lot to him, and his spirits are considerably lifted.
1766	56	The Fountains	°
1767	57		During a February visit to the library of King George III, Johnson encounters George III himself. During the conversation, the King "expressed a desire to have the literary biography of his country ably executed," says Boswell.
1770	60	The False Alarm	°
1771	61	Thoughts on the Late Transactions Respecting Falklands Islands	°
1773	63	4th edition of	J and Boswell tour Scotland,

		his *Dictionary*	August 18 - November 22.
1774	64	The first "*Collected Edition*" of J's works published. (The genesis of the edition is curious: Davies, in financial difficulties, started it without J's authorization, rounding out the second volume [of an intended 2 volumes] with the works of others; the whole idea incenses J, but his temper is dissipated on seeing Davies' financial straits, and they publish more.) The Patriot	J visits Wales with the Thrales.
1775	65	A Journey to the Western Islands of Scotland; Taxation No Tyranny	Visits France with the Thrales.
1781	71	The Lives of the Poets; the full title is *Prefaces Biographical and Critical to the Works of the most eminent English Poet s*	Friend Henry Thrale dies. J is one of four executors of his estate.

1784	74	°	The Thrale Brewery is sold, providing Hester with somewhat of a release. She marries Gabriel Piozzi, an Italian musician. This upsets J, who has become extraordinarily fond of Hester over the years. J dies on December 13. (We have Hawkins account ofJohnson's last years and George Steevens' account of Johnson's funeral.
1785	°	°	Boswell's *Journal of a Tour to the Hebrides* appears in September. Some are shocked by the explicit, detailed retelling of conversations.
1786	°	°	Mrs. Piozzi's *Anecdotes of the Late Samuel Johnson* published.
1787	°	°	Sir John Hawkins' *Life of Samuel Johnson, LL.D.* published. I've posted an extract covering Johnson's Last Years.
1788	°	*Sermons Left For Publication By John Taylor, LL.D.* (Sermon 4) These sermons are generally accepted as having been written by Johnson. Johnson's name first appeared on an 1812 edition. Hester Piozzi's Letters To And From the Late Samuel	

		Johnson published. This is the first estate.edition of his letters, and includes her letters to him as well as his to her.	
1791	°	°	Boswell's *Life of Samuel Johnson, LL.D.* published. This is pretty much the only endeavor at which Boswell is successful. Boswell will die in 1795.

Chapter 7

The Restoration Period and the 18th Century

This period extends from 1660, the year Charles II was restored to the throne, until about 1789. The prevailing characteristic of the literature of the Renaissance had been its reliance on poetic inspiration or what today might be called imagination. The inspired conceptions of Marlowe, Shakespeare, and Milton, the true originality of Spenser, and the daring poetic style of Donne all support this generalization. Furthermore, although nearly all these poets had been far more bound by formal and stylistic conventions than modern poets are, they had developed a large variety of forms and of rich or exuberant styles into which individual poetic expression might fit. In the succeeding period, however, writers reacted against both the imaginative flights and the ornate or startling styles and forms of the previous era. The quality of the later age is suggested by its writers' admiration for Ben Johnson and his disciples; the transparent and apparently effortless poetic medium of the "school of Ben," along with its emphasis on good taste, moderation, and the Greek and Latin classics as models, appealed profoundly to the new generation.

Thus, the restoration of Charles II ushered in a literature characterized by reason, moderation, good taste, deft management, and simplicity. The historical parallel between the early imperialism of Rome and the restored English monarchy, both of which had replaced republican institutions, was not lost on the ruling and learned classes. Their appreciation of the literature of the time of the Roman emperor

Augustus led to a widespread acceptance of the new English literature and encouraged grandeur of tone in the poetry of the period, the later phase of which is often referred to as Augustan. In addition, the ideals of impartial investigation and scientific experimentation promulgated by the newly founded Royal Society of London for Improving Natural Knowledge (established in 1662) were influential in the development of clear and simple prose as an instrument of rational communication.

Finally, the great philosophical and political treatises of the time emphasize rationalism. Even in the earlier 17th century, Francis Bacon had moved in this direction by advocating reasoning and scientific investigation in Advancement of Learning (1605) and The New Atlantis (1627). Essay Concerning Human Understanding (1690), by John Locke, is the product of a belief in experience as the exclusive basis of knowledge, a view pushed to its logical extreme in An Enquiry Concerning Human Understanding (1748) by David Hume. Locke himself continued to profess faith in divine revelation, but this residual belief was weakened among the similarly rationalist Deists, who tended to base religion on what reason could find in the world God had created around humans.

In political thought, the arbitrary acceptance of the monarch's divine right to rule (a conception popular in the Renaissance) had so nearly succumbed to skeptical criticism that Thomas Hobbes in his Leviathan (1651) found it necessary to defend the idea of political absolutism with a rationally conceived sanction. According to him, the monarch should rule not by divine right but by an original and indissoluble social contract in order to secure universal peace and material gratification. Similarly rationalistic, but opposed to this rigorous subordination of all organs of the state to central control, were Locke's two Treatises on Government (1690), in which he stated that the authority of the governor is derived from the always revocable consent of the governed and that the people's welfare is the only proper object of that authority.

Perhaps the greatest historical work in English is The

History of the Decline and Fall of the Roman Empire (6 volumes, 1776-1788), by Edward Gibbon. Notable for its stately, balanced style, it is permeated with rationalistic skepticism and distrust of emotion, particularly religious emotion.

The successive stages of literary taste during the period of the Restoration and the 18th century are conveniently referred to as the ages of Dryden, Pope, and Johnson, after the three great literary figures that, one after another, carried on the so-called classical tradition in literature. The age as a whole is sometimes called the Augustan age, or the classical or neoclassical period.

Age of Dryden

The poetry of John Dryden possesses a grandeur, force, and fullness of tone that were eagerly received by readers still having something in common with the Elizabethans. At the same time, however, his poetry set the tone of the new age in achieving a new clarity and in establishing a self-limiting, somewhat impersonal canon of moderation and good taste. His polished heroic couplet (a unit of two rhyming lines of iambic pentameter, generally end-stopped), which he inherited from less accomplished predecessors and then developed, became the dominant form in the composition of longer poems.

In a number of critical works, Dryden defined the stylistic restraint, compression, clarity, and common sense that he exemplified in his own poetry and that he showed to be lacking in much of the poetry of the preceding age, particularly in the exuberant and mechanically complex metaphorical wit of the older metaphysical school. His reputation rests primarily on satire.

This form became the dominant poetic genre of the age, both because of the religious and political factionalism of the times and because mocking denunciation of the ludicrousness or rascality of the opposition comes naturally to an age with so strong a public sense of norms of behaviour. Absalom and Achitophel (1681-1682) and Mac Flecknoe (1682) are the most remarkable of Dryden's political satires. Among his other poetic works are noteworthy translations of Roman satirists and of the works of Virgil, and the Pindaric ode "Alexander's Feast," a tour de force of varied cadences, which was published in 1697.

The bulk of Dryden's work was in drama. By means of it, following the new mode of living of the professional literary man, he could derive his support from a large public rather than from private patrons. In his heroic tragedies The Conquest of Granada (1670) and All for Love; or, The World Well Lost (1678), a rewriting of Shakespeare's Antony and Cleopatra in the new taste, Dryden showed a different and not always satisfying side of his talent and exemplified the dominant quality of all Restoration tragedy.

In order to achieve splendor and surprise on the stage, he sacrificed reality of characterization and consistency in motivation for sensual display in exotic locales and extravagance in plot and situation, presented in a style verging on the bombastic. The affinities of this kind of drama are with Beaumont and Fletcher rather than with the great Elizabethan age; and the indirect influence of Ben Johnson is apparent also, for these two men were Johnson's disciples. Probably the best example of this genre of tragedy was produced by Thomas Otway, whose Venice Preserved (1682) avoids the worst excesses to which this form is liable and also possesses considerable tenderness and sensibility. By this time, however, the vogue of heroic tragedy was coming to an end; the style already had been successfully parodied in The Rehearsal (1671), by George Villiers, 2nd duke of Buckingham, and his collaborators.

The comedy of the time is much more successful than the tragedy. It is derived directly from the comedies of Ben Johnson but tries for more refinement while displaying less strength. In a cool, satiric spirit, it criticizes middle-class ambition and other variations from the courtly social norm, of which the canons are aristocratic good taste and good sense, rarely conventional morality. In the eyes of succeeding generations, the chief defects of Restoration comedy are its reduction of sentiment and emotion to silliness and its frequent amorality. Reaction against this type of comedy, known as the comedy of manners, already had developed by the time that its greatest practitioner, William Congreve, was displaying his subtle artistry in Love For Love (1695) and The Way of the World (1700).

Just as Dryden's poetry defined the tone of his time, so too did his easy, informal, clear prose style, notably in his Essay of Dramatic Poesie (1668) and in various prefaces to his plays and translations. Noteworthy prose of a rather different nature was produced by two other figures of the age, Samuel Pepys and John Bunyan. The appetite of the period for life at all levels, but particularly for the life of the senses, is suggested by the secret diary of Samuel Pepys, a high official of the Admiralty Office.

This extraordinary work, valuable as it is as a document of contemporary taste, has much to say of the private, unheroic life and longings of people of all times. A figure in stronger contrast to Pepys could hardly be imagined than John Bunyan, a Puritan preacher, completely alien to the aristocratic and professional world of letters. Bunyan wrote The Pilgrim's Progress from This World to That Which Is to Come (1st part published in 1678; 2nd part, 1684) and The Life and Death of Mr. Badman (1680), two rough-hewn, moving, allegorical narratives of the human journey at the level of the fundamental verities of life, death, and religion. The first of these is now a literary classic, but in spite of the penetrating characterization and vitality of both works, they initially attained popularity only among artisans, merchants, and the poor.

Age of Pope

In the age of Alexander Pope (dated from about the death of Dryden in 1700 to Pope's death in 1744), the classical spirit in English literature reached its highest point, and at the same time other forces became manifest. Dryden's poetry had achieved grandeur, amplitude, and sublimity within a particular definition of good taste and good sense and under the tutelage of the Roman and Greek classics. To the poetry of Pope this characterization applies even more stringently. More than any other English poet, he submitted himself to the requirement that the expressive force of poetic genius should issue forth only in a formulation as reasonable, lucid, balanced, compressed, final, and perfect as the power of human reason can make it. Pope did not have Dryden's majesty. Perhaps, given his predilection for correctness of detail, he could not have had it. Also, the readers of succeeding times have concluded that the dictates of reason do not all converge on only one poetic formula, just as the heroic couplet, which Pope brought to final perfection, is not necessarily the most generally suitable of English poetic forms. Nevertheless, the ease, harmony, and grace of Pope's poetic line are still impressive, and his quality of precise but never labored expression of thought remains unequaled.

Pope's reputation rests in large part on his satires, but his didactic bent led him to formulate in verse An Essay on Criticism (1711) and An Essay on Man (1732-1734). The former attempts to show that poetry must be modeled on nature; but his conception of nature, a traditional one shared by all his contemporaries, differs from that of succeeding generations. For Pope, nature meant the rules that right reason has discovered to be immanent in all things, so that what the experience of reasonable minds through the ages has shown to be the greatest poetry-namely, that of classical antiquity-provides a perfect model for modern times. A similar conservatism reappears in An Essay on Man, which concludes with the much debated generalization that "Whatever is, is right."

Pope's brilliant satiric masterpiece, The Rape of the Lock (1712; revised edition 1714), makes an epic theme of a trifling drawing-room episode: the contention arising from a young lord's having covertly snipped a lock of hair from a young lady's head. His most sustained satire, The Dunciad (1728; final version 1743), follows Dryden's Mac Flecknoe in its elegantly pointed, often malicious but always high-spirited mockery of the literary dullards who were Pope's enemies.

Like Dryden, Pope made translations of classical works, notably of the Iliad, which was a great popular and financial success. His edition of Shakespeare's works bears witness to a range of taste not usually ascribed to him.

It is only natural that the 18th-century preoccupation with the power of reason and good sense should have produced a large number of works in the more sober medium of prose. Jonathan Swift, who was, like Pope, a Tory conservative for the latter half of his life and a satirist, wrote a number of mordantly satirical prose narratives in which a profound and despairing perception of human stupidities and evil are in contrast with the social criticism of his great contemporaries. Swift's Tale of a Tub (1704) reduces the quarrels among three important religious divisions of his day to an allegory of three disreputable brothers.

His generous anger on behalf of the poor of Ireland produced "A Modest Proposal" (1729), in which, with horrifying mock seriousness, he proposed that the children of the poor should be raised for slaughter as food for the rich. His best-known work, Gulliver's Travels (1726), purports to be a ship doctor's account of his voyages into strange places, but in reality it is a castigation of the human race. The accounts of Gulliver's first two voyages are often read as a children's book. The last part abandons, however, delicate fancy and unmasks the selfish and sick bestiality of humanity in the guise of the so-called Yahoos, who are the savage and improvident servants of a race of apparently reasonable and noble horses, called Houyhnhnms. This work, like all of Swift's, is written in a prose of unrivaled lucidity, energy, and polemical skill.

Similarly noteworthy for the quality of their prose are the Spectator papers (1711-1712; 1714), written mainly by Joseph Addison and Richard Steele. Published daily, these essays, like many others, corresponded to the newly felt need of the day for popular journalism, but their enlightened comment and their criticism of contemporary society separate them from the mass of similar publications. The main intent of Addison and Steele may be defined in their own words: "To enliven morality with wit, and to temper wit with morality." In a series of informal, conversational essays describing the activities of various ideal representatives of social groups, such as the Tory country squire Sir Roger de Coverley and the Whig merchant Sir Andrew Freeport, Addison and Steele salvaged and united some of the best sides of the contemporary English character. The lightly borne, free-and-easy manners of the court and the older landed classes should, according to these papers, exist side by side with the industry, uprightness, and deeply felt morality of the newly rich city merchants. The amorality associated with the one and the stubborn narrowness of the other should disappear. The emphasis on public decorum and individual rectitude and on sympathy with one's fellow beings in the Spectator papers is a measure of their distance from the cool indifference and frequent licentiousness of much Restoration literature, particularly comedy, although the purpose of both was to represent reason, moderation, and common sense.

A quite different kind of journalism is represented by the work of the middle-class adventurer, hack writer, and political agent Daniel Defoe. Separated from the life of the upper classes and their erudite writers, as Bunyan had been before him, he produced, among many pieces of commissioned writing, a series of purportedly true but actually fictitious memoirs and confessions. The first of these, and the greatest, is Robinson Crusoe (1719), which reports the life and adventures of a shipwrecked sailor.

Age of Johnson

The age of Samuel Johnson, from 1744 to about 1784, was a time of changing literary ideals. The developed classicism and literary conservatism associated with Johnson fought a rearguard action against the cult of sentiment and feeling associated in various ways with the harbingers of the coming age of romanticism. Johnson composed poetry that continued the traditions and forms of Pope, but he is best known as a prose writer and as an extraordinarily gifted conversationalist and literary arbiter in the cultivated urban life of his time. His conservatism and sturdy common sense are what might be expected given his intellectual tradition, but his individual quality has little to do with literary tendencies. His curiously lovable and upright personality, along with his intellectual preeminence and idiosyncrasies, have been preserved in the most famous of English biographies, the Life of Samuel Johnson (1791), by James Boswell, a Scottish writer with an appetite for literary celebrities.

Johnson worked his way up from poverty by honest literary labors, among which was his Dictionary of the English Language (1755). A great success, it was the first such work prepared according to modern standards of lexicography. Like Addison and Steele, Johnson produced a series of journalistic essays, The Rambler (1750-1752), but because of their somewhat pedantic style and Latinate vocabulary, they lack the easy informality of the Spectator papers and serve to accentuate the opposition between his neoclassical formality and the succeeding romantic ideal of heart-to-heart communication. Johnson's philosophical tale Rasselas (1759), of which the moral is that "human life is everywhere a state in which much is to be endured, and little to be enjoyed," is reminiscent of Swift (as well as of his contemporary the French writer Voltaire in his tale Candide) in its perception of the vanity of human wishes. For all his pessimism, however, the amazing detail, independence, and intellectual facility of Johnson's critical biographies of English poets since 1600 (Lives of the Poets, 1779-1781), written in his old age, show what critical discrimination and intellectual integrity can accomplish.

Johnson's friend Oliver Goldsmith was a curious mixture of the old and the new. His novel The Vicar of Wakefield (1766) begins with dry humour but passes quickly into tearful calamity. His poem The Deserted Village (1770) is in form reminiscent of Pope, but in the tenderness of its sympathy for the lower classes it foreshadows the romantic age. In such plays as She Stoops to Conquer (1773) Goldsmith, like the younger Richard Sheridan in his School for Scandal (1777), demonstrated an older tradition of satirical quality and artistic adroitness that was to be anathema to a younger generation.

The signs of this newer feeling, which resulted in romanticism, can be traced in the poetry of William Cowper and of Thomas Gray. The cultivation of a pensive and melancholy sensibility and the interruption of the rule of the heroic couplet, as in Gray's "Elegy Written in a Country Churchyard" (1751), hint at the period to come, as does Gray's interest in medieval, non-classical literature. New interests are even more obvious in the highly original poetry of the self-educated artist and engraver William Blake.

His work consists in part of simple, almost childlike lyrics (Songs of Innocence, 1789), as well as of powerful but lengthy and obscure declarations of a new mythological vision of life (The Book of Thel, 1789). All Blake's poetry expresses a revolt against the ideal of reason (which he considered destructive to life) and advocates the life of feeling-but in a more vital and assertive sense than is the case with the other previously mentioned pre-romantics. Similarly robust and passionate are the lyrics of the Scottish poet Robert Burns, which are characterized by his use of regional Scottish vernacular. The simplicity, forcefulness, and powerful emotion of the ancient ballads of the Scottish-English border region, as revealed in Reliques of Ancient English Poetry (1765), by Bishop Thomas Percy, were likewise influential in the development of romanticism.

Among writers of the novel-a newly popular form in this period-an advocate of sentiment and simple, innocent feelings had already appeared in the person of Samuel Richardson. In his sentimental novel Clarissa (1747-1748), the plight of a young, innocent girl, destroyed by the man she loves, is represented through lengthy letters interchanged among the characters. This device permits an unprecedented revelation of motives and feelings. Richardson's contemporary Henry Fielding evinced his connection with the earlier satirical spirit in his novel Joseph Andrews (1742), which parodies Richardson's other novel of virtue besieged, Pamela (1740). Fielding's greatest novel, Tom Jones (1749), reveals a robust and healthy spirit of good sense and comedy, in which well-intentioned vigor wins out over excessive hypocrisy. Fielding's contemporary, the Scottish-born Tobias Smollett, wrote a number of novels of picaresque adventure, the last and probably best of which is Humphry Clinker (1771). The Life and Opinions of Tristram Shandy, Gentleman (1759-1767), the masterpiece of another great British novelist of the century, Laurence Sterne, indulges in the new cult of sentiment, but by reason of its cast of eccentric characters and the skilled weaving of the most extraordinary behaviour into the depiction of their personalities, this novel lies outside the usual historical categories.

Chapter 8

Introduction: Shakespeare

Hakespeare's Ancestry

As a brief introductory detail, it should be mentioned that, during the sixteenth century, there were many families with the name Shakespeare in and around Stratford. "Shakespeare" appears countless times in town minutes and court records, spelled in a variety of ways, from Shags ere to Casper. Unfortunately, very few records reveal William Shakespeare's relationship to or with the many other Stratford Shakespeare's. Genealogists claim to have discovered one man related to Shakespeare who was hanged in Gloucestershire for theft in 1248, and Shakespeare's father, in an application for a coat of arms, claimed that his grandfather was a hero in the War of the Roses and was granted land in Warwickshire in 1485 by Henry VII.

No historical evidence has been discovered to corroborate this story of the man who would be William Shakespeare's great-grandfather, but, luckily, we do have information regarding his paternal and maternal grandfathers. The Bard's paternal grandfather was Richard Shakespeare (1561), a farmer in Snitterfield, a village four miles northeast of Stratford. There is no record of Richard Shakespeare before 1529, but details about his life after this reveal that he was a tenant farmer, who, on occasion, would be fined for grazing too many cattle on the common grounds and for not attending manor court. There is no record of Richard Shakespeare's wife, but together they had two sons (possibly more), John and Henry. Richard Shakespeare worked on several different sections of land during his lifetime, including the land owned by the wealthy Robert Arden of Wilmecote, Shakespeare's maternal grandfather. Robert Arden (1556) was the son of Thomas Arden of Wilmecote, Shakespeare's maternal great-grandfather, who probably belonged to the aristocratic family of the Arden's of Park Hall. He was catholic and married more than once (we know the name of his second wife — Agnes Hill) and he fathered no fewer than eight daughters. He became the stepfather of Agnes' four children. Robert Arden had accumulated much property, and when he died, he named his daughter (Shakespeare's mother) Mary, only sixteen at the time, one of his executors. He left Mary some money and, in his own words, "all my land in Willmecote cawlide As byes and the crop apone the grounde, sowne and tyllide as hitt is".

Shakespeare's Parents

Shakespeare's father, John, came to Stratford from Snitterfield before 1532 as an apprentice glover and tanner of leathers. John Shakespeare prospered and began to deal in farm products and wool. It is recorded that he bought a house in 1552 (the date that he first appears in the town records), and bought more property in 1556. Because John Shakespeare owned one house on Greenhill Street and two houses on Henley Street, the exact location of William's birth cannot be known. Sometime between 1556 and 1558, John Shakespeare married Mary Arden, the daughter of the wealthy Robert Arden of Wilmecote and owner of the sixty-acre farm called Asbies.

The wedding would have most likely taken place in Mary Arden's parish church at Aston Cantlow, the burial place of Robert Arden, and, although there is no evidence of strong piety on either side of the family, it would have been a Catholic service, since Queen Mary I was the reigning monarch. We assume neither John nor Mary could write — John used a pair of glovers' compasses as his signature while Mary used a running horse — but it did not prevent them from becoming important members of the community. John Shakespeare was elected to a multitude of civic positions, including ale-taster of the borough (Stratford had a long-reaching reputation for its brewing) in 1557, chamberlain of the borough in 1561, alderman in 1565, (a position which came with free education for his children at the Stratford Grammar School), high bailiff, or mayor, in 1568, and chief alderman in 1571. Due to his important civic duties, he rightfully sought the title of gentleman and applied for his coat-of-arms in 1570.

However, for unspecific reasons the application was abruptly withdrawn, and within the next few years, for reasons just as mystifying, John Shakespeare would go from wealthy business owner and dedicated civil servant to debtor and absentee council member. By 1578, he was behind in his taxes and stopped paying the statutory aldermanic subscription for poor relief. In 1579, he had to mortgage Mary Shakespeare's estate, Asbies, to pay his creditors. In 1580, he was fined 40 pounds for missing a court date and in 1586, the town removed him from the board of aldermen due to lack of attendance.

By 1590, John Shakespeare owned only his house on Henley Street and, in 1592, he was fined for not attending church. However, near the very end of John Shakespeare's life, it seems that his social and economic standing was again beginning to flourish. He once again applied to the College of Heralds for a coat-of-arms in 1596, and, due likely to the success of William in London, this time his wish was granted. On October 20 of that year, by permission of the Garter King of Arms (the Queen's aid in such matters) "the said John Shakespeare, Gentlemen, and...His children, issue and posterity" were lawfully entitled to display the gold coat-of-arms, with a black banner bearing a silver spear (a visual representation of the family name "Shakespeare"). The coat-of-arms could then be displayed on their door and all their personal items.

The motto was "Non sans droict" or "not without right. The reason cited for granting the coat-of-arms was John Shakespeare's grandfather's faithful service to Henry VII, but no specifics were given as to what service he actually performed. The coat-of-arms appears on Shakespeare's tomb in Stratford. In 1599, John Shakespeare was reinstated on the town council, but died a short time later, in 1601. He was probably near seventy years old and he had been married for forty-four years. Mary Shakespeare died in 1608 and was buried on September 9.

Shakespeare's Birth

The baptismal register of the Holy Trinity parish church, in Stratford, shows the following entry for April 26, 1564: Gulielmus filius Johannes Shakespeare. The actual date of Shakespeare's birth is not known, but, traditionally, April 23, St George's Day has been Shakespeare's accepted birthday, and a house on Henley Street in Stratford, owned by William's father, John, is accepted as Shakespeare's birthplace. However, the reality is that no one really knows when the great dramatist was born. According to the Book of Common Prayer, it was required that a child be baptized on the nearest Sunday or holy day following the birth, unless the parents had a legitimate excuse. As Dennis Kay proposes in his book Shakespeare.

If Shakespeare were indeed born on Sunday, April 23, the next feast day would have been St. Mark's Day on Tuesday the 25. There might well have been some cause, both reasonable and great — or perhaps, as has been suggested, St. Mark's Day was still held to be unlucky, as it had been before the Reformation, when altars and crucifixes used to be draped in black cloth, and when some claimed to see in the churchyard the spirits of those doomed to die in that year....but that does not help to explain the christening on the twenty-sixth.

No doubt, Shakespeare's true birthday will remain a mystery forever. However, the assumption that the Bard was born on the same day of the month that he died lends an exciting esoteric highlight to the otherwise mundane details of Shakespeare's life.

Shakespeare's Siblings

William Shakespeare was indeed lucky to survive to adulthood in sixteenth-century England. Waves of the plague swept across the countryside, and pestilence ravaged Stratford during the hot summer months. Mary and John Shakespeare became parents for the first time in September of 1558, when their daughter Joan was born. Nothing is known of Joan Shakespeare except for the fact that she was baptized in Stratford on September 15, and succumbed to the plague shortly after.

Their second child, Margaret, was born in 1562 and was baptized on December 2. She died one year later. The Shakespeare's' fourth child, Gilbert, was baptized on October 13, 1566, at Holy Trinity. It is likely that John Shakespeare named his second son after his friend and neighbour on Henley Street, Gilbert Bradley, a glover and the burgess of Stratford for a time. Records show that Gilbert Shakespeare survived the plague and reached adulthood, becoming a haberdasher, working in London as of 1597, and spending much of his time back in Stratford. In 1609, he appeared in Stratford court in connection with a lawsuit, but we know no details regarding the matter.

Gilbert Shakespeare seems to have had a long and successful career as a tradesman, and he died a bachelor in Stratford on February 3, 1612. In 1569, John and Mary Shakespeare gave birth to another girl, and named her after her first-born sister, Joan. Joan Shakespeare accomplished the wondrous feat of living to be seventy-seven years old — outliving William and all her other siblings by decades. Joan married William Hart the hatter and had four children but two of them died in childhood. Her son William Hart (1600-1639) followed in his famous uncle's footsteps and became an actor, performing with the King's Men in the mid-1630s. His most noted role was that of Falstaff. William Hart never married, but the leading actor of the restoration period, Charles Hart, is believed to have been William Hart's illegitimate son and grandnephew to Shakespeare.

Due to the fact that Shakespeare's children and his other siblings did not carry on the line past the seventeenth century, the descendants of Joan Shakespeare Hart possess the only genetic link to the great playwright. Joan Shakespeare lost her husband William a week before she lost her brother William in 1616, and she lived the rest of her life in Shakespeare's birthplace. Joan died in 1646, but her descendants stayed in

Stratford until 1806. Undoubtedly already euphoric that Joan had survived the precarious first few years of childhood, the Shakespeare's' joy was heightened with the birth of their fourth daughter, Anne, in 1571, when William was seven years old.

Unfortunately, tragedy befell the family yet again when Anne died at the age of eight. The sorrow felt by the Shakespeare's' over the loss of Anne was profound, and even though they were burdened by numerous debts at the time of her death, they arranged an unusually elaborate funeral for their cherished daughter.

Anne Shakespeare was buried on April 4, 1579. In 1574, Mary and John Shakespeare had another boy and they named him Richard, probably after his paternal grandfather. Richard was baptized on March 11 of that year, and nothing else is known about him, except for the fact that he died, unmarried, and was buried on February 4, 1613 — a year and a day after the death of Gilbert Shakespeare. Mary gave birth to one more child in 1580.

They christened him on May 3 and named him Edmund, probably in honor of his uncle Edmund Lambert. Edmund was eager to follow William into the acting profession, and when he was old, enough he joined William in London to embark on a career as a "player". Edmund did not make a great reputation for himself as an actor, but, in all fairness, cruel fate, and not his poor acting abilities, was likely the reason. Edmund died in 1607—not yet thirty years old.

He was buried in St. Savior's Church, in Southwark, on December 31 of that year. His funeral was costly and magnificent, with tolling bells heard across the Thames. It is most likely that William planned the funeral for his younger brother because William would have been the only Shakespeare wealthy enough to afford such an expensive tribute to Edmund.

In addition, records show that the funeral was held in the morning, and as Dennis Kay points out, funerals were usually held in the afternoon. It is probable that the morning funeral was arranged so that Shakespeare's fellow actors could attend the burial of Edmund.

Shakespeare's Education and Childhood

Shakespeare probably began his education at the age of six or seven at the Stratford grammar school, which is still standing only a short distance from his house on Henley Street and is in the care of the Shakespeare Birthplace Trust. Although we have no record of Shakespeare attending the school, due to the official position held by John Shakespeare it seems likely that he would have decided to educate young William at the school, which was under the care of Stratford's governing body. The Stratford grammar school had been built some two hundred years before Shakespeare was born and in that time the lessons taught there were, of course dictated primarily by the beliefs of the reigning monarch.

In 1553, due to a charter by King Edward VI, the school became known as the King's New School of Stratford-upon-Avon. During the years that Shakespeare attended the school, at least one and possibly three headmasters stepped down because of their devotion to the Catholic religion proscribed by Queen Elizabeth. One of these masters was Simon Hunt (1551), who, in 1578, according to tradition, left Stratford to pursue his more spiritual goal of becoming a Jesuit, and relocated to the seminary at Rheims. Hunt had found his true vocation: when he died in Rome seven years later he had raised to the position of Grand Penitentiary.

Like all of the great poets and dramatists of the time, Shakespeare learned his basic reading and writing skills from an ABC, or hornbook. Robert Speight in his book, Shakespeare: The Man and His Achievement, describes this book as

a primer framed in wood and covered with a thin plate of transparent horn. It included the alphabet in small letters and in capitals, with combinations of the five vowels with b, c, and d, and the Lord's Prayer in English. The first of these alphabets, which ended with the abbreviation for 'and' began with the mark of the cross. Hence the alphabet was known as 'Christ cross row' — the cross-row of Richard III, I, i, 55. A short catechism was often included in the ABC book.

In 'The Merry Wives of Windsor', there is a comical scene in which the Welsh headmaster tests his pupil's knowledge, who is appropriately named William. There is little doubt that Shakespeare was recalling his own experiences during his early school years. As was the case in all Elizabethan grammar schools, Latin was the primary language of learning. Although Shakespeare likely had some lessons in English, Latin composition and the study of Latin authors like Seneca, Cicero, Ovid, Virgil, and Horace would have been the focus of his literary training. One can see that Shakespeare absorbed much that was taught in his grammar school, for he had an impressive familiarity with the stories by Latin authors, as is evident when examining his plays and their sources. Even though scholars, basing their argument on a story told more than a century after the fact, accept that Shakespeare was removed from school around age thirteen because of his father's financial and social difficulties.

There is no reason whatsoever to believe that he had not acquired a firm grasp of both English and Latin and that he had continued his studies elsewhere. The famous quotation from Nicholas Rowe's notoriously inaccurate biography of Shakespeare (written in 1709), where he claims that Shakespeare "acquired that little Latin he was Master of" and that Shakespeare was prevented by his father's poor fortune from "further Proficiency in that Language", should be read with an extremely critical eye.

There are other fragmented and dubious details about Shakespeare's life growing up in Stratford. He is supposed to have worked for a butcher, in addition to helping run his father's business. There is a fable that Shakespeare stole a deer from Sir Thomas Lucy at Charlecote, and instead of serving a prison sentence, fled from Stratford. Although this surely is a fictitious incident, a few verses of a humorous ballad mocking Lucy have been connected to Shakespeare. "Edmond Malone records a version of two verses of the Lucy Ballad collected by one of the few great English classical scholars, Joshua Barnes, at Stratford between 1687 and 1690. Barnes stopped overnight at an inn and heard an old woman singing it. He gave her a new gown for the two stanzas which were all she remembered":

Sir Thomas was so covetous

To covet so much deer
When horns enough upon his head
Most plainly did appear
Had not his worship one deer left?
What then? He had a wife
Took pains enough to find him horns
Should last him during life.

Shakespeare's daily activities after he left school and before he re-emerged as a professional actor in the late 1580s are impossible to trace. Suggestions that he might have worked as a schoolmaster or lawyer or glover with his father and brother, Gilbert, are all plausible. So too is the argument that Shakespeare studied intensely to become a master at his literary craft, and honed his acting skills while traveling and visiting playhouses outside of Stratford. However, it is from this period known as the "lost years" that we obtain one vital piece of information about Shakespeare: he married a pregnant orphan named Anne Hathaway.

Shakespeare's Marriage and Children

Recordings in the Episcopal register at Worcester on the dates of November 27 and 28, 1582, reveal that Shakespeare desired to marry a young girl named Anne. There are two different documents regarding this matter, and their contents have raised a debate over just whom Shakespeare first intended to wed. Were there two Anne's? Was Shakespeare in love with one but in lust with the other? Was Shakespeare ready to join in matrimony with the Anne of his dreams only to have an attack of conscience and marry the Anne with whom he had carnal relations? To discuss the controversy properly we should look at the documents in question. The first entry in the register is the following record of the issue of a marriage license to one Wm Shakespeare:

Anno Domini 1582...Novembers...27 die eiusdem mensis. Item eodem die supradicto emanavit Licentia inter Wm Shaxpere et Annam Whateley de Temple Grafton.1

The next entry in the episcopal register records the marriage bond granted to one Wm Shakespeare:

Noverint universi per praesentes nos Fulconem Sandells de Stratford in comitatu Warwici agricolam et Johannem Rychardson ibidem agricolam, teneri et firmiter obligari Ricardo Cosin generoso et Roberto Warmstry notario publico in quadraginta libris bonae et legalis monetae Angliae solvend. eisdem Ricardoet Roberto haered. execute. et assign at. suis ad quam quidem solucionem bene et fideliter faciend. obligamus nos et utrumque nostrum per se pro toto et in solid. haired. executor. et administrator. nostros firmiter per praesentes sigillis nostris sigillat.

Dat. 28 die Novem. Anno regni dominae nostrae Eliz. Dei gratia Angliae Franc. et Hiberniae Reginae fidei defensor &c.25.2 The condition of this obligation is such that if hereafter there shall not appear any lawful let or impediment by reason of any precontract, consanguinity, affinity or by any other lawful means whatsoever, but that William Shagspere on the one party and Anne Hathwey of Stratford in the diocese of Worcester, maiden, may lawfully solemnize matrimony together, and in the same afterwards remain and continue like man and wife according unto the laws in that behalf provided...

Three possible conclusions can be reached from the above records: 1) The Anne Whateley in the first record and the Anne Hathwey in the second record are the same woman. Some scholars believe that the name Whateley was substituted accidentally for Hathwey into the register by the careless clerk. "The clerk was a nincompoop: he wrote Baker for Barber in his register and Darby for Bradley, and Dock for Lock and Anne Whitely for Anne Hathaway. A lot of ingenious ink has been spilt over this error, but it is surely a simple one: the name whitely occurs in a tithe appeal by a vicar on the same page of the register; the clerk could not follow his own notes, or he was distracted" Moreover, some believe that the couple selected Temple Grafton as the place for the wedding for reasons of privacy and that is why it is recorded in the register instead of Stratford. 2) The Wm Shaper and the Anna Whateley who wished to marry in Temple Grafton were two different people entirely from the Wm Shagspere and Anne Hathwey who were married in Stratford.

This argument relies on the assumption that there was a relative of Shakespeare's living in Temple Grafton, or a man unrelated but sharing Shakespeare's name (which would be extremely unlikely), and that there is no trace of this relative after the issue of his marriage license. 3) The woman Shakespeare loved and the woman Shakespeare finally married were two different Anne's. Not many critics support this hypothesis, but those that do use it to portray Shakespeare as a young man torn between the love he felt for Anne Whateley and the obligation he felt toward Anne Hathwey and the child she was carrying, which was surely his. In Shakespeare, Anthony Burgess constructs a vivid scenario to this effect:

It is reasonable to believe that Will wished to marry a girl named Anne Whateley. The name is common enough in the Midlands and is even attached to a four-star hotel in Horse Fair, Banbury. Her father may have been a friend of John Shakespeare's, he may have sold kidskin cheap, there are various reasons why the Shakespeare's and the Whateleys, or their nubile children, might become friendly. Sent on skin-buying errands to Temple Grafton, Will could have fallen for a comely daughter, sweet as May and shy as a fawn. He was eighteen and highly susceptible.

Knowing something about girls, he would know that this was the real thing. Something, perhaps, quite different from what he felt about Mistress Hathaway of Shottery. But why, attempting to marry Anne Whateley, had he put himself in the position of having to marry the other Anne? I suggest that, to use the crude but convenient properties of the old women's-magazine morality-stories, he was exercised by love for the one and lust for the other. I find it convenient to imagine that he knew Anne Hathaway carnally, for the first time, in the spring of 1582...

Whichever argument one chooses to accept, it is fact that Shakespeare, a minor at the time, married Anne Hathaway, who was twenty-six and already several months pregnant. Anne was the eldest daughter, and one of the seven children of Richard Hathaway, a twice-married farmer in Shottery.

When Richard died in 1581, he requested his son, Bartholomew, move into the house we now know as Anne Hathaway's Cottage, and maintain the property for his mother, Richard's second wife and Anne's stepmother. Anne lived in the cottage with Bartholomew, her stepmother, and her other siblings.

No doubt, she was bombarded with a barrage of household tasks to fill her days at Hew land Farm, as it was then called. After her marriage to Shakespeare, Anne left Hew land Farm to live in John Shakespeare's house on Henley Street, as was the custom of the day. Preparations for the new bride were made, and for reasons unknown, her arrival greatly bothered John Shakespeare's current tenant in the house, William Burbage. A heated fight ensued, and John refused to release Burbage from his lease, so Burbage decided to take the matter to a London court. On July 24, 1582, lawyers representing both sides met and resolved the matter — John would release William Burbage from his lease.

The Shakespeare's' first child was Susanna, christened on May 26, 1583, and twins arrived in January 1585. They were baptized on February 2 of that year and named after two very close friends of William — the baker Hamnet Sadler and his wife, Judith. The Sadlers became the goarents of the twins and, in 1598, they, in turn, named their own son William. Not much information is known about the life of Anne and her children after this date, except for the tragic fact that Hamnet Shakespeare died of an unknown cause on August 11, 1596, at the age of eleven. By this time, Shakespeare had long since moved to London to realise his dreams on the English stage (a time in the Bard's life that will be covered in depth later on) and we do not know if he was present at Hamnet's funeral in Stratford. We can only imagine how deeply the loss of his only son touched the sensitive poet, but his sorrow is undeniably reflected in his later work, and, particularly, in a passage from King John, written between 1595 and 1597:

Young Arthur is my son, and he is lost:
I am not mad: I would to heaven I were!
For then, 'tis like I should forget myself:

O, if I could, what grief should I forget!
Preach some philosophy to make me mad,
And thou shalt be canonized, cardinal;
For being not mad but sensible of grief,
My reasonable part produces reason
How I may be deliver'd of these woes,
And teaches me to kill or hang myself:
If I were mad, I should forget my son,
Or madly think a babe of clouts were he:
I am not mad; too well, too well I feel
The different plague of each calamity....
I tore them from their bonds and cried aloud
'O that these hands could so redeem my son,
As they have given these hairs their liberty!'
But now I envy at their liberty,
And will again commit them to their bonds,
Because my poor child is a prisoner.
And, father cardinal, I have heard you say
That we shall see and know our friends in heaven:
If that be true, I shall see my boy again;
For since the birth of Cain, the first male child,
To him that did but yesterday suspire,
There was not such a gracious creature born.
But now will canker-sorrow eat my bud
And chase the native beauty from his cheek
And he will look as hollow as a ghost,
As dim and meagre as an ague's fit,
And so he'll die; and, rising so again,
When I shall meet him in the court of heaven
I shall not know him: therefore never, never
Must I behold my pretty Arthur more.

Chapter 9

Shakespeare as Actor and Play Wright

We know very little about Shakespeare's life during two major spans of time, commonly referred to as the "lost years." The lost years fall into two periods: 1578-82 and 1585-92. The first period covers the time after Shakespeare left grammar school until his marriage to Anne Hathaway in November of 1582. The second period covers the seven years of Shakespeare's life in which he must have been perfecting his dramatic skills and collecting sources for the plots of his plays. "What could such a genius accomplish in this direction during six or eight years? The histories alone must have required unending hours of labour to gather facts for the plots and counter-plots of these stories.

When we think of the time he must have spent in reading about the pre-Tudor dynasties, we are at a loss to estimate what a day's work meant to him. Perhaps he was one of those singular geniuses who absorb books. George Douglas Brown, when discussing Shakespeare, often used to say he knew how to 'pluck the guts' out of a tome".

No one knows for certain how Shakespeare first started his career in the theatre, although several London players would visit Stratford regularly, and so, sometime between 1585 and 1592, it is probable that young Shakespeare could have been recruited by the Leicester's or Queen's men. Whether an acting troupe recruited Shakespeare in his hometown or he was forced on his own to travel to London to begin his career, he was nevertheless an established actor in the great city by the end of 1592. In this year came the first reference to Shakespeare in the world of the theatre. The dramatist Robert Greene declared in his death-bed autobiography that "There is an upstart crow, beautified with our feathers, that with his Tigers heart wrap in a Players hide supposes he is as well able to bombast out a blank verse as the best of you; and, being an absolute Johannes Factotum, is in his own conceit the only Shake-scene in a country." After Green's death, his editor, Henry Chettle, publicly apologized to Shakespeare in the Preface to his Kind-Heart's Dream:

About three months since died M. Robert Greene, leaving many papers in sundry booksellers' hands, among other his Groatsworth of Wit, in which a letter written to divers play-makers is offensively by one or two of them taken, and because on the dead they cannot be avenged, they willfully forge in their conceits a living author....With neither of them that take offence was I acquainted, and with one of them I care not if I never be. The other, whom at that time I did not so much spare as since I wish I had, for that, as I have moderated the heat of living writers and might have used my own discretion (especially in such a case, the author being dead), that I did not I am as sorry as if the original fault had been my fault, because myself have seen his demeanor no less civil than he excellent in the quality he professes. Besides, the divers of worship have reported his uprightness of dealing, which argues his honesty and his facetious grace in writing that approves his art. Such an apology indicates that Shakespeare was already a respected player in London with influential friends and connections. Records also tell us that several of Shakespeare's plays were popular by this time, including Henry VI, The Comedy of Errors, and Titus Andronicus.

The company that staged most of the early productions of these plays was Pembroke's Men, sponsored by the Earl of Pembroke, Henry Herbert. The troupe was very popular and performed regularly at the court of Queen Elizabeth. Most critics conclude that Shakespeare spent time as both a writer and an actor for Pembroke's Men before 1592. The turning point in Shakespeare's career came in 1593. The theatres had been closed since 1592 due to an outbreak of the plague and, although it is possible that Shakespeare toured the outlying areas of London with acting companies like Pembroke's Men or Lord Strange's Men, it seems more likely that he left the theatre entirely during this time to work on his non-dramatic poetry. The hard work paid off, for by the end of 1593, Shakespeare had caught the attention of the Earl of Southampton.

Southampton became Shakespeare's patron, and on April 18, 1593, Venus and Adonis were entered for publication. Shakespeare had made his formal debut as a poet. The dedication Shakespeare wrote to Southampton at the beginning of the poem is impassioned and telling, "phrased with courtly deference"

TO THE RIGHT HONORABLE HENRY WRIOTHESLEY, EARL OF SOUTHAMPTON, AND BARON OF TICHFIELD. RIGHT HONORABLE,

I Know not how I shall offend in dedicating my unpolished lines to your lordship, nor how the world will censure me for choosing so strong a prop to support so weak a burden only, if your honour seem but pleased, I account myself highly praised, and vow to take advantage of all idle hours, till I have honoured you with some graver labour. But if the first heir of my invention prove deformed, I shall be sorry it had so noble a god-father, and never after ear so barren a land, for fear it yield me still so bad a harvest. I leave it to your honourable survey, and your honour to your heart's content; which I wish may always answer your own wish and the world's hopeful expectation. Your honour's in all duty, Although there is no concrete proof that Shakespeare had a long and close friendship with Southampton, most scholars agree that this was the case, based on Shakespeare's writings, particularly the early sonnets.

Shakespeare returned to the theatre in 1594, and became a leading member of the Lord Chamberlain's Men, formally known as Lord Strange's Men. The manuscript account of the treasurer of the royal chamber in the public records office tells us the following:

To William Kempe, William Shakespeare, and Richard Burbage, servants to the Lord Chamberlain, upon the council's warrant dated at Whitehall xv die March 1594 for two several comedies or interludes showed by them before her Majesty in Christmas time last past, viz; upon St. Stephan's day and Innocent's day, xiiij li. vj s. viij d. and by way of her Majesty's reward...

This is proof that Shakespeare had performed with the Chamberlain's Men before Elizabeth I on several occasions. As payment for their performance, the actors each received 10 pounds. During his time with the Chamberlain's Men Shakespeare wrote many plays, including Romeo and Juliet, Richard II, King John, and Love's Labour's Lost. As G.E. Bentley points out in Shakespeare and the Theatre, Shakespeare had by this time become immersed in his roles as actor and writer.

He was "more completely and more continuously involved in theatres and acting companies than any other Elizabethan dramatist. Shakespeare is "the only one known who not only wrote plays for his company, acted in the plays, and shared the profits, but who was also one of the housekeepers who owned the building. For seventeen years he was one of the owners of the Globe theatre and for eight years he was one of the housekeepers of the company's second theatre, the Black friars, as well". During the years Shakespeare performed with the Chamberlain's Men, before their purchase of the Globe in 1599, they played primarily at the well-established theatres like the Swan, the Curtain, and the Theatre. The troupe would also give regular performances before Elizabeth I and her court, and tour the surrounding areas of London. Some important events in Shakespeare's personal life also take place during this period.

The Shakespeare has finally received a coat of arms 1596 (see "Shakespeare's Parents" for more information on the coat-of-arms), and on August 11 of the same year, Shakespeare's son, Hamnet, died at the age of eleven. Shakespeare no doubt returned to Stratford for the burial, although we have no documented proof. In 1597, Shakespeare purchased the second largest house in Stratford: New Place. The house stood at the corner of Chapel Lane and Chapel Street, north of the Guild Chapel and right across from the very school he attended in his youth. He bought it from William Underhill for the low price of 60 pounds. And below is the actual deed (translated from the original Latin) transferring New Place from Underhill to Shakespeare on May 4, 1597.

Between William Shakespeare, complainant, and William Underhill, deforciant wrongful occupier, supposed by the legal fiction on which the fine method of transfer was based to be keeping the complainant out of his rightful property, concerning one dwelling house, two barns, and two gardens with their appurtenances in Stratford-on-Avon, in regard to which a plea of agreement was broached in the same court: Namely, that the said William Underhill acknowledged the said tenements with their appurtenances to be the right of W. Shakespeare as being those which the same William Shakespeare has by gift of the said W. U., and remitted and waived claim to them from himself and his heirs to the said W.S. and his heirs forever....and agreement the same W.S. has given the foresaid W./U. sixty pounds sterling.

Many theorize that Shakespeare renewed his interest in Stratford only after the death of Hamnet and that, for the many years he was away in London, he neglected his family back home. However, it is just as likely that he made frequent yet unrecorded trips to Stratford while he was trying to find success in London.

Shakespeare's Fellow Actors

Richard Burbage (b.1567? d.1619)

Richard Burbage is considered to be the first great actor in the English theatre. He was the son of James Burbage, the theatrical entrepreneur who built "the Theatre" in Shore ditch on the outskirts of London, and the brother of another famous actor of the day, Cuthbert Burbage. Richard Burbage achieved success as performer by the age of 20 and during his career, he appeared in plays by Jonson, Kyd, Beaumont and Fletcher, and

John Webster. He also played many of the major Shakespearean characters, including Othello, Hamlet, Lear, and Richard III. "It is likely that Richard III was the most popular of all Shakespeare's plays with the Elizabethan public; it provided a superlative part for Burbage". Legend tells us that a woman fell in love with Burbage when she saw him play Richard III and begged him to come to her chambers that night under the name of King Richard. But Shakespeare overheard the proposition and, as a joke, left the theatre early to take Burbage's place. Shakespeare was 'at his game ere Burbage came.

Then, message being brought that Richard III was at the door, Shakespeare caused return to be made that "William the Conqueror" was before Richard III". Early in his career Burbage probably would have been a member of both Lord Strange's Men and the Admiral's Men. Both companies performed at James Burbage's Theatre between 1590 and 1591. We do know that Burbage was a member of the Chamberlain's Men after 1594 and stayed with the group through its evolution into the King's Men in 1603. Although his last recorded performance was in 1610, he remained with the King's Men until his death in 1619.

In addition to acting, Richard Burbage was also an entrepreneur much like his father. When James Burbage died in 1597, he left the Theatre to Richard and his brother. Together they disassembled the Theatre and built the Globe in 1599. The Burbages kept half the shares in the new theatre and the rest were assigned equally to Shakespeare and other members of the Chamberlain's Men.

James Burbage also left another theatre to Richard - the Blackfriars Theatre. Richard Burbage leased it to an acting company called the Children of the Chapel, but, after they could not make the payments, Burbage bought back the lease with his brother and four new partners from the King's Men - Shakespeare, Henry Condell, William Sly, and John Heminge. Richard Burbage was also a wonderful painter.

Some believe that the anonymous oil painting of Burbage seen above is actually a self-portrait, and he has often been credited with painting the Chandos portrait of Shakespeare, seen on the right. Burbage's skills as an artist were often in demand. With Shakespeare as his partner, providing the commemorative words, Burbage designed an impresa, or personal badge, for the Earl of Rutland (1578-1632). The badge was to be worn on the Earl's shield at a tournament on March 24, 1613 to honor James I. When Shakespeare died in 1616, he left his dear friend Burbage money to buy a mourning-ring in his memory. Burbage died on March 9, 1619, and "the true sound of Shakespeare's lines, as he had conceived them and Burbage had interpreted them, was silenced forever".

William Kempe (b.1560? d.1603)

William Kempe was one of the most beloved clowns in the Elizabethan theatre. Records tell us that Kempe was an actor with Leicester's Men on a tour of the Netherlands and Denmark in 1585-86. By 1593, Kempe was a member of Strange's Men, and theatregoers and fellow actors were beginning to recognize his comedic talent. Thomas Nashe declared him the successor to the great Elizabethan performer, Richard Tarlton. Kempe joined the Chamberlain's Men in 1594 and acted in many of Shakespeare's plays. He was the original portrayer of Dogberry in Much Ado about Nothing, Peter in Romeo and Juliet, and possibly Falstaff. He also likely played Lancelot Gobbo in The Merchant of Venice and Bottom in A Midsummer Night's Dream. However, it appears that Kempe suddenly left the Chamberlain's Men in 1599. The reason for his departure is not documented, although many believe that he was asked to leave due to his chronic improvising, and that Shakespeare referred to this in Hamlet:

And let those that play
your clowns speak no more than is
set down for them;
for there be of them that will themselves laugh, to
set on some quantity of barren spectators to laugh
too (3.2.40-5)

Once Kempe left the troupe, Shakespeare's comic characters changed dramatically, indicating that earlier parts were written to fit Kempe's unique style. Examining

Shakespeare's changes provides us with even more information about Kempe's stage presence. "He was a big man who specialized in Plebian clowns who spoke in earthly language...Kempe's characters have a tendency to confuse and mispronounce their words, and contemporary references to his dancing and ability to "make a scurvy face" suggest a physical brand of humour."Now finished with Shakespeare's troupe and looking for another way to entertain the people of London, Kempe planned a wild publicity stunt.

In 1600, he danced a morris dance from London to Norwich, almost 100 miles north. He wrote his own account of the event called Kempe's Nine Days Wonder, and the picture above is from the cover of the original copy. Kempe returned to acting in 1601 when he left England to tour Europe. When he arrived home in 1602 he joined Worchester's Men, but he disappears from the records shortly after. Some scholars conclude that he died from the 1603 plague in London - the year of one of the largest outbreaks of the disease during Shakespeare's life.

Chapter 10

William Shakespeare Timeline

1564 Born in Stratford-upon-Avon to tanner and glove maker, John Shakespeare and his wife, Mary (Arden). His actual birthday is unknown but assumed to be April the 23 rd. His baptism was recorded in the Parish register of Holy Trinity Church on April the 26th.

1571 If Shakespeare went to school this is when he would have started because children in Stratford began their schooling at the age of seven. He would have gone to the local grammar school.

1582 Shakespeare marries Anne Hathaway November the 27th at Temple Grafton, a village near Stratford.

1583 Susanna, his first child is born

1585 Judith and Hamnet, twins, are born, February 2 nd. Shakespeare goes to London and starts his theatrical career.

1589 -92 Shakespeare establishes his career and begins to make a name for himself. Henry VI, 1,2,3 The Comedy of Errors Titus Andronicus The Taming of the Shrew Richard III

1593 Dedicates *Venus and Adonis* and *The Rape of Lucrece* to Henry Wriothsley, Earl of Southampton - thought to be the beautiful youth of the Sonnets 1 5 9 3 Venus and Adonis Begins writing the Sonnets, Two Gentlemen of Verona Love's Labour's Lost

1594 Founding member of the Lord Chamberlain's Men, an acting company. The Rape of Lucrece (published)

1596-97 Hamnet dies 1597Shakespeare purchases New Place, a large house in Stratford, 1597. A Midsummer Night's Dream Romeo and Juliet Richard II Merchant of Venice

1597-99	The Globe Theater built on Bankside 1599. Shakespeare is a shareholder. Henry IV,1,2 The Merry Wives of Windsor As You Like It Much Ado About Nothing Henry V Julius Caesar
1600-08	The Great Tragedies 1601 Shakespeare's father dies 1603 The Lord Chamberlain's Men become The King's Men and perform regularly at court. 1607 Susanna Shakespeare marries Dr. John Hall 1608 The King's Men begin playing at the Blackfriars 1608 Shakespeare's mother dies. Twelfth Night Hamlet Troilus & Cressida Alls Well That Ends Well Measure for Measure Othello King Lear Macbeth Antony and Clepatra Coriolanus Timon of Athens
1609-11	1609 the Sonnets published. The Romances Pericles Prince of Tyre Cymbeline The Winter's Tale The Tempest
1612-16	Shakespeare retires from the theatre and returns to live in Stratford. Works on new plays with his friend, John Fletcher 1616 Judith Shakespeare married Thomas Quiney. Henry VIII The Two Noble Kinsmen Cardenio
1616	Shakespeare dies 23 rd April (on his birthday) and is buried in Holy Trinity Church.

Chapter 11

William Shakespeare-List of Works

Comedy

- All's Well That Ends Well
- As You Like It
- The Comedy of Errors
- Cymbeline
- Love's Labours Lost
- Measure for Measure
- The Merry Wives of Windsor
- The Merchant of Venice
- A Midsummer Night's Dream
- Much Ado About Nothing
- Pericles, Prince of Tyre
- Taming of the Shrew
- The Tempest
- Troilus and Cressida
- Twelfth Night
- Two Gentlemen of Verona
- Winter's Tale

History

- Henry IV, part 1
- Henry IV, part 2
- Henry V
- Henry VI, part 1
- Henry VI, part 2
- Henry VI, part 3
- Henry VIII
- King John
- Richard II
- Richard III

Tragedy

- Antony and
- Cleopatra
- Coriolanus
- Hamlet
- Julius Caesar
- King Lear
- Macbeth
- Othello
- Romeo and Juliet
- Timon of Athens
- Titus Andronicus

Poetry

- The Sonnets
- A Lover's
- Complaint
- The Rape of
- Lucrece
- Venus and Adonis
- Funeral Elegy by W.S.

Chapter 12

Important Aspects of Elizabethan Drama

The Elizabethan Age in the world occurred in the sixteenth and seventeenth century in England. It is named for Queen Elizabeth, who is known mainly for her love of religion of the arts. The Elizabethan Age was most influential through its drama. The Elizabethan Age in England showered the world with a burst of brilliant playwrights. Four of the most well known of early Elizabethan playwrights were John Lyly, Thomas Kyd, Robert Greene, and Christopher Marlowe. John Lyly's most famous work is "Endimion, Man in Moon." Thomas Kyd is the author of "Spanish Tragedy." Robert Greene is best known for "Friar Bacon Friar Bungay." Many people think that Christopher Marlowe was the greatest of early Elizabethan writers. His most well known play is "Doctor Faustus." This play is about a man named Faustus who sells his soul to the devil in exchange for power on earth. Christopher Marlowe was born shortly before William Shakespeare. He was supposed to be a shoemaker.

The Archbishop of Canterbury offered him a scholarship to Cambridge University, but Christopher avoided becoming shoemaker to enter the theater. He started writing plays for an acting company called the Admiral's Men. His major literary works were tragedies, as lots of Elizabethan dramas were. Other than "Doctor Faustus", his other two greatest works were "Tamburlaine" and "Jew of Malta." Marlowe's major literary achievements are the use of refined blank verse, spiritual drama, dramatic action, and the Renaissance hero.

He loved learning and hated ignorance. This was apparent in many of his literary works. Marlowe was a friend of Sir Walter Raleigh and a favourite of Queen Elizabeth, even though records show that Marlowe was not gentleman. Christopher Marlowe's roommate accused him of atheism and treason, which were crimes in that time. Records show that he was involved in two tavern brawls. In one of the brawls, a man lost his life. In the other brawl, Marlowe was stabbed in the eye. He died three days later. Conspiracy has been suspected about his death. Marlowe, Lyly, Kyd, Greene are known as the University Wits. They defined the London Theater.

William Shakespeare wrote in the middle of the Elizabethan Period, and he is the most famous writer in the era; maybe the greatest of all time. His plays have very good plots, characterization, and backgrounds. Other than tragedy, which was the most common drama of the time, Shakespeare wrote great comedies, tragicomedies, and histories. His characters come alive, and they are admired and even envied by people. His plots are full of action. "Hamlet" was the most popular of his tragedies. Shakespeare's most successful comedy was "A Midsummer Night's Dream." Perhaps his most famous tragicomedy was "The Tempest". "Richard III" and Henry V" are two of Shakespeare's histories that have been made into motion pictures. Shakespeare combined the best aspects of Elizabethan drama with classic drama. This enriched his imagination and humour. The age of Shakespeare was a great time in English history.

There are many important events that occurred during the Elizabethan Period. In approximately 1477, Caxton set up a printing press, and he printed the first books in England. Around 1500, "Everyman", a morality play, was written and performed. In 1533, John Heywood's "The Play of the Weather" was performed. A poetry collection called "Tottle's Miscellany" was published in 1557. This work included Wyatt and Surrey's sonnets. Besides drama, the sonnet is the epitome of literature in the Elizabethan period. In 1564, William Shakespeare and Christopher Marlowe were born. "The Theatre", the first permanent structure for plays in England, was constructed in 1576. Christopher Marlowe directed his first play, "Tamburlaine", in 1587. In 1590, Shakespeare directed his first play, "The Comedy of Errors." Christopher Marlowe wrote "The Jew of Malta"a year later. He was killed in 1593. Shakespeare wrote "The Merchant of Venice" in 1597. In 1599, the Globe Theater was constructed. Shakespeare wrote "Macbeth" in 1605. He died in 1616.

Another very important aspect of Elizabethan Drama was the audiences. The audiences were always large and very excited at plays. The common people paid an equivalent to one penny to sit in the front of the theater. Unless it was raining, these people had the best seats in the theater. The audience would participate in the play by cheering, hissing, or even throwing rotten vegetables. The audience would know that plays were about to be performed by a flag that rose over the theater. The theater played an important role in this era. Without theaters, there would be nowhere for the play to be performed. There were two types of theaters: indoor and outdoor. Outdoor theaters were public theaters. "The Theatre" is an example of an outdoor theater. Indoor theaters were private theaters.

Elizabethan Actors were all male. Females were not allowed to act in the theater. All female parts were played by men whose voices had not changed yet. Actors had to have good memories, strong voices, and the ability to fence. Actors also had to have the ability to sing and dance. The costumes that the actors wore were very elaborate, but not historic.

Many special effects were used in the theater. Death scenes were very gory and realistic. To show an eye falling out, a grape would fall to the floor. Animal organs were used to show scenes where organs fell out of actors' bodies.

The stage was the centre of the theater. It had several levels. The lowest level of the stage was used for a number of things. Devils, ghosts, graves, and ditched are a few of them. The second level was the main stage. This is where the most important scenes were. The third level of the stage was a balcony. It was used for a number of things such as mountains or city walls. The fourth level of the stage was a series of pulleys where angels, birds, and thunderbolts could be sent down from the main stage. The highest level was a room where the musicians were. There is one aspect of Elizabethan Drama that still remains a mystery. Vocabulary in the Elizabethan Era was very different than it is now. Modern historians are not sure about all of the word meanings. This is why some of the phrases used are hard to understand.

Elizabethan Drama is a very important addition to the literature world and to England. Drama is part of England's heritage, and helps make them who they are. The most important aspects of Elizabethan Drama are is playwrights, events, audiences, theaters, actors, speech, special effects, and the stage. These things make it up, and help keep it alive. Elizabethan Drama is very important in literature.

Chapter 13

The History of the Globe Theater

The first proper theater as we know it was called the Theatre, built at Shoreditch, London in 1576 and the owner was James Burbage. James Burbage had obtained a 21 year lease with permission to build the first playhouse, aptly named ' The Theatre '.

Before this time plays were performed in the courtyard of inns or inn-yards, or sometimes, in the houses of noblemen or in extreme circumstances on open ground. After the Theatre, further open-air playhouses (theaters) opened in the London area, including the Rose Theatre (1587), and the Hope Theatre (1613). The most famous Elizabethan playhouse (theater) was the Globe Theatre (1599) built by the company in which Shakespeare had a stake - now often referred to as the Shakespearean Globe.

The Lease of the 'Theatre' Expires

The 21 year lease for the ground upon which The Theatre had been built was due to expire at the end of 1597. The ground landlord of The Theater was called Giles Allen. A grasping man, he disapproved of theatrical productions, the theatre in general, and raised the price of the lease of The Theatre to an exorbitant level.

The troupe failed to agree new terms and when the lease of The Theatre finally expired, the Chamberlain's men were forced to move to The Curtain Theater, another public playing house near The Theatre. All attempts to negotiate the new tenancy and lease agreement of The Theatre failed and Giles Allen planned to pull down the Theatre and capitalize on the building materials. But Burbage found a clause in their former lease allowing them to dismantle the Theatre building.

The players decided to pull down The Theatre and transport the timber to a new Theater site on Bankside in Southwark. The work of demolishing the Theatre and transporting the timber across the River Thames was noisily undertaken by the Acting Troupe themselves. Giles Allen was absolutely furious. A new theatre would be built learning from both the mistakes and successes of the original ' Theatre '. The new theater was called The Globe.

The Globe Theater, Bankside in Southward, London

The Globe, built by carpenter Peter Smith and his workers, was the most magnificent theater that London had ever seen and built in 1597 -1598. This theatre could hold several thousand people! The Globe Theatre didn't just show plays. It was also reputed to be a brothel and gambling house. It was situated on the South bank of the river Thames in Southward. The old Globe Theatre was a magnificent amphitheàtre, as shown in the picture at the top of the page. Maps of London clearly show the architecture of the Globe Theatre, and these have enabled an approximate picture of the old Globe Theatre to be drawn.

Not one inside picture of the old Globe Theatre is in existence, however, a picture of another amphitheatre, the Swan, has survived. The amphitheatres were similar in design, so the picture of the Swan Theatre can be used a good guide to the structure of the old Globe.

The Globe Theater is a huge success

The Globe Theatre was a huge success and as it had been built in close proximity to the Bear Garden. The profits of the Bear Garden slumped and in 1614, Henslowe and Edward Alleyn (the most famous actor in Elizabethan England) had it demolished and replaced with a new playhouse, which they called The Hope Theatre (aptly named!). Edward Alleyn returned to the stage in an attempt to lure the crowds from The Globe Theatre.

The Globe Theater the Plays

Plays were big! There was money to be made! There was a constant demand for new material! Rivalry between the Theatres Playhouses was enormous! As soon as a play had been written it was immediately produced - printing followed productions! So the actors initially used 'foul papers' or prompts. Rival theater companies would send their members to attend plays to produce unauthorized copies of plays - notes were made and copied as quickly as possible. In Shakespeare's time, copyright did not exist. Alternative versions of Shakespearean plays were produced! These unauthorized and inferior text copies of Shakespeare's plays are called Quarto Texts. The success of the Elizabethan theaters, including the Globe, was such that other forms of Elizabethan entertainment were being seriously affected. In 1591, the growing popularity of theatres led to a law closing all theaters on Thursdays so that the bull and bear bating industries would not be neglected!

The Globe Theater the Event

Days out at the Globe Theater would have been an exciting event. The grounds surrounding the Globe Theater would have been bustling with people. There would be Stalls selling merchandise and refreshments creating a market day atmosphere. Non-playgoers would flock to the Globe Theater to go to the market stalls and 'soak in ' the holiday-like atmosphere. The Globe would have particularly attracted young people and the were many complaints of apprentices avoiding work in order to go to the theater. A trumpet was sounded to announce to people that the play was about to begin at the Globe Theatre in order for people to take their final places.

Elizabethan Advertising

Towering above the Globe was a small tower with a flagpole. Flags were used as a form of Elizabethan Advertising! Flags were erected on the day of the performance, which sometimes displayed a picture advertising the next play to be performed. Colour-coding was also used - a black flag meant a tragedy, white a comedy and red a history. Elizabethan and Shakespearean Advertising

The Globe Theatre's crest and motto

To announce the arrival of the new playhouse, the Lord Chamberlain's Men flew a flag featuring the figure of Hercules carrying a Globe on his shoulders to announce the imminent performance of their first performance, Julius Caesar. This theme was displayed above the main entrance of the Globe Theater. A crest displaying Hercules bearing the globe on his shoulders together with the motto "Totus mundus agit histrionem" (the whole world is a playhouse). This phrase was slightly re-worded in the William Shakespeare play As You Like It - "All the world's a stage" which was performed at the Globe Theater.

The Globe Theater the Productions

The purpose built Globe theatre allowed stage productions to become quite sophisticated with the use of massive props such as fully working canons, although it would of course had to be left on stage for the entire performance of the play. Special effects at the Globe were also a spectacular addition at the theater allowing for smoke effects, the firing of a real canon, fireworks (for dramatic battle scenes) and spectacular 'flying' entrances from the rigging in the 'heavens'. The stage floor had trap doors allowing for additional surprising incidents. Music was another addition to the Globe productions. It was no wonder that the Globe Theater and this form of Elizabethan entertainment were so popular. The sight of Shakespearean actors apparently flying must have been quite amazing to the discerning Elizabethan Theater audiences.

The Globe Theater the Actors

The Globe Theater audience never had time to get bored. In just two weeks, Elizabethan theaters could often present "eleven performances of ten different plays". The Shakespearean Actors generally only got their lines as the play was in progress. Parts were often allocated on the day of the performance. Many times the actors didn't even get their own lines. They did "cue acting ", which meant that there was a person backstage who whispered the lines to the actor just before he was going to say them. This rapid turnover led to another technique called "cue scripting", where each actor was given only his own lines.

The complete scene of the play was not explained to the actors until it was actually being performed. This technique allowed for zero rehearsal time, thus enabling a fast turnover in terms of new productions at the Globe Theater and a huge portfolio of different roles. There were no actresses. Female characters had to be played by young boys. The acting profession was not a credible one and it was unthinkable that any woman would appear in a play. Two of the most notable actors of the Elizabethan era were Edward Alleyn and Will Kempe. Edward Alleyn became immensely wealthy due to stake holding in a theatre company (the Admiral's men).

The Globe Theater Audiences

The Elizabethan general public (the Commoners) referred to, as groundlings would pay 1 penny to stand in the 'Pit' of the Globe Theater. The gentry would pay to sit in the galleries often using cushions for comfort! Rich nobles could watch the play from a chair set on the side of the Globe stage itself. Theatre performances were held in the afternoon, because, of course, there was no artificial lighting. Men and women attended plays, but often the prosperous women would wear a mask to disguise their identity. The plays were extremely popular and attracted vast audiences to the Globe. The audiences only dropped during outbreaks of the bubonic plague, which was unfortunately an all too common occurrence during the Elizabethan era. This happened in 1593, 1603 and 1608 when all theaters were closed due to the Bubonic Plague (The Black Death). The Shakespearean actors were therefore temporary out of work and left London to stay in other parts of England. William Shakespeare no doubt used these periods of closure to write more plays and go home to Stratford.

The 'Box Office'

Globe audiences had to put one penny in a box by the door, which would pay for a view of the play by standing on the ground, in front of the stage. To sit on the first gallery would cost another penny in the box, which was held by a collector on the front of the stairs. To sit on the second gallery, you put another penny in the box held by the man at the second flight of stairs.

Then when the show started, the men went and put the boxes in a room backstage - the Elizabethan box office. Profits there were shared between members of the Globe company as such and the owners of the theatre (called "housekeepers"), who included the James and his son the actor Richard Burbage and five others, one of them was William Shakespeare. Shakespeare received approximately 10% of the profit although he had a 20% stake holding in the troupe, as James Burbage owned the lease for the land that the Globe Theater was built on.

Shakespeare the Actor

William Shakespeare had a stake holding in the Globe Theatre and also acted in some of the productions of the plays. It is not known exactly how many roles Shakespeare played himself, although we do have some documented information. Shakespeare had began his career on the stage by 1592, because there is a surviving document by Robert Greene' Groatsworth. It is probable that Shakespeare played the title role in Edward I (a play by Edward Peele) in 1593.

It is also assumed that Shakespeare played smaller roles in a variety of his own plays, including As You Like It (Adam), Macbeth (King Duncan), Henry IV (King Henry), and Hamlet (Hamlet's father). Shakespeare's first biographer, Nicholas Rowe, referring to a role by William Shakespeare as "the Ghost in his own Hamlet" and was "the top of his performance".

Plays and Propaganda

Strolling players of actors had been popular for centuries in England but as there were no initial regulations it was possible to use plays as a vehicle for propaganda. Plays could be used to encourage criticism of the state and freedom of thought in terms of both religion and politics. Queen Elizabeth, ever concerned about her popularity with the people, realized that although it would be prudent to enforce some regulations that it would be foolhardy to apply too many restrictions. She had controlled the troupes of strolling players in 1572 by granting a license by royal patent to organized acting companies, thus initiating legitimate troupes such as Earl of Leicester's Men. Any Elizabethan players might at any time be required to show their credentials. And under Queen Elizabeth, political and religious subjects were forbidden on the stage. Plays still however often led to heated debates in the theaters and arguments erupted. The subject matter of the plays would often be vulgar and bawdy. The behaviour of some the audience was the worse! The theatres didn't just show plays. Some also served as a bear pit, brothel and gambling house. Crime increased at the theaters and following the performances, the crowds were noisy and unruly. The vast crowds and the popularity of the London Theaters needed some additional controls. Published plays soon required a license, which provided a form of censorship by the state.

The Theaters are banned from London City Limits

The objections to the theaters escalated and the Church, London Officials and respectable citizens raised even more objections to the theatres. Theaters were not only used to show plays. There was gambling and in some there was even bear baiting. Not only were there objections about the bawdy nature of some of the plays, the rise in crime but there was also the real risk of the crowded theatres encouraging the spread of the plague. The reputation of actors was remained disreputable, a legacy from the rogues and vagabonds who had previously roamed the country putting on plays and their classification as "vagabonds and sturdy beggars," in a 1572 act of Parliament. In December 1574, the Common Council of London, under the influences of puritanical factions, issued a statement describing:

" great disorder rampant in the city by the inordinate haunting of great multitudes of people, especially youth, to plays, interludes, namely occasion of frays and quarrels, evil practices of incontinency in great inns having chambers and secret places adjoining to their open stages and galleries, inveigling and alluring of maids, especially of orphans and good citizens' children under age, to privy and unmeet contracts, the publishing of unchaste, uncomely, and unshamefast speeches and doings... uttering of popular, busy, and seditious matters, and many other corruptions of youth and other enormities... Thus from henceforth no play, comedy, tragedy, interlude, not public show shall be openly played or showed within the liberties of the City... and that no innkeeper, tavernkeeper, nor other person whatsoever within the liberties of this City shall openly show or play... any interlude, comedy, tragedy, matter, or show which shall not be first perused and allowed..."

The outcry continued and grew so much that in 1596 London's authorities banned the public presentation of plays and all theaters within the city limits of London. All theaters located in the City were forced to move to the South side of the River Thames.

The Globe Theater the Fire and the re-building of the Globe Theatre

The Globe was only in use until 1613, when on June 29 a fire broke out at the Globe Theatre. The canon used for special affects, such as heralding great entrances, was loaded with gunpowder and wadding. The thatched roof caught on fire and the Globe Theatre burned to the ground. It is not known whether there were any casualties but there must have been some panic. In 1614, the Globe Theatre was rebuilt (referred to as Globe 2).

The End of the Globe Theater - the Puritans

In 1642, under the force of the Puritans, the English Parliament issued an ordinance suppressing all stage plays in the theatres. The Puritans were a religious faction and the term came into general usage at the end of the reign of Queen Mary I (Bloody Mary). A broad definition of the puritans is 'those who wanted to completely change the Church of England, with its Roman Catholic type of structure and traditions, for another reformed and plain church model'. This strict religious view spread to encompass many social activities within England moving to a stricter code of conduct, which deplored any kind of finery or flippant behaviours. 1642 was a truly eventful year for England.

The Puritans, lead by Oliver Cromwell, who had been elected to Parliament came into total conflict with the Royalists lead by King Charles I. The English Civil war broke out. In 1644, the Puritans demolished the Globe Theatre. In 1647, even stricter rules were passed regarding stage plays and theatres. This culminated in 1648 when all playhouses were ordered to be pulled down. All players were to be seized and whipped, and anyone caught attending a play to be fined five shillings. In 1649, the Civil War finally leads to the terrible execution of King Charles I. In 1653, Oliver Cromwell becomes Lord Protector of England. In 1658, Cromwell dies and the power of the Puritan starts to decline. In 1660, King Charles II is restored to the throne of England. With the Restoration of the English monarchy and, and the demise in the power of the Puritans in 1660 the theatres finally open again. But the Globe is never re-built.

Chapter 14

William Shakespeare and Existentialism

One may find it ridiculous to contrast between Shakespeare and existentialism in its 20th century form, however one must keep in mind, that existentialism does not appear as a single philosophical system. It is more an attitude of life, a General vision - existentialist Jean-Paul Sartre is known to have stated that existentialism was never invented, it has always existed as the ultimate foundation. Upon that light, why not seek the foundations from the work of the forefather of all dramatists?

It is above all naïve to claim Prospero's epilogue in Shakespeare's play The Tempest a mere conventional appeal for applause or the stripping of the imaginary glamour built up by the plays magic. Even the greatest of artists would rather give away his life than surrender his art to be judged solely by the public. Art for an artistic genius is practiced for its own sake, art for the purpose of art. Existence for the sake of existence itself - stripped of meaning, of value and of subjective interpretation. In its bear meaningless form, something still remains the necessary Natural Law, a philosophical concept considered the basis of human well-being, a system of the values that determine human existence.

Throughout The Tempest Prospero's character portrays an image of a nearly Nietzchean superhuman capable of disclaiming authority, killing God. He is in control of every situation and event as if the chain of causes and effects would be a conductible melody waiting for an artist's touch. On the other hand, he is very human: a wronged duke and a father, a symbiosis which Shakespeare displayed with the use of Prospero's garment as a theatrical tool. An artist is the creator, the maker of realities yet he remains human, an animal with feelings and urges, ties only waiting to be cut. The view implied is not far from the ideologies that emerged from the great suffering of the second world war: a man is capable of constructing himself a framework of personal and social meaning, but his true animal nature remains unchanged. In the heart of existence, life has no predefined meaning, it is a mere passage of survival from necessary birth to necessary death. Prospero's and his daughter's situation on the island was hopeless, however Prospero had chosen a function for his life - revenge.

Prospero created a meaning for his life, built a synthetic reality to keep him sane on the path towards the finality of human death. Early existentialism begins to appear.

The literatory image behind The Epilogue of The Tempest greatly involves the attitude and interpretation of art. Having constructed a window or more or less a door to an imaginary world for the audience, Shakespeare has succeeded in fusing art and reality. Upon that light, it is incomprehensible to assume his need to address the subjective yet neutral third party, the audience - shatter the synthetic reality. However, The Epilogue is a beautiful and humble ending to a story filled with strong magical elements - the control is given to the audience, they are given Prospero's magical garment. The passive third party is given a choice of interaction, chance to rise beyond spectatorship. An interesting aspect to The Epilogue of The Tempest is the fact that it was Shakespeare's last play - the final words of a great artist. Due to the lack of historically trustworthy biographical information of Shakespeare's character, it is difficult if not impossible to determine the effect of his life situation to the message itself. Whether justified or not, The Epilogue seems like a farewell - a humble artist handing over his life to the audience to which he has dedicated his entire life.

When examining The Epilogue with the restriction of

intertextuality, one is forced to focus on the character of Prospero. Why does he leave a farewell, why does he become the ultimate link from the world of the play to the world of the third party, the audience. His importance as the narrator of The Epilogue creates a third dimension to his character traits, he becomes the God-figure that seems limited to living on an island yet he can Perform metaphysical leaps between dimensions. The person speaking is the author himself, for in his art he has become God.

Rhythmically and structurally, The Epilogue follows the same style and pattern as the entire play, rich in Rhyme and in wording. The passage can be more or less distinctly separated into three equal parts. However, every detail gives space for wide interpretation.

Now my charms are all o'erthrown, / And what strength I have's mine own, Whish is most faint: now, 'tis true, / I must be here confin'd by you, Or sent to Naples. Let me not, / Since I have my dukedom got, The main structure of The Epilogue can be interpreted as the passage of a life. First the narrator enters the game of existence, appears from the womb: "And what strength I have's my own." As strongly claimed by Jean-Paul Sartre's metaphysics, birth to a person is a subjectively chosen process, emerged from the "charms" that are now, after birth "all o'erthrown". Using the presented division birth is followed by life itself, a search for a meaning and true freedom: "But release me from my bands." The narrator realizes his situation on the island of life, in the world derived of meaning and purpose. He wants to be released from his misery - the only way he can achieve that is making his life worthwhile - giving up life would be a crime against Natural Law.

And pardon'd the deceiver, dwell / In this bear island by your spell; But release me from my bands / With the help of your good hands: The last segment of The Epilogue requests freedom by final death. The narrator has realized the purpose he has constructed for his life has been fully fulfilled. He wants to die with peace - he seeks acknowledgement for his life's successful passage. "As you from crimes would pardon'd be, / Let your indulgence set me free." Gentle breathe of yours my sails / Must fill, or else my project fails, Which was to please. Now I want / Spirits to enforce, Art to enchant;

And my ending in despair, / Unless I be reliev'd by prayer, Which pierces so, that it assaults / Mercy itself, and frees all faults. As you from crimes would pardon'd be, / Let your indulgence set me free.

One view The Epilogue can be examined upon is the fact that the artist, be it Shakespeare or Prospero as his creation declares himself detached from moral ties directed to towards the third party and, with reference to Prospero's use of power, the other characters of the play. This is a very important aspect in both the general basis of human nature and as the driving force of the artist, in this case Shakespeare. The Epilogue clearly claims that the cause-effect event-chain created by the artist was built free of ties - therefore to be judged with the appropriate honesty and freedom of attitude. One may question the necessity for such a statement, but considering the importance of theatre during Shakespeare's era, it has certain logicality. Just as a true human, the human of the Natural Laws, is justified to assume a superhuman position, an artist, the creator, is justified to practice unconditional freedom.

Freedom is and element of the Natural Law - the system of necessities to justify a meaningful existence. However, as the French philosopher Jean-Paul Sartre stated, freedom necessarily involves the property of responsibility. Man has unconditional freedom and self-defined moral ties yet he is responsible for following his own will with regard to his own value system. If responsibility is not utilized, man takes s step towards animal qualities, he does not fulfill the Natural Law. A similar pattern of freedom and responsibilities is presented in The Epilogue. Shakespeare has utilized unconditional freedom not only in his art but also in giving respect to the audience as the object of amusement: "Gentle breathe of yours my sails / Must fill, or else my project fails, / which was to please. Now I want / Spirits to enforce, Art to enchant."

Chapter 15

Preface to Shakespeare: Text

That praises are without reason lavished on the dead, and that the honours due only to excellence are paid to antiquity, is a complaint likely to be always continued by those, who, being able to add nothing to truth, hope for eminence from the heresies of paradox; or those, who, being forced by disappointment upon consolatory expedients, are willing to hope from posterity what the present age refuses, and flatter themselves that the regard which is yet denied by envy, will be at last bestowed by time.

Antiquity, like every other quality that attracts the notice of mankind, has undoubtedly votaries that reverence it, not from reason, but from prejudice. Some seem to admire indiscriminately whatever has been long preserved, without considering that time has sometimes co-operated with chance; all perhaps are more willing to honour past than present excellence; and the mind contemplates genius through the shades of age, as the eye surveys the sun through artificial opacity. The great contention of criticism is to find the faults of the moderns, and the beauties of the ancients. While an author is yet living we estimate his powers by his worst performance, and when he is dead we rate them by his best. avour.

As among the works of nature no man can properly call a river deep or a mountain high, without the knowledge of many mountains and many rivers; so in the productions of genius, nothing can be stilled excellent till it has been compared with other works of the same kind. Demonstration immediately displays its power, and has nothing to hope or fear from the flux of years; but works tentative and experimental must be estimated by their proportion to the general and collective ability of man, as it is discovered in a long succession of endeavours.

Of the first building that was raised, it might be with certainty determined that it was round or square, but whether it was spacious or lofty must have been referred to time. The Pythagorean scale of numbers was at once discovered to be perfect; but the poems of Homer we yet know not to transcend the common limits of human intelligence, but by remarking, that nation after nation, and century after century, has been able to do little more than transpose his incidents, new name his characters, and paraphrase his sentiments.

The reverence due to writings that have long subsisted arises therefore not from any credulous confidence in the superior wisdom of past ages, or gloomy persuasion of the degeneracy of mankind, but is the consequence of acknowledged and indubitable positions, that what has been longest known has been most considered, and what is most considered is best understood.

The Poet, of whose works I have undertaken the revision, may now begin to assume the dignity of an ancient, and claim the privilege of established fame and prescriptive veneration. He has long outlived his century, the term commonly fixed as the test of literary merit. Whatever advantages he might once derive from personal allusions, local customs, or temporary opinions, have for many years been lost; and every topic of merriment or motive of sorrow, which the modes of artificial life afforded him, now only obscure the scenes which they once illuminated.

The effects of favour and competition are at an end; the tradition of his friendships and his enmities has perished; his works support no opinion with arguments, nor supply any faction with invectives; they can neither indulge vanity nor gratify malignity, but are read without any other reason than the desire of pleasure, and are therefore praised only as pleasure is obtained; yet, thus unassisted by interest or passion, they have past through variations of taste and changes of manners, and, as they devolved from one generation to another, have received new honours at every transmission.

But because human judgment, though it be gradually gaining upon certainty, never becomes infallible; and approbation, though long continued, may yet be only the approbation of prejudice or fashion; it is proper to inquire, by what peculiarities of excellence Shakespeare has gained and kept the favour of his countrymen.

Nothing can please many, and please long, but just representations of general nature. Particular manners can be known to few, and therefore few only can judge how nearly they are copied. The irregular combinations of fanciful invention may delight a-while, by that novelty of which the common satiety of life sends us all in quest; but the pleasures of sudden wonder are soon exhausted, and the mind can only repose on the stability of truth. Shakespeare is above all writers, at least above all modern writers, the poet of nature; the poet that holds up to his readers a faithful mirrour of manners and of life. His characters are not modified by the customs of particular places, unpracticed by the rest of the world; by the peculiarities of studies or professions, which can operate but upon small numbers; or by the accidents of transient fashions or temporary opinions: they are the genuine progeny of common humanity, such as the world will always supply, and observation will always find.

His persons act and speak by the influence of those general passions and principles by which all minds are agitated, and the whole system of life is continued in motion. In the writings of other poets a character is too often an individual; in those of Shakespeare it is commonly a species. It is from this wide extension of design that so much instruction is derived. It is this which fills the plays of Shakespeare with practical axioms and domestic wisdom. It was said of Euripides, that every verse was a precept and it may be said of Shakespeare, that from his works may be collected a system of civil and economical prudence. Yet his real power is not shown in the splendor of particular passages, but by the progress of his fable, and the tenor of his dialogue; and he that tries to recommend him by select quotations, will succeed like the pedant in Hierocles, who, when he offered his house to sale, carried a brick in his pocket as a specimen.

It will not easily be imagined how much Shakespeare excels in accommodating his sentiments to real life, but by comparing him with other authors. It was observed of the ancient schools of declamation, that the more diligently they were frequented, the more was the student disqualified for the world, because he found nothing there which he should ever meet in any other place. The same remark may be applied to every stage but that of Shakespeare.

The theatre, when it is under any other direction, is peopled by such characters as were never seen, conversing in a language which was never heard, upon topics which will never arise in the commerce of mankind. But the dialogue of this author is often so evidently determined by the incident which produces it, and is pursued with so much ease and simplicity, that it seems scarcely to claim the merit of fiction, but to have been gleaned by diligent selection out of common conversation, and common occurrences. Upon every other stage the universal agent is love, by whose power all good and evil is distributed, and every action quickened or retarded. To bring a lover, a lady and a rival into the fable; to entangle them in contradictory obligations, perplex them with oppositions of interest, and harass them with violence of desires inconsistent with each other; to make them meet in rapture and part in agony; to fill their mouths with hyperbolical joy and outrageous sorrow; to distress them as nothing human ever was distressed; to deliver them as nothing human ever was delivered, is the business of a modern dramatist.

For this probability is violated, life is misrepresented, and language is depraved. But love is only one of many passions, and as it has no great influence upon the sum of life, it has little operation in the dramas of a poet, who caught his ideas from the living world, and exhibited only what he saw before him. He knew, that any other passion, as it was regular or exorbitant, was a cause of happiness or calamity.

Characters thus ample and general were not easily

discriminated and preserved, yet perhaps no poet ever kept his personages more distinct from each other. I will not say with Pope, that every speech may be assigned to the proper speaker, because many speeches there are which have nothing characteristical; but, perhaps, though some may be equally adapted to every person, it will be difficult to find, any that can be properly transferred from the present possessor to another claimant.

The choice is right, when there is reason for choice. Other dramatists can only gain attention by hyperbolical or aggravated characters, by fabulous and unexampled excellence or depravity, as the writers of barbarous romances invigorated the reader by a giant and a dwarf; and he that should form his expectations of human affairs from the play, or from the tale, would be equally deceived. Shakespeare has no heroes; his scenes are occupied only by men, who act and speak as the reader thinks that he should himself have spoken or acted on the same occasion: Even where the agency is supernatural the dialogue is level with life.

Other writers disguise the most natural passions and most frequent incidents: so that he who contemplates them in the book will not know them in the world: Shakespeare approximates the remote, and familiarizes the wonderful; the event which he represents will not happen, but if it were possible, its effects would be probably such as he has assigned; and it may be said, that he has not only shown human nature as it acts in real exigences, but as it would be found in trials, to which it cannot be exposed.

This therefore is the praise of Shakespeare, that his drama is the mirrour of life; that he who has mazed his imagination, in following the phantoms which other writers raise up before him, may here be cured of his delirious extasies, by reading human sentiments in human language; by scenes from which a hermit may estimate the transactions of the world, and a confessor predict the progress of the passions.

His adherence to general nature has exposed him to the censure of critics, who form their judgments upon narrower principles. Dennis and Rhymer think his Romans not sufficiently Roman; and Voltaire censures his kings as not completely royal. Dennis is offended, that Menenius, a senator of Rome, should play the buffoon; and Voltaire perhaps thinks decency violated when the Danish Usurper is represented as a drunkard. But Shakespeare always makes nature predominate over accident; and if he preserves the essential character, is not very careful of distinctions super induced and adventitious.

His story requires Romans or kings, but he thinks only on men. He knew that Rome, like every other city, had men of all dispositions; and wanting a buffoon, he went into the senate-house for that which the senate-house would certainly have afforded him. He was inclined to show an usurper and a murderer not only odious but despicable, he therefore added drunkenness to his other qualities, knowing that kings love wine like other men, and that wine exerts its natural power upon kings. These are the petty cavils of petty minds; a poet overlooks the casual distinction of country and condition, as a painter, satisfied with the figure, neglects the drapery.

The censure which he has incurred by mixing comic and tragic scenes, as it extends to all his works, deserves more consideration. Let the fact be first stated, and then examined. Shakespeare's plays are not in the rigorous and critical sense either tragedies or comedies, but compositions of a distinct kind; exhibiting the real state of sublunary nature, which partakes of good and evil, joy and sorrow, mingled with endless variety of proportion and innumerable modes of combination; and expressing the course of the world, in which the loss of one is the gain of another; in which, at the same time, the reveler is hasting to his wine, and the mourner burying his friend; in which the malignity of one is sometimes defeated by the frolic of another; many mischiefs and many benefits are done and hindered without design.

Out of this chaos of mingled purposes and casualties the ancient poets, according to the laws which custom had prescribed, selected some the crimes of men, and some their absurdities; some the momentous vicissitudes of life, and some the lighter occurrences; some the terrors of distress, and some the gayeties of prosperity. Thus rose the two modes of imitation, known by the names of tragedy and comedy, compositions intended to promote different ends by contrary means, and considered as so little allied, that I do not recollect among the Greeks or Romans a single writer who attempted both. Shakespeare has united the powers of exciting laughter and sorrow not only in one mind, but in one composition. Almost all his plays are divided between serious and ludicrous characters, and, in the successive evolutions of the design, sometimes produce seriousness and sorrow, and sometimes levity and laughter.

That this is a practice contrary to the rules of criticism will be readily allowed; but there is always an appeal open from criticism to nature. The end of writing is to instruct; the end of poetry is to instruct by pleasing. That the mingled drama may convey all the instruction of tragedy or comedy cannot be denied, because it includes both in its alterations of exhibition, and approaches nearer than either to the appearance of life, by showing how great machinations and slender designs may promote or obviate one another, and the high and the low co-operate in the general system by unavoidable concatenation.

It is objected, that by this change of scenes the passions are interrupted in their progression, and that the principal event, being not advanced by a due gradation of preparatory incidents, wants at last the power to move, which constitutes the perfection of dramatic poetry. This reasoning is so specious, that it is received as true even by those who in daily experience feel it to be false. The interchanges of mingled scenes seldom fail to produce the intended vicissitudes of passion. Fiction cannot move so much, but that the attention may be easily transferred; and though it must be allowed that pleasing melancholy be sometimes interrupted by unwelcome levity, yet let it be considered likewise, that melancholy is often not pleasing, and that the disturbance of one man may be the relief of another; that different auditors have different habitudes; and that, upon the whole, all pleasure consists in variety.

The players, who in their edition divided our author's

works into comedies, histories, and tragedies, seem not to have distinguished the three kinds, by any very exact or definite ideas.

An action, which ended happily to the principal persons, however serious or distressful through its intermediate incidents, in their opinion constituted a comedy. This idea of a comedy continued long amongst us, and plays were written, which, by changing the catastrophe, were tragedies to-day and comedies to-morrow.

Tragedy was not in those times a poem of more general dignity or elevation than comedy; it required only a calamitous conclusion, with which the common criticism of that age was satisfied, whatever lighter pleasure it afforded in its progress.

History was a series of actions, with no other than chronological succession, independent of each other, and without any tendency to introduce or regulate the conclusion. It is not always very nicely distinguished from tragedy. There is not much nearer approach to unity of action in the tragedy of "Antony and Cleopatra", than in the history of "Richard the Second". But a history might be continued through many plays; as it had no plan, it had no limits.

Through all these denominations of the drama, Shakespeare's mode of composition is the same; an interchange of seriousness and merriment, by which the mind is softened at one time, and exhilarated at another. But whatever be his purpose, whether to gladden or depress, or to conduct the story, without vehemence or emotion, through tracts of easy and familiar dialogue, he never fails to attain his purpose; as he commands us, we laugh or mourn, or sit silent with quiet expectation, in tranquility without indifference. When Shakespeare's plan is understood, most of the criticisms of Rhymer and Voltaire vanish away.

The play of "Hamlet" is opened, without impropriety, by two sentinels; Iago bellows at Brabantio's window, without injury to the scheme of the play, though in terms which a modern audience would not easily endure; the character of Polonius is seasonable and useful; and the Grave-diggers themselves may be heard with applause. Shakespeare engaged in dramatic poetry with the world open before him; the rules of the ancients were yet known to few; the public judgment was unformed; he had no example of such fame as might force him upon imitation, nor critics of such authority as might restrain his extravagance: He therefore indulged his natural disposition, and his disposition, as Rhymer has remarked, led him to comedy.

In tragedy he often writes with great appearance of toil and study, what is written at last with little felicity; but in his comic scenes, he seems to produce without labour, what no labour can improve. In tragedy he is always struggling after some occasion to be comic, but in comedy he seems to repose, or to luxuriate, as in a mode of thinking congenial to his nature. In his tragic scenes there is always something wanting, but his comedy often surpasses expectation or desire. His comedy pleases by the thoughts and the language, and his tragedy for the greater part by incident and action. His tragedy seems to be skill, his comedy to be instinct. The force of his comic scenes has suffered little diminution from the changes made by a century and a half, in manners or in words.

As his personages act upon principles arising from genuine passion, very little modified by particular forms, their pleasures and vexations are communicable to all times and to all places; they are natural, and therefore durable; the adventitious peculiarities of personal habits, are only superficial dies, bright and pleasing for a little while, yet soon fading to a dim tinct, without any remains of former luster; but the discriminations of true passion are the colours of nature; they pervade the whole mass, and can only perish with the body that exhibits them. The accidental compositions of heterogeneous modes are dissolved by the chance which combined them; but the uniform simplicity of primitive qualities neither admits increase, nor suffers decay.

The sand heaped by one flood is scattered by another, but the rock always continues in its place. The stream of time, which is continually washing the dissoluble fabricsf of other poets, passes without injury by the adamant of Shakespeare. If there be, what I believe there is, in every nation, a stile which never becomes obsolete, a certain mode of phraseology so consonant and congenial to the analogy and principles of its respective language as to remain settled and unaltered; this stile is probably to be sought in the common intercourse of life, among those who speak only to be understood, without ambition of elegance.

The polite are always catching modish innovations, and the learned depart from established forms of speech, in hope of finding or making better; those who wish for distinction forsake the vulgar, when the vulgar is right; but there is a conversation above grossness and below refinement, where propriety resides, and where this poet agreeable to the ears of the present age than any other author equally remote, and among his other excellencies deserves to be studied as one of the original masters of our language.

These observations are to be considered not as unexceptionably constant, but as containing general and predominant truth. Shakespeare's familiar dialogue is affirmed to be smooth and clear, yet not wholly without ruggedness or difficulty; as a country may be eminently fruitful, though it has spots unfit for cultivation: His characters are praised as natural, though their sentiments are sometimes forced, and their actions improbable; as the earth upon the whole is spherical, though its surface is varied with protuberances and cavities.

Shakespeare with his excellencies has likewise faults, and faults sufficient to obscure and overwhelm any other merit. I shall show them in the proportion in which they appear to me, without envious malignity or superstitious veneration. No question can be more innocently discussed than a dead poet's pretensions to renown; and little regard is due to that bigotry which sets candour higher than truth. His first defect is that to which may be imputed most of the evil in books or in men. He sacrifices virtue to convenience, and is so much more careful to please than to instruct, that he seems to write without any moral purpose. From his writings indeed a system of social duty may be selected, for he that thinks reasonably must think morally; but his precepts and axioms drop casually from him;

he makes no just distribution of good or evil, nor is always careful to show in the virtuous a disapprobation of the wicked; he carries his persons indifferently through right and wrong, and at the close dismisses them without further care, and leaves their examples to operate by chance.

This fault the barbarity of his age cannot extenuate; for it is always a writer's duty to make the world better, and justice is a virtue independent on time or place. The plots are often so loosely formed, that a very slight consideration may improve them, and so carelessly pursued, that he seems not always fully to comprehend his own design. He omits opportunities of instructing or delighting which the train of his story seems to force upon him, and apparently rejects those exhibitions which would be more affecting, for the sake of those which are more easy.

It may be observed, that in many of his plays the latter part is evidently neglected. When he found himself near the end of his work, and, in view of his reward, he shortened the labour, to snatch the profit. He therefore remits his efforts where he should most vigorously exert them, and his catastrophe is improbably produced or imperfectly represented. He had no regard to distinction of time or place, but gives to one age or nation, without scruple, the customs, institutions, and opinions of another, at the expanse not only of likelihood, but of possibility.

These faults Pope has endeavoured, with more zeal than judgment, to transfer to his imagined in interpolators. We need not wonder to find Hector quoting Aristotle, when we see the loves of Theseus and Hippolyta combined with the Gothic mythology of fairies. Shakespeare, indeed, was not the only violator of chronology, for in the same age Sidney, who wanted not the advantages of learning, has, in his "Arcadia", confounded the pastoral with the feudal times, the days of innocence, quiet and security, with those of turbulence, violence and adventure.

In his comic scenes he is seldom very successful, when he engages his characters in reciprocations of smartness and contest of sarcasm; their jests are commonly gross, and their pleasantry licentious; neither his gentlemen nor his ladies have much delicacy, nor are sufficiently distinguished from his clowns by any appearance of refined manners. Whether he represented the real conversation of his time is not easy to determine; the reign of Elizabeth is commonly supposed to have been a time of stateliness, formality and reserve, yet perhaps the relaxations of that severity were not very elegant.

There must, however, have been always some modes of gayety preferable to others, and a writer ought to choose the best. In tragedy, his performance seems constantly to be worse, as his labour is more. The effusions of passion which exigence forces out are for the most part striking and energetic; but whenever he solicits his invention, or strains his faculties, the offspring of his throes is tumor, meanness, tediousness, and obscurity. In narration he affects a disproportionate pomp of diction and a wearisome train of circumlocution, and tells the incident imperfectly in many words, which might have been more plainly delivered in few. Narration in dramatic poetry is, naturally tedious, as it is unanimated and inactive, and obstructs the progress of the action; it should therefore always be rapid, and enlivened by frequent interruption. Shakespeare found it an encumbrance, and instead of lightening it by brevity, endeavoured to recommend it by dignity and splendour.

His declamations or set speeches are commonly cold and weak, for his power was the power of nature; when he endeavoured, like other tragic writers, to catch opportunities of amplification, and instead of inquiring what the occasion demanded, to show how much his stores of knowledge could supply, he seldom escapes without the pity or resentment of his reader. It is incident to him to be now and then entangled with an unwieldy sentiment, which he cannot well express, and will not reject; he struggles with it a while, and if it continues stubborn, comprises it in words such as occur, and leaves it to be disentangled and evolved by those who have more leisure to bestow upon it.

Not that always where the language is intricate the thought is subtle, or the image always great where the line is bulky; the equality of words to things is very often neglected, and trivial sentiments and vulgar ideas disappoint the attention, to which they are recommended by sonorous epithets and swelling figures. But the admirers of this great poet have never less reason to indulge their hopes of supreme excellence, than when he seems fully resolved to sink them in dejection, and mollify them with tender emotions by the fall of greatness, the danger of innocence, or the crosses of love. He is not long soft and pathetic without some idle conceit, or contemptible equivocation. He no sooner begins to move, than he counteracts himself; and terror and pity, as they are rising in the mind, are checked and blasted by sudden frigidity.

A quibble is to Shakespeare, what luminous vapours are to the traveller; he follows it at all adventures, it is sure to lead him out of his way, and sure to engulf him in the mire. It has some malignant power over his mind, and its fascinations are irresistible. Whatever be the dignity or profundity of his disquisition, whether he be enlarging knowledge or exalting affection, whether he be amusing attention with incidents, or enchaining it in suspense, let but a quibble spring up before him, and he leaves his work unfinished. A quibble is the golden apple for which he will always turn aside from his career, or stoop from his elevation.

A quibble poor and barren as it is, gave him such delight, that he was content to purchase it, by the sacrifice of reason, propriety and truth. A quibble was to him the fatal Cleopatra for which he lost the world, and was content to lose it. It will be thought strange, that, in enumerating the defects of this writer, I have not yet mentioned his neglect of the unities; his violation of those laws which have been instituted and established by the joint authority of poets and of critics. For his other deviations from the art of writing, I resign him to critical justice, without making any other demand in his favour, than that which must be indulged to all human excellence; that his virtues be rated with his failings: But, from the censure which this irregularity may bring upon him, I shall, with due reverence to that learning which I must oppose, adventure to try how I can defend him.

His histories, being neither tragedies nor comedies, are not subject to any of their laws; nothing more is necessary to all the praise which they expect, than that the changes of action be so prepared as to be understood, that the incidents be various and affecting, and the characters consistent, natural and distinct. No other unity is intended, and therefore none is to be sought. In his other works hc has well enough preserved the unity of action.

He has not, indeed, an intrigue regularly perplexed and regularly unraveled; he does not endeavour to hide his design only to discover it, for this is seldom the order of real events, and Shakespeare is the poet of nature: But his plan has commonly what Aristotle requires, a beginning, a middle, and an end; one event is concatenated with another, and the conclusion follows by easy consequence. There are perhaps some incidents that might be spared, as in other poets there is much talk that only fills up time upon the stage; but the general system makes gradual advances, and the end of the play is the end of expectation.

To the unities of time and place he has shown no regard, and perhaps a nearer view of the principles on which they stand will diminish their value, and withdraw from them the veneration which, from the time of Corneille, they have very generally received by discovering that they have given more trouble to the poet, than pleasure to the auditor. The necessity of observing the unities of time and place arises from the supposed necessity of making the drama credible. The criticks hold it impossible, that an action of months or years can be possibly believed to pass in three hours; or that the spectator can suppose himself to sit in the theatre, while ambassadors go and return between distant kings, while armies are levied and towns besieged, while an exile wanders and returns, or till he whom they saw courting his mistress, shall lament the untimely fall of his son.

The mind revolts from evident falsehood, and fiction loses its force when it departs from the resemblance of reality. From the narrow limitation of time necessarily arises the contraction of place. The spectator, who knows that he saw the first act at

Alexandria, cannot suppose that he sees the next at Rome, at a distance to which not the dragons of Medea could, in so short a time, have transported him; he knows with certainty that he has not changed his place; and he knows that place cannot change itself; that what was a house cannot become a plain; that what was Thebes can never be Persepolis. Such is the triumphant language with which a critic exults over the misery of an irregular poet, and exults commonly without resistance or reply. It is time therefore to tell him, by the authority of Shakespeare, that he assumes, as an unquestionable principle, a position, which, while his breath is forming it into words, his understanding pronounces to be false. It is false, that any representation is mistaken for reality; that any dramatic fable in its materiality was ever credible, or, for a single moment, was ever credited.

The objection arising from the impossibility of passing the first hour at Alexandria, and the next at Rome, supposes, that when the play opens the spectator really imagines himself at Alexandria, and believes that his walk to the theatre has been a voyage to Egypt, and that he lives in the days of Antony and Cleopatra. Surely he that imagines this, may imagine more. He that can take the stage at one time for the palace of the Ptolemies, may take it in half an hour for the promontory of Actium. Delusion, if delusion be admitted, has no certain limitation; if the spectator can be once persuaded, that his old acquaintance are Alexander and Caesar, that a room illuminated with candles is the plain of Pharsalia, or the bank of Granicus, he is in a state of elevation above the reach of reason, or of truth, and from the heights of empyrean poetry, may despise the circumscriptions of terrestrial nature.

There is no reason why a mind thus wandering in ecstasy should count the clock, or why an hour should not be a century in that calenture of the brains that can make the stage a field. The truth is, that the spectators are always in their senses, and know, from the first act to the last, that the stage is only a stage, and that the players are only players. They come to hear a certain number of lines recited with just gesture and elegant modulation.

The lines relate to some action, and an action must be in some place; but the different actions that complete a story may be in places very remote from each other; and where is the absurdity of allowing that space to represent first Athens, and then Sicily, which was always known to be neither Sicily nor Athens, but a modern theatre? By supposition, as place is introduced, time may be extended; the time required by the fable elapses for the most part between the acts; for, of so much of the action as is represented, the real and poetical duration is the same. If, in the first act, preparations for war against Mithridates are represented to be made in Rome, the event of the war may, without absurdity, be represented, in the catastrophe, as happening in Pontus; we know that there is neither war, nor preparation for war; we know that we are neither in Rome nor Pontus; that neither Mithridates nor Lucullus are before us.

The drama exhibits successive imitations of successive actions, and why may not the second imitation represent an action that happened years after the first; if it be so connected with it, that nothing but time can be supposed to intervene? Time is, of all modes of existence, most obsequious to the imagination; a lapse of years is as easily conceived as a passage of hours. In contemplation we easily contract the time of real actions, and therefore willingly permit it to be contracted when we only see their imitation. It will be asked, how the drama moves, if it is not credited. It is credited with all the credit due to a drama.

It is credited, whenever it moves, as a just picture of a real original; as representing to the auditor what he would himself feel, if he were to do or suffer what is there feigned to be suffered or to be done. The reflection that strikes the heart is not, that the evils before us are real evils, but that they are evils to which we ourselves may be exposed. If there be any fallacy, it is not that we fancy the players, but that we fancy ourselves unhappy for a moment; but we rather lament the possibility than suppose the presence of misery, as a mother weeps over her babe, when she remembers that death may take it from her.

The delight of tragedy proceeds from our consciousness of fiction; if we thought murders and treasons real, they would please no more. Imitations produce pain or pleasure, not because they are mistaken for realities, but because they bring realities to mind. When the imagination is recreated by a painted landscape, the trees are not supposed capable to give us shade, or the fountains coolness; but we consider, how we should be pleased with such fountains playing beside us, and such woods waving over us. We are agitated in reading the history of "Henry the Fifth", yet no man takes his book for the field of Agencourt. A dramatic exhibition is a book recited with concomitants that increase or diminish its effect. Familiar comedy is often more powerful on the theatre, than in the page; imperial tragedy is always less.

The humour of Petruchio may be heightened by grimace; but what voice or what gesture can hope to add dignity or force to the soliloquy of Cato. A play read, affects the mind like a play acted. It is therefore evident, that the action is not supposed to be real, and it follows that between the acts a longer or shorter time may be allowed to pass, and that no more account of space or duration is to be taken by the auditor of a drama, than by the reader of a narrative, before whom may pass in an hour the life of a hero, or the revolutions of an empire. Whether Shakespeare knew the unities, and rejected them by design, or deviated from them by happy ignorance, it is, I think, impossible to decide, and useless to inquire. We may reasonably suppose, that, when he rose to notice, he did not want the counsels and admonitions of scholars and critics, and that he at last deliberately persisted in a practice, which he might have begun by chance.

As nothing is essential to the fable, but unity of action, and as the unities of time and place arise evidently from false assumptions, and, by circumscribing the extent of the drama, lessen its variety, I cannot think it much to be lamented, that they were not known by him, or not observed: Nor, if such another poet could arise, should I very vehemently reproach him, that his first act passed at Venice, and his next in Cyprus. Such violations of rules merely positive, become the comprehensive genius of Shakespeare, and such censures are suitable to the minute and slender criticism of Voltaire: Non usque adeo permiscuit imis Longus summa dies, ut non, si voce Metelli Serventur leges, malint a Caesare tolli.

Yet when I speak thus slightly of dramatic rules, I cannot but recollect how much wit and learning may be produced against me; before such authorities I am afraid to stand, not that I think the present question one of those that are to be decided by mere authority, but because it is to be suspected, that these precepts have not been so easily received but for better reasons than I have yet been able to find. The result of my enquiries, in which it would be ludicrous to boast of impartiality, is, that the unities of time and place are not essential to a just drama, that though they may sometimes conduce to pleasure, they are always to be sacrificed to the nobler beauties of variety and instruction; and that a play, written with nice observation of critical rules, is to be contemplated as an elaborate curiosity, as the product of superfluous and ostentatious art, by which is shown, rather what is possible, than what is necessary.

He that, without diminution of any other excellence, shall preserve all the unities unbroken, deserves the like applause with the architect, who shall display all the orders of architecture in a citadel, without any deduction from its strength; but the principal beauty of a citadel is to exclude the enemy; and the greatest graces of a play, are to copy nature and instruct life. Perhaps, what I have here not dogmatically but deliberately written, may recall the principles of the drama to a new examination. I am almost frightened at my own temerity; and when I estimate the fame and the strength of those that maintain the contrary opinion, am ready to sink down in reverential silence; as Aeneas withdrew from the defence of Troy, when he saw Neptune shaking the wall, and Juno heading the besiegers.

Those whom my arguments cannot persuade to give their approbation to the judgment of Shakespeare, will easily, if they consider the condition of his life, make some allowance for his ignorance. Every man's performances, to be rightly estimated, must be compared with the state of the age in which he lived, and with his own particular opportunities; and though to the reader a book be not worse or better for the circumstances of the author, yet as there is always a silent reference of human works to human abilities, and as the enquiry, how far man may extend his designs, or how high he may rate his native force, is of far greater dignity than in what rank we shall place any particular performance, curiosity is always busy to discover the instruments, as well as to survey the workmanship, to know how much is to be ascribed to original powers, and how much to casual and adventitious help.

The palaces of Peru or Mexico were certainly mean and incommodious habitations, if compared to the houses of European monarchs; yet who could forbear to view them with astonishment, who remembered that they were built without the use of iron? The English nation, in the time of Shakespeare, was yet struggling to emerge from barbarity. The philology of Italy had been transplanted hither in the reign of Henry the Eighth; and the learned languages had been successfully cultivated by Lilly and More; by Pole, Cheke, and Gardiner; and afterwards by Smith, Clerk, Haddon, and Ascham. Greek was now taught to boys in the principal schools; and those who united elegance with learning, read, with great diligence, the Italian and Spanish poets.

But literature was yet confined to professed scholars, or to men and women of high rank. The public was gross and dark; and to be able to read and write, was an accomplishment still valued for its rarity. Nations, like individuals, have their infancy. A people newly awakened to literary curiosity, being yet unacquainted with the true state of things, knows not how to judge of that which is proposed as its resemblance. Whatever is remote from common appearances is always welcome to vulgar, as to childish credulity; and of a country unenlightened by learning, the whole people is the vulgar. The study of those who then aspired to plebeian learning was laid out upon adventures, giants, dragons, and enchantments.

The Death of Arthur was the favourite volume. The mind, which has feasted on the luxurious wonders of fiction, has no taste of the insipidity of truth. A play which imitated only the common occurrences of the world, would, upon the admirers of Palmerin and Guy of Warwick, have made little impression; he that wrote for such an audience was under the necessity of looking round for strange events and fabulous transactions, and that incredibility, by which maturer knowledge is offended, was the chief recommendation of writings, to unskillful curiosity. Our author's plots are generally borrowed from novels, and it is reasonable to suppose, that he chose the most popular, such as were read by many, and related by more; for his audience could not have followed him through the intricacies of the drama, had they not held the thread of the story in their hands.

The stories, which we now find only in remoter authors, were in his time accessible and familiar. The fable of "As You Like It", which is supposed to be copied from Chaucer's Gamelyn, was a little pamphlet of those times; and old Mr. Cibber remembered the tale of Hamlet in plain English prose, which the critics have now to seek in Saxo Grammaticus. His English histories he took from English chronicles and English ballads; and as the ancient writers were made known to his countrymen by versions, they supplied him with new subjects; he dilated some of Plutarch's lives into plays, when they had been translated by North.

His plots, whether historical or fabulous, are always crouded with incidents, by which the attention of a rude people was more easily caught than by sentiment or argumentation; and such is the power of the marvelous even over those who despise it, that every man finds his mind more strongly seized by the tragedies of Shakespeare than of any other writer; others please us by particular speeches, but he always makes us anxious for the event, and has perhaps excelled all but Homer in securing the first purpose of a writer, by exciting restless and unquenchable curiosity, and compelling him that reads his work to read it through.

The shows and bustle with which his plays abound have the same original. As knowledge advances, pleasure passes from the eye to the ear, but returns, as it declines, from the ear to the eye. Those to whom our author's labours were exhibited had more skill in pomps or processions than in poetical language, and perhaps wanted some visible and discriminated events, as comments on the dialogue.

He knew how he should most please; and whether his practice is more agreeable to nature, or whether his example has prejudiced the nation, we still find that on our stage something must be done as well as said, and inactive declamation is very coldly heard, however musical or elegant, passionate or sublime. Voltaire expresses his wonder, that our author's extravagancies are endured by a nation, which has seen the tragedy of Cato.

Let him be answered, that Addison speaks the language of poets, and Shakespeare, of men. We find in Cato innumerable beauties which enamor us of its author, but we see nothing that acquaints us with human sentiments or human actions; we place it with the fairest and the noblest progeny which judgment propagates by conjunction with learning, but "Othello" is the vigorous and vivacious offspring of observation impregnated by genius. Cato affords a splendid exhibition of artificial and fictitious manners, and delivers just and noble sentiments, in diction easy, elevated and harmonious, but its hopes and fears communicate no vibration to the heart; the composition refers us only to the writer; we pronounce the name of Cato, but we think on Addison.

The work of a correct and regular writer is a garden accurately formed and diligently planted, varied with shades, and scented with flowers; the composition of Shakespeare is a forest, in which oaks extend their branches, and pines tower in the air, interspersed sometimes with weeds and brambles, and sometimes giving shelter to myrtles and to roses; filling the eye with awful pomp, and gratifying the mind with endless diversity. Other poets display cabinets of precious rarities, minutely finished, wrought into shape, and polished unto brightness.

Shakespeare opens a mine which contains gold and diamonds in inexhaustible plenty, though clouded by incrustations, debased by impurities, and mingled with a mass of meaner minerals. It has been much disputed, whether Shakespeare owed his excellence to his own native force, or whether he had the common helps of scholastic education, the precepts of critical science, and the examples of ancient authors. There has always prevailed a tradition that Shakespearc wanled learning, that he had no regular education, nor much skill in the dead languages. Johnson, his friend, affirms, that "He had small Latin and no Greek."; who, besides that he had no imaginable temptation to falsehood, wrote at a time when the character and acquisitions of Shakespeare were known to multitudes. His evidence ought therefore to decide the controversy, unless some testimony of equal force could be opposed.

Some have imagined, that they have discovered deep learning in many imitations of old writers; but the examples which I have known urged, were drawn from books translated in his time; or were such easy coincidences of thought, as will happen to all who consider the same subjects; or such remarks on life or axioms of morality as float in conversation, and are transmitted through the world in proverbial sentences. I have found it remarked, that, in this important sentence, "Go before, I'll follow," we read a translation of, I prae, sequar.

I have been told, that when Caliban, after a pleasing dream, says, "I cry'd to sleep again," the author imitates Anacreon, who had, like every other man, the same wish on the same occasion. There are a few passages, which may pass for imitations, but so few, that the exception only confirms the rule; he obtained them from accidental quotations, or by oral communication, and as he used what he had, would have used more if he had obtained it.

The "Comedy of Errors" is confessedly taken from the Menaechmi of Plautus; from the only play of Plautus which was then in English. What can be more probable, than that he who copied that, would have copied more; but that those which were not translated were inaccessible? Whether he knew the modern languages is uncertain. That his plays have some French scenes proves but little; he might easily procure them to be written, and probably, even though he had known the language in the common degree, he could not have written it without assistance. In the story of "Romeo and Juliet" he is observed to have followed the English translation, where it deviates from the Italian; but this on the other part proves nothing against his knowledge of the original.

He was to copy, not what he knew himself, but what was known to his audience. It is most likely that he had learned Latin sufficiently to make him acquainted with construction, but that he never advanced to an easy perusal of the Roman authors. Concerning his skill in modern languages, I can find no sufficient ground of determination; but as no imitations of French or Italian authors have been discovered, though the Italian poetry was then high in esteem, I am inclined to believe, that he read little more than English, and chose for his fables only such tales as he found translated. That much knowledge is scattered over his works is very justly observed by Pope, but it is often such knowledge as books did not supply. He that will understand Shakespeare, must not be content to study him in the closet, he must look for his meaning sometimes among the sports of the field, and sometimes among the manufactures of the shop.

There is however proof enough that he was a very diligent reader, nor was our language then so indigent of books, but that he might very liberally indulge his curiosity without excursion into foreign literature. Many of the Roman authors were translated, and some of the Greek; the reformation had filled the kingdom with theological learning; most of the topicks of human disquisition had found English writers; and poetry had been cultivated, not only with diligence, but success.

This was a stock of knowledge sufficient for a mind so capable of appropriating and improving it. But the greater part of his excellence was the product of his own genius. He found the English stage in a state of the utmost rudeness; no essays either in tragedy or comedy had appeared, from which it could be discovered to what degree of delight either one or other might be carried. Neither character nor dialogue were yet understood. Shakespeare may be truly said to have introduced them both amongst us, and in some of his happier scenes to have carried them both to the utmost height.

By what gradations of improvement he proceeded, is not easily known; for the chronology of his works is yet unsettled. Rowe is of opinion, that "perhaps we are not to look for his beginning, like those of other writers, in his least perfect works; art had so little, and nature so large a share in what he did, that for ought I know," says he, "the performances of his youth, as they were the most vigorous, were the best." But the power of nature is only the power of using to any certain purpose the materials which diligence procures, or opportunity supplies. Nature gives no man knowledge,

and when images are collected by study and experience, can only assist in combining or applying them. Shakespeare, however favoured by nature, could impart only what he had learned; and as he must increase his ideas, like other mortals, by gradual acquisition, he, like them, grew wiser as he grew older, could display life better, as he knew it more, and instruct with more efficacy, as he was himself more amply instructed. There is a vigilance of observation and accuracy of distinction which books and precepts cannot confer; from this almost all original and native excellence proceeds. Shakespeare must have looked upon mankind with perspicacity, in the highest degree curious and attentive.

Other writers borrow their characters from preceding writers, and diversify them only by the accidental appendages of present manners; the dress is a little varied, but the body is the same. Our author had both matter and form to provide; for except the characters of Chaucer, to whom I think he is not much indebted, there were no writers in English, and perhaps not many in other modern languages, which showed life in its native colours.

The contest about the original benevolence or malignity of man had not yet commenced. Speculation had not yet attempted to analyse the mind, to trace the passions to their sources, to unfold the seminal principles of vice and virtue, or sound the depths of the heart for the motives of action.

All those enquiries, which from that time that human

nature became the fashionable study, have been made sometimes with nice discernment, but often with idle subtlety, were yet unattempted. The tales, with which the infancy of learning was satisfied, exhibited only the superficial appearances of action, related the events but omitted the causes, and were formed for such as delighted in wonders rather than in truth. Mankind was not then to be studied in the closet; he that would know the world, was under the necessity of gleaning his own remarks, by mingling as he could in its business and amusements.

Boyle congratulated himself upon his high birth, because it favoured his curiosity, by facilitating his access. Shakespeare had no such advantage; he came to London a needy adventurer, and lived for a time by very mean employments. Many works of genius and learning have been performed in states of life, that appear very little favourable to thought or to enquiry; so many, that he who considers them is inclined to think that he sees enterprise and perseverance predominating over all external agency, and bidding help and hindrance vanish before them.

The genius of Shakespeare was not to be depressed by the weight of poverty, nor limited by the narrow conversation to which men in want are inevitably condemned; the encumbrances of his fortune were shaken from his mind, "as dewdrops from a lion's mane." Though he had so many difficulties to encounter, and so little assistance to surmount them, he has been able to obtain an exact knowledge of many modes of life, and many casts of native dispositions; to vary them with great multiplicity; to mark them by nice distinctions; and to show them in full view by proper combinations. In this part of his performances He had none to imitate, but has himself been imitated by all succeeding writers; and it may be doubted, whether from all his successors more maxims of theoretical knowledge, or more rules of practical prudence, can be collected, than he alone has given to his country.

Nor was his attention confined to the actions of men; he was an exact surveyor of the inanimate world; his descriptions have always some peculiarities, gathered by contemplating things as they really exist. It may be observed, that the oldest poets of many nations preserve their reputation, and that the following generations of wit, after a short celebrity, sink into oblivion. The first, whoever they be, must take their sentiments and descriptions immediately from knowledge; the resemblance is therefore just, their descriptions are verified by every eye, and their sentiments acknowledged by every breast. Those whom their fame invites to the same studies, copy partly them, and partly nature, till the books of one age gain such authority, as to stand in the place of nature to another, and imitation, always deviating a little, becomes at last capricious and casual. Shakespeare, whether life or nature be his subject, shows plainly, that he has seen with his own eyes; he gives the image which he receives, not weakened or distorted by the intervention of any other mind; the ignorant feel his representations to be just, and the learned see that they are complete.

Perhaps it would not be easy to find any author, except Homer, who invented so much as Shakespeare, who so much advanced the studies which he cultivated, or effused so much novelty upon his age or country. The form, the characters, the language, and the shows of the English drama are his. "He seems," says Dennis, "to have been the very original of our English tragical harmony, that is, the harmony of blank verse, diversified often by dissyllable and trissyllable terminations. For the diversity distinguishes it from heroic harmony, and by bringing it nearer to common use makes it more proper to gain attention, and more fit for action and dialogue.

Such verse we make when we are writing prose; we make such verse in common conversation." I know not whether this praise is rigorously just. The dissyllable termination, which the critic rightly appropriates to the drama, is to be found, though, I think, not in Gorboduc which is confessedly before our author; yet in Hieronnymo, of which the date is not certain, but which there is reason to believe at least as old as his earliest plays. This however is certain, that he is the first who taught either tragedy or comedy to please, there being no theatrical piece of any older writer, of which the name is known, except to antiquaries and collectors of books, which are sought because they are scarce, and would not have been scarce, had they been much esteemed.

To him we must ascribe the praise, unless Spenser may divide it with him, of having first discovered to how much smoothness and harmony the English language could be softened. He has speeches, perhaps sometimes scenes, which have all the delicacy of Rowe, without his effeminacy. He endeavours indeed commonly to strike by the force and vigour of his dialogue, but he never executes his purpose better, than when he tries to sooth by softness.

Yet it must be at last confessed, that as we owe every thing to him, he owes something to us; that, if much of his praise is paid by perception and judgment, much is likewise given by custom and veneration. We fix our eyes upon his graces, and turn them from his deformities, and endure in him what we should in another loath or despise. If we endured without praising, respect for the father of our drama might excuse us; but I have seen, in the book of some modern critic, a collection of anomalies which show that he has corrupted language by every mode of depravation, but which his admirer has accumulated as a monument of honour.

He has scenes of undoubted and perpetual excellence, but perhaps not one play, which, if it were now exhibited as the work of a contemporary writer, would be heard to the conclusion. I am indeed far from thinking, that his works were wrought to his own ideas of perfection; when they were such as would satisfy the audience, they satisfied the writer. It is seldom that authors, though more studious of fame than Shakespeare, rise much above the standard of their own age; to add a little of what is best will always be sufficient for present praise, and those who find themselves exalted into fame, are willing to credit their encomiasts, and to spare the labour of contending with themselves.

It does not appear, that Shakespeare thought his works worthy of posterity, that he levied any ideal tribute upon future times, or had any further prospect, than of present popularity and present profit. When his plays had been acted, his hope was at an end; he solicited no addition of honour from the reader. He therefore made no scruple to repeat the same jests in many dialogues, or to entangle different plots by the same knot of perplexity, which may be at least forgiven him, by those who recollect, that of Congreve's four comedies, two are concluded by a marriage in a mask, by a deception, which perhaps never happened, and which, whether likely or not, he did not invent.

So careless was this great poet of future fame, that, though he retired to ease and plenty, while he was yet little "declined into the vale of years," before he could be disgusted with fatigue, or disabled by infirmity, he made no collection of his works, nor desired to rescue those that had been already published from the depravations that obscured them, or secure to the rest a better destiny, by giving them to the world in their genuine state.

Of the plays which bear the name of Shakespeare in the late editions, the greater part were not published till about seven years after his death, and the few which appeared in his life are apparently thrust into the world without the care of the author, and therefore probably without his knowledge. Of all the publishers, clandestine or professed, their negligence and unskilfulness has by the late revisers been sufficiently shown. The faults of all are indeed numerous and gross, and have not only corrupted many passages perhaps beyond recovery, but have brought others into suspicion, which are only obscured by obsolete phraseology, or by the writer's unskilfulness and affectation.

To alter is more easy than to explain, and temerity is a more common quality than diligence. Those who saw that they must employ conjecture to a certain degree, were willing to indulge it a little further. Had the author published his own works, we should have sat quietly down to disentangle his intricacies, and clear his obscurities; but now we tear what we cannot loose, and eject what we happen not to understand. The faults are more than could have happened without the concurrence of many causes. The stile of Shakespeare was in itself ungrammatical, perplexed and obscure; his works were transcribed for the players by those who may be supposed to have seldom understood them; they were transmitted by copiers equally unskillful, who still multiplied errors; they were perhaps sometimes mutilated by the actors, for the sake of shortening the speeches; and were at last printed without correction of the press.

In this state they remained, not as Dr. Warburton supposes, because they were unregarded, but because the editor's art was not yet applied to modern languages, and our ancestors were accustomed to so much negligence of English printers, that they could very patiently endure it. At last an edition was undertaken by Rowe; not because a poet was to be published by a poet, for Rowe seems to have thought very little on correction or explanation, but that our author's works might appear like those of his fraternity, with the appendages of a life and recommendatory preface.

Rowe has been clamorously blamed for not performing what he did not undertake, and it is time that justice be done him, by confessing, that though he seems to have had no thought of corruption beyond the printer's errors, yet he has made many emendations, if they were not made before, which his successors have received without acknowledgment, and which, if they had produced them, would have filled pages and pages with censures of the stupidity by which the faults were committed, with displays of the absurdities which they involved, with ostentatious exposition of the new reading, and self congratulations on the happiness of discovering it.

Of Rowe, as of all the editors, I have preserved the preface and have likewise retained the author's life, though not written with much elegance or spirit; it relates however what is now to be known, and therefore deserves to pass through all succeeding publications. The nation had been for many years content enough with Mr. Rowe's performance, when Mr. Pope made them acquainted with the true state of Shakespeare's text, showed that it was extremely corrupt, and gave reason to hope that there were means of reforming it.

He collated the old copies, which none had thought to examine before, and restored many lines to their integrity; but, by a very compendious criticism, he rejected whatever he disliked, and thought more of amputation than of cure.

I know not why he is commended by Dr. Warburton for distinguishing the genuine from the spurious plays. In this choice he exerted no judgment of his own; the plays which he received, were given by Hemings and Condel, the first editors; and those, which he rejected, though, according to the licentiousness of the press in those times, they were printed during Shakespeare's life, with his name, had been omitted by his friends, and were never added to his works before the edition of 1664, from which they were copied by the later printers. This was a work which Pope seems to have thought unworthy of his abilities, being not able to suppress his contempt of "the dull duty of an editor". He understood but half his undertaking. The duty of a collator is indeed dull, yet, like other tedious tasks, is very necessary; but an emendatory critic would ill discharge his duty, without qualities very different from dullness. In perusing a corrupted piece, he must have before him all possibilities of meaning, with all possibilities of expression.

Such must be his comprehension of thought, and such his copiousness of language. Out of many readings possible, he must be able to select that which best suits with the state, opinions, and modes of language prevailing in every age, and with his author's particular cast of thought, and turn of expression. Such must be his knowledge, and such his taste. Conjectural criticism demands more than humanity possesses, and he that exercises it with most praise has very frequent need of indulgence. Let us now be told no more of the dull duty of an editor.

Confidence is the common consequence of success. They whose excellence of any kind has been loudly celebrated, are ready to conclude, that their powers are universal. Pope's edition fell below his own expectations, and he was so much offended, when he was found to have left any thing for others to do, that he past the latter part of his life in a state of hostility with verbal criticism. I have retained all his notes, that no fragment of so great a writer may be lost; his preface, valuable alike for elegance of composition and justness of remark, and containing a general criticism on his author, so extensive that little can be added, and so exact, that little can be disputed, every editor has an interest to suppress, but that every reader would demand its insertion.

Pope was succeeded by Theobald, a man of narrow comprehension and small acquisitions, with no native and intrinsic splendor of genius, with little of the artificial light of learning, but zealous for minute accuracy, and not negligent in pursuing it. He collated the ancient copies, and rectified many errors. A man so anxiously scrupulous might have been expected to do more, but what little he did was commonly right. In his report of copies and editions he is not to be trusted, without examination. He speaks sometimes indefinitely of copies, when he has only one. In his enumeration of editions, he mentions the two first folios as of high, and the third folio as of middle authority; but the truth is, that the first is equivalent to all others, and that the rest only deviate from it by the printer's negligence. Whoever has any of the folios has all, excepting those diversities which mere reiteration of editions will produce.

I collated them all at the beginning, but afterwards used only the first. Of his notes I have generally retained those which he retained himself in his second edition, except when they were confuted by subsequent annotators, or were too minute to merit preservation. I have sometimes adopted his restoration of a comma, without inserting the panegyric in which he celebrated himself for his achievement. The exuberant excrescence of diction I have often lopped, his triumphant exultations over Pope and Rowe I have sometimes suppressed, and his contemptible ostentation I have frequently concealed; but I have in some places shown him, as he would have shown himself, for the reader's diversion, that the inflated emptiness of some notes may justify or excuse the contraction of the rest.

Theobald, thus weak and ignorant, thus mean and faithless, thus petulant and ostentatious, by the good luck of having Pope for his enemy, has escaped, and escaped alone, with reputation, from this undertaking. So willingly does the world support those who solicit favour, against those who command reverence; and so easily is he praised, whom no man can envy.

Our author fell then into the hands of Sir Thomas Hanmer, the Oxford editor, a man, in my opinion, eminently qualified by nature for such studies. He had, what is the first requisite to emendatory criticism, that intuition by which the poet's intention is immediately discovered, and that dexterity of intellect which dispatches its work by the easiest means. He had undoubtedly read much; his acquaintance with customs, opinions, and traditions, seems to have been large; and he is often learned without show.

He seldom passes what he does not understand, without an attempt to find or to make a meaning, and sometimes hastily makes what a little more attention would have found. He is solicitous to reduce to grammar, what he could not be sure that his author intended to be grammatical. Shakespeare regarded more the series of ideas, than of words; and his language, not being designed for the reader's desk, was all that he desired it to be, if it conveyed his meaning to the audience. Hanmer's care of the meter has been too violently censured. He found the measures reformed in so many passages, by the silent labours of some editors, with the silent acquiescence of the rest, that he thought himself allowed to extend a little further the license, which had already been carried so far without reprehension; and of his corrections in general, it must be confessed, that they are often just, and made commonly with the least possible violation of the text.

But, by inserting his emendations, whether invented or borrowed, into the page, without any notice of varying copies, he has appropriated the labour of his predecessors, and made his own edition of little authority. His confidence indeed, both in himself and others, was too great; he supposes all to be right that was done by Pope and Theobald; he seems not to suspect a critic of fallibility, and it was but reasonable that he should claim what he so liberally granted.

As he never writes without careful enquiry and diligent

consideration, I have received all his notes, and believe that every reader will wish for more. Of the last editor it is more difficult to speak. Respect is due to high place, tenderness to living reputation, and veneration to genius and learning; but he cannot be justly offended at that liberty of which he has himself so frequently given an example, nor very solicitous what is thought of notes, which he ought never to have considered as part of his serious employments, and which, I suppose, since the ardour of composition is remitted, he no longer numbers among his happy effusions.

The original and predominant error of his commentary, is acquiescence in his first thoughts; that precipitation which is produced by consciousness of quick discernment; and that confidence which presumes to do, by surveying the surface, what labour only can perform, by penetrating the bottom. His notes exhibit sometimes perverse interpretations, and sometimes improbable conjectures; he at one time gives the author more profundity of meaning than the sentence admits, and at another discovers absurdities, where the sense is plain to every other reader.

But his emendations are likewise often happy and just; and his interpretation of obscure passages learned and sagacious. Of his notes, I have commonly rejected those, against which the general voice of the public has exclaimed, or which their own incongruity immediately condemns, and which, I suppose, the author himself would desire to be forgotten. Of the rest, to part I have given the highest approbation, by inserting the offered reading in the text; part I have left to the judgment of the reader, as doubtful, though specious; and part I have censured without reserve, but I am sure without bitterness of malice, and, I hope, without wantonness of insult.

It is no pleasure to me, in revising my volumes, to observe how much paper is wasted in confutation. Whoever considers the revolutions of learning, and the various questions of greater or less importance, upon which wit and reason have exercised their powers, must lament the unsuccessfulness of enquiry, and the slow advances of truth, when he reflects, that great part of the labour of every writer is only the destruction of those that went before him.

The first care of the builder of a new system, is to demolish the fabrics which are standing. The chief desire of him that comments an author, is to show how much other commentators have corrupted and obscured him. The opinions prevalent in one age, as truths above the reach of controversy, are confuted and rejected in another, and rise again to reception in remoter times. Thus the human mind is kept in motion without progress. Thus sometimes truth and error, and sometimes contrarieties of error, take each other's place by reciprocal invasion.

The tide of seeming knowledge which is poured over one generation, retires and leaves another naked and barren; the sudden meteors of intelligence which for a while appear to shoot their beams into the regions of obscurity, on a sudden withdraw their lustre, and leave mortals again to grope their way. These elevations and depressions of renown, and the contradictions to which all improvers of knowledge must for ever be exposed, since they are not escaped by the highest and brightest of mankind, may surely be endured with patience by critics and annotators, who can rank themselves but as the satellites of their authors.

How canst thou beg for life, says Achilles to his captive, when thou knowest that thou art now to suffer only what must another day be suffered by Achilles? Dr. Warburton had a name sufficient to confer celebrity on those who could exalt themselves into antagonists, and his notes have raised a clamour too loud to be distinct. His chief assailants are the authors of the Canons of Criticism and of the Review of Shakespeare's Text; of whom one ridicules his errors with airy petulance, suitable enough to the levity of the controversy; the other attacks them with gloomy malignity, as if he were dragging to justice an assassin or incendiary.

The one stings like a fly, sucks a little blood, takes a gay flutter, and returns for more; the other bites like a viper, and would be glad to leave inflammations and gangrene behind him. When I think on one, with his confederates, I remember the danger of Coriolanus, who was afraid that "girls with spits, and boys with stones, should slay him in puny battle;" when the other crosses my imagination, I remember the prodigy in "Macbeth", An eagle tow'ring in his pride of place, was by a mousing owl hawk'd at and kill'd. Let me however do them justice. One is a wit, and one a scholar. They have both shown acuteness sufficient in the discovery of faults, and have both advanced some probable interpretations of obscure passages; but when they aspire to conjecture and emendation, it appears how falsely we all estimate our own abilities, and the little which they have been able to perform might have taught them more candour to the endeavours of others.

Before Dr. Warburton's edition, "Critical Observations on Shakespeare" had been published by Mr. Upton, a man skilled in languages, and acquainted with books, but who seems to have had no great vigour of genius or nicety of taste. Many of his explanations are curious and useful, but he likewise, though he professed to oppose the licentious confidence of editors, and adhere to the old copies, is unable to restrain the rage of emendation, though his ardour is ill seconded by his skill. Every cold empiric, when his heart is expanded by a successful experiment, swells into a theorist, and the laborious collator some unlucky moment frolics in conjecture. "Critical, historical and explanatory notes" have been likewise published upon Shakespeare by Dr.

Grey, whose diligent perusal of the old English writers has enabled him to make some useful observations. What he undertook he has well enough performed, but as he neither attempts judicial nor emendatory criticism, he employs rather his memory than his sagacity. It were to be wished that all would endeavour to imitate his modesty who have not been able to surpass his knowledge. I can say with great sincerity of all my predecessors, what I hope will hereafter be said of me, that not one has left Shakespeare without improvement, nor is there one to whom I have not been indebted for assistance and information.

Whatever I have taken from them it was my intention to refer to its original author, and it is certain, that what I have not given to another, I believed when I wrote it to be my own. In some perhaps I have been anticipated; but if I am ever found to encroach upon the remarks of any other commentator, I am willing that the honour, be it more or less, should be transferred to the first claimant, for his right, and his alone, stands above dispute; the second can prove his pretensions only to himself, nor can himself always distinguish invention, with sufficient certainty, from recollection.

They have all been treated by me with candour, which they have not been careful of observing to one another. It is not easy to discover from what cause the acrimony of a scholiast can naturally proceed. The subjects to be discussed by him are of very small importance; they involve neither property nor liberty; nor favour the interest of sect or party. The various readings of copies, and different interpretations of a passage, seem to be questions that might exercise the wit, without engaging the passions. But, whether it be, that "small things make mean men proud," and vanity catches small occasions; or that all contrariety of opinion, even in those that can defend it no longer, makes proud men angry; there is often found in commentaries a spontaneous strain of invective and contempt, more eager and venomous than is vented by the most furious controverts in politics against those whom he is hired to defame.

Perhaps the lightness of the matter may conduce to the vehemence of the agency; when the truth to be investigated is so near to inexistence, as to escape attention, its bulk is to be enlarged by rage and exclamation: That to which all would be indifferent in its original state, may attract notice when the fate of a name is appended to it. A commentator has indeed great temptations to supply by turbulence what he wants of dignity, to beat his little gold to a spacious surface, to work that to foam which no art or diligence can exalt to spirit.

The notes which I have borrowed or written are either illustrative, by which difficulties are explained; or judicial, by which faults and beauties are remarked; or emendatory, by which depravations are corrected. The explanations transcribed from others, if I do not subjoin any other interpretation, I suppose commonly to be right, at least I intend by acquiescence to confess, that I have nothing better to propose. After the labours of all the editors, I found many passages which appeared to me likely to obstruct the greater number of readers, and thought it my duty to facilitate their passage. It is impossible for an expositor not to write too little for some, and too much for others. He can only judge what is necessary by his own experience; and how long so ever he may deliberate, will at last explain many lines which the learned will think impossible to be mistaken, and omit many for which the ignorant will want his help. These are censures merely relative and must be quietly endured.

I have endeavoured to be neither superfluously copious, nor scrupulously reserved, and hope that I have made my author's meaning accessible to many who before were frighted from perusing him, and contributed something to the public, by diffusing innocent and rational pleasure. The complete explanation of an author not systematic and consequential, but desultory and vagrant, abounding in casual allusions and light hints, is not to be expected from any single scholiast.

All personal reflections, when names are suppressed, must be in a few years irrecoverably obliterated; and customs, too minute to attract the notice of law, such as mode of dress, formalities of conversation, rules of visits, disposition of furniture, and practices of ceremony, which naturally find places in familiar dialogue, are so fugitive and unsubstantial that they are not easily retained or recovered. What can be known, will be collected by chance, from the recesses of obscure and obsolete papers, perused commonly with some other view. Of this knowledge every man has some, and none has much; but when an author has engaged the public attention, those who can add any thing to his illustration, communicate their discoveries, and time produces what had eluded diligence.

To time I have been obliged to resign many passages, which, though I did not understand them, will perhaps hereafter be explained, having, I hope, illustrated some, which others have neglected or mistaken, sometimes by short remarks or marginal directions, such as every editor has added at his will, and often by comments more laborious than the matter will seem to deserve; but that which is most difficult is not always most important, and to an editor nothing is a trifle by which his author is obscured.

The poetical beauties or defects I have not been very diligent to observe. Some plays have more, and some fewer judicial observations, not in proportion to their difference of merit, but because I gave this part of my design to chance and to caprice. The reader, I believe, is seldom pleased to find his opinion anticipated; it is natural to delight more in what we find or make, than in what we receive. Judgement, like other faculties, is improved by practice, and its advancement is hindered by submission to dictatorial decisions, as the memory grows torpid by the use of a table book.

Some initiation is however necessary; of all skill, part is infused by precept, and part is obtained by habit; I have therefore shown so much as may enable the candidate of criticism to discover the rest. To the end of most plays, I have added short strictures, containing a general censure of faults, or praise of excellence; in which I know not how much I have concurred with the current opinion; but I have not, by any affectation of singularity, deviated from it.

Nothing is minutely and particularly examined, and therefore it is to be supposed, that in the plays which are condemned there is much to be praised, and in these which are praised much to be condemned. The part of criticism in which the whole succession of editors has laboured with the greatest diligence, which has occasioned the most arrogant ostentation, and excited the keenest acrimony, is the emendation of corrupted passages, to which the public attention having been first drawn by the violence of contention between Pope and Theobald, has been continued by the persecution, which, with a kind of conspiracy, has been since raised against all the publishers of Shakespeare.

That many passages have passed in a state of depravation through all the editions is indubitably certain; of these the restoration is only to be attempted by collation of copies or sagacity of conjecture. The collator's province is safe and easy, the conjecturer's perilous and difficult. Yet as the greater part of the plays are extant only in one copy, the peril must not be avoided, nor the difficulty refused.

Of the readings which this emulation of amendment has hitherto produced, some from the labours of every publisher have advanced into the text; those are to be considered as in my opinion sufficiently supported; some I have rejected without mention, as evidently erroneous; some I have left in the notes without censure or approbation, as resting in equipoise between objection and defence; and some, which seemed specious but not right, I have inserted with a subsequent animadversion. Having classed the observations of others, I was at last to try what I could substitute for their mistakes, and how I could supply their omissions.

I collated such copies as I could procure, and wished for more, but have not found the collectors of these rarities very communicative. Of the editions which chance or kindness put into my hands I have given an enumeration, that I may not be blamed for neglecting what I had not the power to do. By examining the old copies, I soon found that the late publishers, with all their boasts of diligence, suffered many passages; to stand unauthorized, and contented themselves with Rowe's regulation of the text, even where they knew it to be arbitrary, and with a little consideration might have found it to be wrong. Some of these alterations are only the ejection of a word for one that appeared to him more elegant or more intelligible.

These corruptions I have often silently rectified; for the history of our language, and the true force of our words, can only be preserved, by keeping the text of authors free from adulteration. Others, and those very frequent, smoothed the cadence, or regulated the measure; on these I have not exercised the same rigour; if only a word was transposed, or a particle inserted or omitted, I have sometimes suffered the line to stand; for the inconstancy of the copies is such, as that some liberties may be easily permitted. But this practice I have not suffered to proceed far, having restored the primitive diction wherever it could for any reason be preferred.

The emendations, which comparison of copies supplied, I have inserted in the text; sometimes where the improvement was slight, without notice, and sometimes with an account of the reasons of the change. Conjecture, though it be sometimes unavoidable, I have not wantonly nor licentiously indulged. It has been my settled principle, that the reading of the ancient books is probably true, and therefore is not to be disturbed for the sake of elegance, perspicuity, or mere improvement of the sense.

For though much credit is not due to the fidelity, nor any to the judgment of the first publishers, yet they who had the copy before their eyes were more likely to read it right, than we who only read it by imagination. But it is evident that they have often made strange mistakes by ignorance or negligence, and that therefore something may be properly attempted by criticism, keeping the middle way between presumption and timidity. Such criticism I have attempted to practice, and where any passage appeared inextricably perplexed, have endeavoured to discover how it may be recalled to sense, with least violence. But my first labour is, always to turn the old text on every side, and try if there be any interstice, through which light can find its way; nor would Huetius himself condemn me, as refusing the trouble of research, for the ambition of alteration. In this modest industry I have not been unsuccessful.

I have rescued many lines from the violations of temerity, and secured many scenes from the inroads of correction. I have adopted the Roman sentiment that it is more honourable to save a citizen, than to kill an enemy, and have been more careful to protect than to attack. I have preserved the common distribution of the plays into acts, though I believe it to be in almost all the plays void of authority. Some of those which are divided in the later editions have no division in the first folio, and some that are divided in the folio have no division in the preceding copies.

The settled mode of the theatre requires four intervals in the play, but few, if any, of our author's compositions can be properly distributed in that manner. An act is so much of the drama as passes without intervention of time or change of place. A pause makes a new act.

In every real, and therefore in every imitative action, the intervals may be more or fewer, the restriction of five acts being accidental and arbitrary. This Shakespeare knew, and this he practiced; his plays were written, and at first printed in one unbroken continuity, and ought now to be exhibited with short pauses, interposed as often as the scene is changed, or any considerable time is required to pass.

This method would at once quell a thousand absurdities. In restoring the author's works to their integrity, I have considered the punctuation as wholly in my power; for what could be their care of colons and commas, who corrupted words and sentences.

Whatever could be done by adjusting points is therefore silently performed, in some plays with much diligence, in others with less; it is hard to keep a busy eye steadily fixed upon evanescent atoms, or a discursive mind upon evanescent truth. The same liberty has been taken with a few particles, or other words of slight effect. I have sometimes inserted or omitted them without notice. I have done that sometimes, which the other editors have done always, and which indeed the state of the text may sufficiently justify.

The greater part of readers, instead of blaming us for passing trifles, will wonder that on mere trifles so much labour is expended, with such importance of debate, and such solemnity of diction. To these I answer with confidence, that they are judging of an art which they do not understand; yet cannot much reproach them with their ignorance, nor promise that they would become in general, by learning criticism, more useful, happier or wiser. As I practiced conjecture more, I learned to trust it less; and after I had printed a few plays, resolved to insert none of my own readings in the text. Upon this caution I now congratulate myself, for every day increases my doubt of my emendations.

Since I have confined my imagination to the margin, it must not be considered as very reprehensible, if I have suffered it to play some freaks in its own dominion. There is no danger in conjecture, if it be proposed as conjecture; and while the text remains uninjured, those changes may be safely offered, which are not considered even by him that offers them as necessary or safe. If my readings are of little value, they have not been ostentatiously displayed or importunately obtruded. I could have written longer notes, for the art of writing notes is not of difficult attainment.

The work is performed, first by railing at the stupidity, negligence, ignorance, and asinine tastelessness of the former editors, and showing, from all that goes before and all that follows, the inelegance and absurdity of the old reading; then by proposing something, which to superficial readers would seem specious, but which the editor rejects with indignation; then by producing the true reading, with a long paraphrase, and concluding with loud acclamations on the discovery, and a sober wish for the advancement and prosperity of genuine criticism. All this may be done, and perhaps done sometimes without impropriety.

But I have always suspected that the reading is right, which requires many words to prove it wrong; and the emendation wrong, that cannot without so much labour appear to be right. The justness of a happy restoration strikes at once, and the moral precept may be well applied to criticism, quod dubitas ne feceris. To dread the shore which he sees spread with wrecks, is natural to the sailor. I had before my eye, so many critical adventures ended in miscarriage, that caution was forced upon me. I encountered in every page Wit struggling with its own sophistry, and Learning confused by the multiplicity of its views.

I was forced to censure those whom I admired, and could not but reflect, while I was dispossessing their emenations, how soon the same fate might happen to my own, and how many of the readings which I have corrected may be some other editor defended and established. Criticks, I saw, that other's names efface, And fix their own, with labour, in the place; Their own, like others, soon their place resign'd, Or disappear'd, and left the first behind.—Pope. That a conjectural critic should often be mistaken, cannot be wonderful, either to others or himself, if it be considered that in his art there is no system, no principal and axiomatical truth that regulates subordinate positions.

His chance of error is renewed at every attempt; an oblique view of the passage a slight misapprehension of a phrase, a casual inattention to the parts connected, is sufficient to make him not only fail but fail ridiculously; and when he succeeds best, he produces perhaps but one reading of many probable, and he that suggests another will always bc able to dispute his claims. It is an unhappy state, in which danger is hid under pleasure.

The allurements of emendation are scarcely resistible. Conjecture has all the joy and all the pride of invention, and he that has once started a happy change, is too much delighted to consider what objections may rise against it. Yet conjectural criticism has been of great use in the learned world; nor is it my intention to depreciate a study, that has exercised so many mighty minds, from the revival of learning to our own age, from the Bishop of Aleria to English Bentley.

The critics on ancient authors have, in the exercise of their sagacity, many assistances, which the editor of Shakespeare is condemned to want. They are employed upon grammatical and settled languages, whose construction contributes so much to perspicuity, that Homer has fewer passages unintelligible than Chaucer. The words have not only a known regimen, but invariable quantities, which direct and confine the choice. There are commonly more manuscripts than one; and they do not often conspire in the same mistakes. Yet Scaliger could confess to Salmasius how little satisfaction his emendations gave him.

Illudunt nobis conjecturae nostrae, quarum nos pudet, posteaquam in meliores cofices incidimus. And Lipsius could complain, that criticks were making faults, by trying to remove them, Ut olim vitiis, ita nunc remediis laboratur. And indeed, where mere conjecture is to be used, the emendations of Scaliger and Lipsius, notwithstanding their wonderful sagacity and erudition, are often vague and disputable, like mine or Theobald's. Perhaps I may not be more censured for doing wrong, than for doing little; for raising in the public expectations, which at last I have not answered.

The expectation of ignorance is indefinite, and that of knowledge is often tyrannical. It is hard to satisfy those who know not what to demand, or those who demand by design what they think impossible to be done. I have indeed disappointed no opinion more than my own; yet I have endeavoured to perform my task with no slight solicitude. Not a single passage in the whole work has appeared to me corrupt, which I have not attempted to restore; or obscure, which I have not endeavoured to illustrate. In many I have failed like others; and from many, after all my efforts, I have retreated, and confessed the repulse.

I have not passed over, with affected superiority, what is equally difficult to the reader and to myself, but where I could not instruct him, have owned my ignorance. I might easily have accumulated a mass of seeming learning upon easy scenes; but it ought not to be imputed to negligence, that, where nothing was necessary, nothing has been done, or that, where others have said enough, I have said no more. Notes are often necessary, but they are necessary evils. Let him, that is yet unacquainted with the powers of Shakespeare, and who desires to feel the highest pleasure that the drama can give, read every play from the first scene to the last, with utter negligence of all his commentators. When his fancy is once on the wing, let it not stoop at correction or explanation. When his attention is strongly engaged, let it disdain alike to turn aside to the name of Theobald and Pope.

Let him read on through brightness and obscurity, through integrity and corruption; let him preserve his comprehension of the dialogue and his interest in the fable. And when the pleasures of novelty have ceased, let him attempt exactness; and read the commentators. Particular passages are cleared by notes, but the general effect of the work is weakened. The mind is refrigerated by interruption; the thoughts are diverted from the principal subject; the reader is weary, he suspects not why; and at last throws away the book, which he has too diligently studied. Parts are not to be examined till the whole has been surveyed; there is a kind of intellectual remoteness necessary for the comprehension of any great work in its full design and its true proportions; a close approach shows the smaller niceties, but the beauty of the whole is discerned no longer.

It is not very grateful to consider how little the succession of editors has added to this author's power of pleasing. He was read, admired, studied, and imitated, while he was yet deformed with all the improprieties which ignorance and neglect could accumulate upon him; while the reading was yet not rectified, nor his allusions understood; yet then did Dryden pronounce "that Shakespeare was the man, who, of all modern and perhaps ancient poets, had the largest and most comprehensive soul.

All the images of nature were still present to him, and he drew them not laboriously, but luckily: When he describes any thing, you more than see it, you feel it too. Those who accuse him to have wanted learning, give him the greater commendation: he was naturally learned: he needed not the spectacles of books to read nature; he looked inwards, and found her there.

I cannot say he is every where alike; were he so, I should do him injury to compare him with the greatest of mankind. He is many times flat and insipid; his comic wit degenerating into clenches, his serious swelling into bombast.

But he is always great, when some great occasion is presented to him: No man can say, he ever had a fit subject for his wit, and did not then raise himself as high above the rest of poets, "Quantum lenta solent inter viburna cupressi." It is to be lamented, that such a writer should want a commentary; that his language should become obsolete, or his sentiments obscure.

But it is vain to carry wishes beyond the condition of human things; that which must happen to all, has happened to Shakespeare, by accident and time; and more than has been suffered by any other writer since the use of types, has been suffered by him through his own negligence of fame, or perhaps by that superiority of mind, which despised its own performances, when it compared them with its powers, and judged those works unworthy to be preserved, which the criticks of following ages were to contend for the fame of restoring and explaining. Among these candidates of inferiour fame, I am now to stand the judgment of the publick; and wish that I could confidently produce my commentary as equal to the encouragement which I have had the honour of receiving.

Every work of this kind is by its nature deficient, and I should feel little solicitude about the sentence, were it to be pronounced only by the skilful and the learned.

Chapter 16

Selected Notes from Some of the Plays

Measure for Measure

There is perhaps not one of Shakespeare's plays more darkened than this by the peculiarities of its Author, and the unskilfulness of its Editors, by distortions of phrase, or negligence of transcription. ACT I. SCENE i. (I. I. 7-9.) Then no more remains: But that to your sufficiency, as your worth is able, And let them work. This is a passage which has exercised the sagacity of the Editors, and is now to employ mine. Sir Tho. Hanmer having caught from Mr. Theobald a hint that a line was lost, endeavours to supply it thus. Then no more remains, But that to your sufficiency you join A will to serve us, as your worth is able.

He has by this bold conjecture undoubtedly obtained a meaning, but, perhaps not, even in his own opinion, the meaning of Shakespeare. That the passage is more or less corrupt, I believe every reader will agree with the Editors. I am not convinced that a line is lost, as Mr. Theobald conjectures, nor that the change of "but" to "put", which Dr. Warburton has admitted after some other Editor, will amend the fault. There was probably some original obscurity in the expression, which gave occasion to mistake in repetition or transcription.

I therefore suspect that the Author wrote thus, —Then no more remains, But that to your sufficiencies your worth is abled, And let them work.

Then nothing remains more than to tell you that your virtue is now invested with power equal to your knowledge and wisdom. let therefore your knowledge and your virtue now work together. It may easily be conceived how "sufficiencies" was, by an inarticulate speaker, or inattentive hearer, confounded with "sufficiency as", and how "abled", a word very unusual, was changed into "able". For "abled", however, an authority is not wanting. Lear uses it in the same sense, or nearly the same, with the Duke.

As for "sufficiencies", D. Hamilton, in his dying speech, prays that "Charles II. may exceed both the VIRTUES and SUFFICIENCIES of his father."

Act I. Scene II. (I. I. 51.)

We have with a leaven'd and prepared choice. "Leaven'd" has no sense in this place: we should read "Level'd choice". The allusion is to archery, when a man has fixed upon his object, after taking good aim.—Warburton. No emendation is necessary. "leaven'd choice" is one of Shakespeare's harsh metaphors. His train of ideas seems to be this. "I have proceeded to you with choice mature, concocted, fermented, leaven'd." When Bread is "leaven'd", it is left to ferment: a "leavn'd" choice is therefore a choice not hasty, but considerate, not declared as soon as it fell into the imagination, but suffered to work long in the mind. Thus explained, it suits better with "prepared" than "levelled".

Act II. Scene IX. (II. III. 11-12.)

Who falling in the flaws of her own youth, Hath blister'd her report. Who doth not see that the integrity of the metaphor requires we should read "flames of her own youth."—Warburton. Who does not see that upon such principles there is no end of correction.

Act III. Scene I. (III. I. 13-15.)

Thou art not noble: For all th' accommodations, that thou bear'st Are nurs'd by baseness. Dr. Warburton is undoubtedly mistaken in supposing that by "baseness" is meant "self-love" here assigned as the motive of all human actions. Shakespeare meant only to observe, that a minute analysis of life at once destroys that splendour which dazzles the imagination. Whatever grandeur can display, or luxury enjoy, is procured by "baseness", by offices of which the mind shrinks from the contemplation. All the delicacies of the table may be traced back to the shambles and the dunghill, all magnificence of building was hewn from the quarry, and all the pomp of ornaments, dug from among the damps and darkness of the mine.

Act III. Scene I. (III. I. 16-17)

The soft and tender fork of a poor worm. "Worm" is put for any creeping thing or "serpent". Shakespeare supposes falsely, but according to the vulgar notion, that a serpent wounds with his tongue, and that his tongue is "forked". He confounds reality and fiction, a serpent's tongue is "soft" but not "forked" nor hurtful. If it could hurt, it could not be soft. In Midsummer-night's Dream he has the same notion. —With doubler tongue Then thine, O serpent, never adder stung.

Act III. Scene I. (III. I. 32-4)

Thou hast nor youth, nor age: But as it were an after dinner's sleep, Dreaming on both. This is exquisitely imagined. When we are young we busy ourselves in forming schemes for succeeding time, and miss the gratifications that are before us; when we are old we amuse the languour of age with the recollection of youthful pleasures or performances; so that our life, of which no part is filled with the business of the present time, resembles our dreams after dinner, when the events of the morning are mingled with the designs of the evening.

Act III Scene I. (III. I. 36-8)

When thou'rt old and rich, Thou hast neither heat, affection, limb, nor beauty To make thy riches pleasant. But how does beauty make "riches pleasant"? We should read "bounty", which compleats the sense, and is this; Thou hast neither the pleasure of enjoying riches thy self, for thou wantest vigour: nor of seeing it enjoyed by others, for thou wantest "bounty". Where the making the want of "bounty" as inseparable from old age as the want of "health", is extremely satyrical tho' not altogether just. —Warburton. I am inclined to believe that neither man nor woman will have much difficulty to tell how "beauty makes riches pleasant". Surely this emendation, though it is elegant and ingenious, is not such as that an opportunity of inserting it should be purchased by declaring ignorance of what every one knows, by confessing insensibility of what every one feels.

Act III. Scene II. (III. I. 137-8)

Is't not a kind of incest, to take life From thine own sister's shame? In Isabella's declamation there is something harsh, and something forced and far-fetched. But her indignation cannot be thought violent when we consider her not only as a virgin but as a nun.

Act IV. Scene VIII. (IV. III. 4-5.)

First here's young Mr. Rash, &c. This enumeration of the inhabitants of the prison affords a very striking view of the practices predominant in Shakespeare's age. Besides those whose follies are common to all times, we have four fighting men and a traveller. It is not unlikely that the originals of these pictures were then known.

Act IV. Scene XIII. (IV. V. 1.)

Duke. These letters at fit time deliver me. Peter never delivers the letters, but tells his story without any credentials. The poet forgot the plot which he had formed.

Act V. Scene VII. (V. I. 448.)

'Till he did look on me. The Duke has justly observed that Isabel is importuned against all sense to solicit for Angelo, yet here against all sense she solicits for him. Her argument is extraordinary. A due sincerity govern'd his deeds, 'Till he did look on me; since it is so, Let him not die. That Angelo had committed all the crimes charged against him, as far as he could commit them, is evident. The only INTENT which his act did not overtake, was the defilement of Isabel.

Of this Angelo was only intentionally guilty. Angelo's crimes were such, as must sufficiently justify punishment, whether its end be to secure the innocent from wrong, or to deter guilt by example; and I believe every reader feels some indignation when he finds him spared. From what extenuation of his crime can Isabel, who yet supposes her brother dead, form any plea in his favour. Since he was good 'till he looked in me, let him not die.

I am afraid our Varlet Poet intended to inculcate, that women think ill of nothing that raises the credit of their beauty, and are ready, however virtuous, to pardon any act which they think incited by their own charms.

ACT V. Secne VIII. (V. I. 479 foll.)

It is somewhat strange, that Isabel is not made to express either gratitude, wonder or joy at the sight of her brother. After the pardon of two murderers Lucio might be treated by the good Duke with less harshness; but perhaps the Poet intended to show, what is too often seen, that men easily forgive wrongs which are not committed against themselves. The novel of Cynthio Giraldi, from which Shakespeare is supposed to have borrowed this fable, may be read in Shakespeare illustrated, elegantly translated, with remarks which will assist the enquirer to discover how much absurdity Shakespeare has admitted or avoided. I cannot but suspect that some other had new modelled the novel of Cynthio, or written a story which in some particulars resembled it, and that Cinthio was not the author whom Shakespeare immediately followed.

The Emperour in Cinthio is named Maximine, the Duke, in Shakespeare's enumeration of the persons of the drama, is called Vincentio. This appears a very slight remark; but since the Duke has no name in the play, nor is ever mentioned but by his title, why should he be called Vincentio among the "Persons", but because the name was copied from the story, and placed superfluously at the head of the list by the mere habit of transcription? It is therefore likely that there was then a story of Vincentio Duke of Vienna, different from that of Maximine Emperour of the Romans. Of this play the light or comic part is very natural and pleasing, but the grave scenes, if a few passages be excepted, have more labour than elegance. The plot is rather intricate than artful.

The time of the action is indefinite; some time, we know not how much, must have elapsed between the recess of the Duke and the imprisonment of Claudio; for he must have learned the story of Mariana in his disguise, or he delegated his power to a man already known to be corrupted. The unities of action and place are sufficiently preserved. HENRY IV None of Shakespeare's plays are more read than the first and second parts of Henry the fourth. Perhaps no author has ever in two plays afforded so much delight.

The great events are interesting, for the fate of kingdoms depends upon them; the slighter occurrences are diverting, and, except one or two, sufficiently probable; the incidents are multiplied with wonderful fertility of invention, and the characters diversified with the utmost nicety of discernment, and the profoundest skill in the nature of man. The prince, who is the hero both of the comic and tragic part, is a young man of great abilities and violent passions, whose sentiments are right, though his actions are wrong; whose virtues are obscured by negligence, and whose understanding is dissipated by levity. In his idle hours he is rather loose than wicked, and when the occasion forces out his latent qualities, he is great without effort, and brave without tumult.

The trifler is roused into a hero, and the hero again reposes in the trifler. This character is great, original, and just. Piercy is a rugged soldier, cholerick, and quarrelsome, and has only the soldier's virtues, generosity and courage. But Falstaff unimitated, unimitable Falstaff, how shall I describe thee? Thou compound of sense and vice; of sense which may be admired but not esteemed, of vice which may be despised, but hardly detested. Falstaff is a character loaded with faults, and with those faults which naturally produce contempt. He is a thief, and a glutton, a coward, and a boaster, always ready to cheat the weak, and prey upon the poor; to terrify the timorous and insult the defenceless. At once obsequious and malignant, he satirises in their absence those whom he lives by flattering.

He is familiar with the prince only as an agent of vice, but of this familiarity he is so proud as not only to be supercilious and haughty with common men, but to think his interest of importance to the duke of Lancaster. Yet the man thus corrupt, thus despicable, makes himself necessary to the prince that despises him, by the most pleasing of all qualities, perpetual gaiety, by an unfailing power of exciting laughter, which is the more freely indulged, as his wit is not of the splendid or ambitious kind, but consists in easy escapes and sallies of levity, which make sport but raise no envy.

It must be observed that he is stained with no enormous or sanguinary crimes, so that his licentiousness is not so offensive but that it may be borne for his mirth. The moral to be drawn from this representation is, that no man is more dangerous than he that with a will to corrupt, hath the power to please; and that neither wit nor honesty ought to think themselves safe with such a companion when they see Henry seduced by Falstaff.

Henry V

ACT. II. Scene IV. (II. III. 27-8.)

Cold as any stone. Such is the end of Falstaff, from whom Shakespeare had promised us in his epilogue to Henry IV. that we should receive more entertainment. It happened to Shakespeare as to other writers, to have his imagination crowded with a tumultuary confusion of images, which, while they were yet unsorted and unexamined, seemed sufficient to furnish a long train of incidents, and a new variety of merriment, but which, when he was to produce them to view, shrunk suddenly from him, or could not be accommodated to his general design. That he once designed to have brought Falstaff on the scene again, we know from himself; but whether he could contrive no train of adventures suitable to his character, or could match him with no companions likely to quicken his humour, or could open no new vein of pleasantry, and was afraid to continue the same strain lest it should not find the same reception, he has here for ever discarded him, and made haste to dispatch him, perhaps for the same reason for which Addison killed Sir Roger, that no other hand might attempt to exhibit him.

Let meaner authors learn from this example, that it is dangerous to sell the bear which is yet not hunted, to promise to the public what they have not written. KING LEAR The Tragedy of Lear is deservedly celebrated among the dramas of Shakespeare. There is perhaps no play, which keeps the attention so strongly fixed; which so much agitates our passions and interests our curiosity. The artful involutions of distinct interests, the striking opposition of contrary characters, the sudden changes of fortune, and the quick succession of events, fill the mind with a perpetual tumult of indignation, pity, and hope. There is no scene which does not contribute to the aggravation of the distress or conduct of the action, and scarce a line which does not conduce to the progress of the scene. So powerful is the current of the poet's imagination, that the mind, which once ventures within it, is hurried irresistibly along. On the seeming improbability of Lear's conduct it may be observed, that he is represented according to histories at that time vulgarly received as true.

And perhaps if we turn our thoughts upon the barbarity and ignorance of the age to which this story is referred, it will appear not so unlikely as while we estimate Lear's manners by our own. Such preference of one daughter to another, or resignation of dominion on such conditions, would be yet credible, if told of a petty prince of Guinea or Madagascar. Shakespeare, indeed, by the mention of his Earls and Dukes, has given us the idea of times more civilised, and of life regulated by softer manners; and the truth that though he so nicely discriminates, and so minutely describes the characters of men, he commonly neglects and confounds the characters of ages, by mingling customs ancient and modern, English and foreign.

My learned friend Mr. Warton, who has in the Adventurer very minutely criticized this play, remarks, that the instances of cruelty are too savage and shocking, and that the intervention of Edmund destroys the simplicity of the story. These objections may, I think, be answered, by repeating, that the cruelty of the daughters is an historical fact, to which the poet has added little, having only drawn it into a series by dialogue and action. But I am not able to apologize with equal plausibility for the extrusion of Gloucester's eyes, which seems an act too horrid to be endured in dramatic exhibition, and such as must always compel the mind to relieve its distress by incredulity. Yet let it be remembered that our author well knew what would please the audience for which he wrote.

The injury done by Edmund to the simplicity of the action is abundantly recompensed by the addition of variety, by the art with which he is made to co-operate with the chief design and the opportunity which he gives the poet of combining perfidy with perfidy, and connecting the wicked son with the wicked daughters, to impress this important moral, that villany is never at a stop, that crimes lead to crimes, and at last terminate in ruin. But though this moral be incidentally enforced, Shakespeare has suffered the virtue of Cordelia to perish in a just cause contrary to the natural ideas of justice, to the hope of the reader, and, what is yet more strange, to the faith of chronicles. Yet this conduct is justified by the Spectator, who blames Tate for giving Cordelia success and happiness in his alteration, and declares, that, in his opinion, the tragedy has lost half its beauty.

Dennis has remarked, whether justly or not, that, to secure the favourable reception of Cato, "the town was poisoned with much false and abominable criticism," and that endeavours had been used to discredit and decry poetical justice. A play in which the wicked prosper, and the virtuous miscarry, may doubtless be good, because it is a just representation of the common events of human life: but since all reasonable beings naturally love justice, I cannot easily be persuaded, that the observation of justice makes a play worse; or, that if other excellencies are equal, the audience will not always rise better pleased from the final triumph of persecuted virtue. In the present case the publick has decided. Cordelia, from the time of Tate, has always retired with victory and felicity. And, if my sensations could add any thing to the general suffrage, I might relate, that I was many years ago so shocked by Cordelia's death, that I know not whether I ever endured to read again the last scenes of the play till I undertook to revise them as an editor.

Romeo and Juliet

Act I. Scene II. (I. I. 181 foll.)

Why then, O brawling love! O loving hate! &c. Of these lines neither the sense nor occasion is very evident. He is not yet in love with an enemy, and to love one and hate another is no such uncommon state, as can deserve all this toil of antithesis.

Act I. Scene III. (I. II. 25.)

Earth-treading stars that make dark HEAVEN's light. This nonsense should be reformed thus, Earth-treading stars that make dark EVEN light. Warburton. But why nonsense? Is anything more commonly said, than that beauties eclipse the sun? Has not Pope the thought and the word? Sol through white curtains shot a tim'rous ray, And ope'd those eyes that must eclipse the day. Both the old and the new reading are philosophical nonsense, but they are both, and both equally poetical sense.

Act I. Scene III. (I. II. 26-8.)

Such comfort as do lusty young men feel, When well-apparel'd April on the heel Of limping winter treads. To say, and to say in pompous words, that a "young man shall feel" as much in an assembly of beauties, "as young men feel in the month of April," is surely to waste sound upon a very poor sentiment. I read, Such comfort as do lusty YEOMEN feel. You shall feel from the sight and conversation of these ladies such hopes of happiness and such pleasure, as the farmer receives from the spring, when the plenty of the year begins, and the prospect of the harvest fills him with delight.

Act I. Scene IV. (I. III. 92.)

That in gold clasps locks in the golden story. The "golden story" is perhaps the "golden legend", a book in the darker ages of popery much read, and doubtless often exquisitely embellished, but of which Canus, one of the popish doctors, proclaims the author to have been homo ferrei oris, plumbei cordis.

Act I. Scene VI. (1. V. 34.)

Good cousin Capulet. This cousin Capulet is "unkle" in the paper of invitation, but as Capulet is described as old, "cousin" is probably the right word in both places.

I know not how Capulet and his lady might agree, their ages were very disproportionate; he has been past masking for thirty years, and her age, as she tells Juliet is but eight and twenty.

Act I. Chorus.. (II. Prologue.)

The use of this chorus is not easily discovered, it conduces nothing to the progress of the play, but relates what is already known or what the next scenes will show; and relates it without adding the improvement of any moral sentiment.

Act II. Scene VI. (II. VI. 15.)

Too swift arrives as tardy as too slow. He that travels too fast is as long before he comes to the end of his journey, as he that travels slow. Precipitation produces mishap.

Act III. Scene I. (III. I. 2.)

The day is hot. It is observed that in Italy almost all assassinations are committed during the heat of summer.

Act III. Scene III. (III. I. 183.)

Affection makes him false. The charge of falshood on Bentivolio, though produced at hazard, is very just. The author, who seems to intend the character of Bentiolio as good, meant perhaps to show, how the best minds, in a state of faction and discord, are detorted to criminal partiality.

Act III. Scene VIII. (III. V. 84.1)

And, yet, no Man like he doth grieve my heart. Juliet's equivocations are rather too artful for a mind disturbed by the loss of a new lover.

Act IV. Scene III. (IV. III. 2-3.)

Leave me to myself to-night; For I have need of many orisons. Juliet plays most of her pranks under the appearance of religion: perhaps Shakespeare meant to punish her hypocrisy.

Act V. Scene I. (V. I. 3.)

My bosom's Lord sits lightly on this throne, &c. These three lines are very gay and pleasing. But why does Shakespeare give Romeo this involuntary cheerfulness just before the extremity of unhappiness? Perhaps to show the vanity of trusting to those uncertain and casual exaltations or depressions, which many consider as certain foretokens of good and evil.

Act V. Scene V. (V. III. 229.)

FRIAR. I will be brief. It is much to be lamented that the Poet did not conclude the dialogue with the action, and avoid a narrative of events which the audience already knew. This play is one of the most pleasing of our Author's performances. The scenes are busy and various, the incidents numerous and important, the catastrophe irresistibly affecting and the process of the action carried on with such probability at least with such congruity to popular opinions, as tragedy requires. Here is one of the few attempts of Shakespeare to exhibit the conversation of gentlemen, to represent the airy sprightliness of juvenile elegance. Mr. Dryden mentions a tradition which might easily reach his time, of a declaration made by Shakespeare, that he was obliged to kill Mercutio in the third act, lest he should have been killed by him. Yet he thinks him no such formidable person, but that he might have lived through the play, and died in his bed, without danger to a poet.

Dryden well knew, had he been in quest of truth, that, in a pointed sentence, more regard is commonly had to the word than the thought, and that it is very seldom to be rigorously understood. Mercutio's wit, gaiety and courage, will always procure him friends that wish him a longer life; but his death is not precipitated, he has lived out the time allotted him in the construction of the play; nor do I doubt the ability of Shakespeare to have continued his existence, though some of his sallies are perhaps out of the reach of Dryden; whose genius was not very fertile of merriment, nor ductile to humour, but acute, argumentative, comprehensive, and sublime.

The Nurse is one of the characters in which the Author delighted: he has, with great subtlety of distinction, drawn her at once loquacious and secret, obsequious and insolent, trusty and dishonest. His comic scenes are happily wrought, but his pathetic strains are always polluted with some unexpected depravations. His persons, however distressed, HAVE A CONCEIT LEFT THEM IN THEIR MISERY, A MISERABLE CONCEIT. HAMLET ACT II. SCENE ii. (II. I. 114-17.) It is as proper to our age To cast beyond ourselves in our opinions, As it is common for the younger sort To lack discretion. This is not the remark of a weak man. The vice of age is too much suspicion. Men long accustomed to the wiles of life "cast" commonly "beyond themselves", let their cunning go further than reason can attend it. This is always the fault of a little mind, made artful by long commerce with the world.

Act II. Scene IV. (II. II.)

Polonius is a man bred in courts, exercised in business, stored with observation, confident of his knowledge, proud of his eloquence, and declining into dotage. His mode of oratory is truly represented as designed to ridicule the practice of those times, of prefaces that made no introduction, and of method that embarrassed rather than explained. This part of his character is accidental, the rest is natural. Such a man is positive and confident, because he knows that his mind was once strong, and knows not that it is become weak. Such a man excels in general principles, but fails in the particular application. He is knowing in retrospect, and ignorant in foresight. While he depends upon his memory, and can draw from his repositories of knowledge, he utters weighty sentences, and gives useful counsel; but as the mind in its enfeebled state cannot be kept long busy and intent, the old man is subject to sudden dereliction of his faculties, he loses the order of his ideas, and entangles himself in his own thoughts, till he recovers the leading principle, and falls again into his former train. This idea of dotage encroaching upon wisdom, will solve all the phenomena of the character of Polonius. If the dramas of Shakespeare were to be characterised, each by the particular excellence which distinguishes it from the rest, we must allow to the tragedy of HAMLET the praise of variety.

The incidents are so numerous, that the argument of the play would make a long tale. The scenes are interchangeably diversified with merriment and solemnity; with merriment that includes judicious and instructive observations, and solemnity, not strained by poetical violence above the natural sentiments of man. New characters appear from time to time in continual succession, exhibiting various forms of life and particular modes of conversation. The pretended madness of HAMLET causes much mirth, the mournful distraction of OPHELIA fills the heart with tenderness, and every personage produces the effect intended, from the apparition that in the first act chills the blood with horror, to the fop in the last that exposes affectation to just contempt. The conduct is perhaps not wholly secure against objections.

The action is indeed for the most part in continual progression, but there are some scenes which neither forward nor retard it. Of the feigned madness of Hamlet there appears no adequate cause, for he does nothing which he might not have done with the reputation of sanity. He plays the madman most, when he treats Ophelia with so much rudeness, which seems to be useless and wanton cruelty. Hamlet is, through the whole play, rather an instrument than an agent. After he has, by the stratagem of the play, convicted the King, he makes no attempt to punish him, and his death is at last effected by an incident which Hamlet has no part in producing. The catastrophe is not very happily produced; the exchange of weapons is rather an expedient of necessity, than a stroke of art. A scheme might easily have been formed, to kill Hamlet with the dagger, and Laertes with the bowl.

The poet is accused of having shown little regard to poetical justice, and may be charged with equal neglect of poetical probability. The apparition left the regions of the dead to little purpose; the revenge which he demands is not obtained but by the death of him that was required to take it; and the gratification which would arise from the destruction of an usurper and a murderer, is abated by the untimely death of Ophelia, the young, the beautiful, the harmless, and the pious.

Othello

Act V. Scene VI. (V. II. 63-5.)

Oh perjur'd woman! Thou dost stone my heart, And mak'st me call, what I intent to do, A murder, which I thought a sacrifice. This line is difficult. Thou hast harden'd my heart, and makest me kill thee with the rage of a MURDERER, when I thought to have sacrificed thee to justice with the calmness of a priest striking a victim. It must not be omitted, that one of the elder quarto's reads, "Thou dost stone THY heart:" which I suspect to be genuine.

The meaning then will be, thou forcest me to dismiss thee from the world in the state of the murdered without preparation for death, when I intended that thy punishment should have been "a sacrifice" atoning for thy crime. I am glad that I have ended my revisal of this dreadful scene. It is not to be endured. The beauties of this play impress themselves so strongly upon the attention of the reader, that they can draw no aid from critical illustration.

The fiery openness of Othello, magnanimous, artless, and credulous, boundless in his confidence, ardent in his affection, inflexible in his resolution, and obdurate in his revenge; the cool malignity of Iago, silent in his resentment, subtle in his designs, and studious at once of his interest and his vengeance; the soft simplicity of Desdemona, confident of merit, and conscious of innocence, her artless perseverance in her suit, and her slowness to suspect that she can be suspected, are such proofs of Shakespeare's skill in human nature, as, I suppose, it is vain to seek in any modern writer.

The gradual progress which Iago makes in the Moor's conviction, and the circumstances which he employs to inflame him, are so artfully natural, that, though it will perhaps not be said of him as he says of himself, that he is "a man not esily jealous," yet we cannot but pity him when at last we find him "perplexed in the extreme." There is always danger lest wickedness conjoined with abilities should steal upon esteem, though it misses of approbation but the character if Iago is so conducted, that he is from the first scene to the last hated and despised.

Event he inferiour characters of this play would be very conspicuous in any other piece, not only for their justness but their strength. Cassio is brave, benevolent, and honest, ruined only by his want of stubbornness to resist an insidious invitation of Rodegigo's suspicious credulity, and impatient submission of the cheats which he sees practiced upon him, and which by persuasion he suffers to be repeated, exhibit a strong picture of a weak mind betrayed by unlawful desires, to a false friend and the virtue of AEmilia is such as we often find, worn loosely but not cast off, easy to commit small crimes, but quickened and alarmed at atrocious villainies.

The Scenes from the beginning to the end are busy, varied but happy interchanges, and regularly promoting the progression of the story; and the narrative in the end, though it tells but what is known already, yet is necessary to produce the death of Othello. Had the scene opened in Cyprus, and the preceding incidents been occasionally related, there had been little wanting of a drama of the most exact and scrupulous regularity.

Chapter 17

Johnson's Preface to Shakespeare: Then and Now

Shakespeare endures. Though four hundred-odd years and countless playwrights have come and gone, the works William Shakespeare continue to enthrall us. Every student studies him. Some love him; many hate him. Still, all know him. Outside the classroom, too, Shakespeare continues to shape the culture of the western world. His plays grace the stage each season, with such diverse company as Sophocles and Jeff Goode. They are produced in every imaginable context. Critics continue to analyse their facets. Indeed, critics dedicate tomes to critiquing their peers' observations of his works. Each year, a new crop of his plays are, with a few intermittent exceptions, butchered by Hollywood. Surprisingly enough, however, those films continue to draw crowds. Surely, Shakespeare's endurance attests to his literary merit. Even in the eighteenth century, the Bard's votaries defended his worth by citing the longevity of his appeal.

Dr. Samuel Johnson, however, warned against such short-sighted estimations of greatness by reminding his contemporaries that all too often "praises are without reason lavished on the dead, and...the honours do only to excellence are paid to antiquity" (Johnson 8). Still, Johnson proclaims Shakespeare's merits. With his publication *The Plays of William Shakespeare* in 1765, Johnson made his contribution to the history of Shakespearean criticism. As with much of his work, Johnson left his own indelible mark on the field. His edition remains relevant today because it continues to affect the way critics approach Shakespeare. Johnson was not the first editor of Shakespeare; nor was he by any means the last. Though he defended the methodology of his edition itself quite well, its legacy in modern literature is, on the whole, indirect. The critical material that accompanies his edition continues to have a much more direct effect on Shakespeare as he is interpreted today.

To use Johnson's own criterion, his Preface and annotation can be called great because "frequent comparisons have confirmed opinion in its favour" (Johnson 9). An understanding of the criticism itself is, of course, necessary to any understanding of its endurance. The notes with which Johnson sprinkled his edition, though indisputably important, are too diverse to be treated with any justice here. Johnson's more comprehensive Preface has retained its influence to the present day. There are four easily distinguished sections in Johnson's Preface; in the first, he explicates Shakespeare's virtues after explaining what merit, if any, can be determined by the Shakespeare's enduring popularity. Johnson walks the middle ground with his critique of antiquity. He neither fully embraces longevity as a litmus test of quality nor rejects it as meaningless. Rather, he points out that those works which have withstood the test of time stand out not because of their age alone, but because, with age, those works have "been compared with other works of the same kind" and can therefore be "stilled excellent" (Johnson 9).

He proceeds thence to elevate Shakespeare as the poet of nature. "Nothing can please many, and please long, but just representations of general nature". It is Shakespeare's realism, Johnson argues, that distinguishes him from other playwrights. In his characterization and dialogue, Shakespeare "overlooks the casual distinction of country and condition," striking at the centre of humanity. The nature captured by Shakespeare's characters is exhibited in the "ease and simplicity" of their dialogues. Indeed, Johnson points out, the distinctions of character stressed by such critics as Voltaire and Rhymer impose only artificial burdens on the natural genius of Shakespeare. Johnson goes further in his defence of the Bard's merit, extending his argument from the characters within his plays to the genre of the plays themselves. In the strictest, classical sense of the terms, Johnson admits, Shakespeare's works cannot be fairly called comedies or tragedies. For this too, his plays earned harsh criticism from Johnson's contemporaries. Johnson, though, sees in the mixture of sorrow and joy a style which "approaches nearer than either to the appearance of life" .

By acknowledging the basis of such criticism, Johnson frees himself to turn the argument on its head. He holds up the tragicomedies of Shakespeare as distinctly natural; in their "interchange of seriousness and merriment," they hold up "a faithful mirrour of manners and of life" (15, 10). This, of course, is paramount to literary success to Johnson. His praise for Shakespeare, which centers on the Bard's sublunary approach to character, dialogue, and plot, does not blind him to the poet of nature's weaknesses. Johnson airs Shakespeare's imperfections without hesitance. In doing so, though, he does not weaken his arguments; he simply establishes his credentials as a critic. As Edward Tomarken points out, "for Johnson, criticism requires, not intrusive sententiae, but evaluative interpretations, decisions about how literature applies to the human dilemma" (Tomarken 2). Johnson is not hesitant to admit Shakespeare's faults: his earlier praise serves to keep those flaws in perspective. Even without that perspective, however, Johnson's censure of Shakespeare is not particularly harsh.

For the most part, Johnson highlights surface-level defects in the Bard's works: his "loosely formed" plots, his "commonly gross" jests, and—most ironically—his "disproportionate pomp of diction and a wearisome train of circumlocution" (Johnson 19, 20). The most egregious fault Johnson finds in Shakespeare, though, is thematic. Unsurprisingly, Johnson exhibits emphatic distaste for Shakespeare's lack of moral purpose. Johnson argues that he "sacrifices virtue to convenience" . In leading "his persons indifferently through right and wrong" and leaving "their examples to operate by chance," Shakespeare has abandoned his duty as an author as the righteous Johnson would have that duty defined. This is, in his eyes, Shakespeare's greatest flaw, though it does not supercede his other merits.

In the third section of his Preface, Johnson ceases his attack on Shakespeare, and returns to his defence. Johnson begins by refuting the reproach wrought by adherents to the unities, which had "elicited from French criticism a tiresome unanimity" (Stock 76). Though they have lost their prominence, Shakespeare's deviation from the unities of action, time, and place earned him substantial censure. Johnson defends Shakespeare's employment of unity of action, though he admits that Shakespeare deviates slightly in to allow his plots to concur with nature. He goes further, though, and summarily dismisses the value of the unities, whose importance, he contends, "arises from the supposed necessity of making the drama credible" (Johnson 23). Such credibility is impossible, however, since the very nature of drama is beyond the reach of reason. "Spectators," Johnson points out, "are always in their senses, and know, from the first act to the last, that the stage is only a stage, and that the players are only players" . The imagination of the audience, stretched by the play itself, is not incapable of further activity.

By reversing the entire paradigm through which the unities are used, Johnson changes Shakespeare's fault into a praiseworthy asset. Johnson also praises Shakespeare within his context. Given the Bard's unimpressive educational background, the quality of his work is astounding. Education alone, however, could not produce Shakespeare's works, which have "a vigilance of distinction which books and precepts cannot offer" . It is that observation which makes him the poet of nature, and frees his works from many forms of criticism. Johnson extends his consideration of context to the national level. At a time in which the English had no model of literary excellence, Shakespeare produced just such a model. In his context, then, Johnson purports that Shakespeare's achievement is phenomenal.

Johnson's defends Shakespeare as having fulfilled the "first purpose of a writer, by exciting restless and unquenchable curiosity, and compelling him that reads his work to read it through" (Johnson 30). His advocacy of Shakespeare in the first section, coupled with his rigorous defence in the third, all but insist that Shakespeare's merits heavily outweigh his faults.

In the final quarter of the Preface, Johnson reviews the work of previous editors of Shakespeare, and after critiquing his predecessors, Johnson explains his own editorial methodology. Clearly, Johnson felt that no extant edition could be considered authoritative, for he undertook to create his own. He opens by lamenting Shakespeare's complete disregard for the preservation of his plays.

Had the Bard released an authorized edition of his works during his lifetime, Johnson points out, the "negligence and unskilfulness" of eighteenth century editors would not have "corrupted many passages perhaps beyond recovery" (Johnson 39, 40). Still, Johnson proves willing add praise to his condemnation as he comments on the particular approaches of Rowe, Pope, Theobald, Hanmer, and Warburton. Rowe, whose edition appeared in 1709, focused little on "correction or explanation," but whose emendations were used by successive editors . Johnson acknowledges that his approach to Shakespeare was suitable for his context. Johnson grants more praise to Pope, who he says illustrated to readers the "true state of Shakespeare's text" . In doing so, Pope edited the plays heavily, even distinguishing between the legitimate and the forgeries. For Pope Johnson retained an editor's notes in full, an indication of the high regard in which Johnson held him.

Not all of Johnson's predecessors faired as well as Pope, though. Johnson is—not altogether surprisingly—harsh with Theobald, who attacked Pope's edition. Johnson characterizes him as "a man of narrow comprehension…with no native and intrinsic splendor of genius" (Johnson 42-43). Still, Johnson acknowledges that "what little he did do was commonly right" . Of his notes, Johnson retains those from his second edition which were not corrected by successive editors. Johnson rigorously defends his fourth predecessor, Hanmer, whose attempts to add form to Shakespeare's meter had been attacked. Johnson, however, stresses Hanmer's great care in annotation, and reaffirms his merit as an editor. Warburton, the most recent of the Bard's editors, earns more sever censure from Johnson's pen. Johnson criticizes, first and foremost, Warburton's overconfidence, "which presumes to do, by surveying the surface, what labour only can perform, by penetrating the bottom" .

Johnson also attacks him for his weak notes and his insight into the plays inconsistent. As to his own edition, Johnson acknowledges his debt to his five predecessors, saying "not one left Shakespeare without improvement" . He also points out that he tended to look before even Rowe's edition in an effort to find the most authoritative text possible. In an effort to maintain plays' integrity, Johnson confines his "imagination to the margin," commenting on the text with as little modification as possible. Still, with a plethora of available sources, Johnson's work as an editor was still significant. In the end, he released the most comprehensive edition of Shakespeare's works of the eighteenth century.

Johnson's edition of Shakespeare was greeted with mix of adulation and criticism. Even from the beginning, however, the Preface "monopolized critical attention" (Sherbo 46). The misconception that the Preface itself constitutes Johnson's edition persists even today. Between Johnson's time and our own the Preface has been both exalted and condemned. Many of his contemporaries showered Johnson's edition with great praise, singling out the Preface as "a fine piece of writing" containing "much truth, good sense, and just criticism" (Colman qtd. in Sherbo 47).

Johnson's "comprehensive views and comprehensive expression...made the essay a classic" (Elledge 1136). Other critics subjected the Preface to further scrutiny, looking beyond the surface criticism at Johnson's methods of approaching Shakespeare. Thus William Kenrick, for example, focused extensively on Johnson's "treatment of the unities and the whole question of dramatic illusion" (Sherbo 48). Kenrick's review was not altogether positive, however. In fact, he bitterly censures Johnson, accusing him of "having acted, in the outrage he hath committed on Shakespeare, just like other sinners, not only by doing those things he ought not to have done, but by leaving undone those things he ought to have done" (Kenrick xv).

In *The Life of Samuel Johnson*, Boswell singles out the Preface, hailing it as a work "in which the excellencies and defects of that immortal bard are displayed with a masterly hand" (130-131). His dismissal of the rest of the work, however, betrays some hint of disappointment in the edition as a whole. Certainly, even in Johnson's lifetime, there were vocal critics besides Kenrick. John Hawkins dismissed it as unimpressive: "Much had been expected from it, and little now appeared to have been performed". Still, Hawkins acknowledges that Johnson's edition of Shakespeare formed the basis of subsequent editions. Critics of the nineteenth century were generally harsh as well. Charles Knight, for example, granted in 1867 that Johnson's work had "influenced the public opinion up to this day;" he immediately adds, though, that "the influence has been for the most part evil". By the end of the nineteenth century, the critical thought on the Preface tended toward the unimpressed.

Johnson has regained some stature in the past hundred years, however. Slowly, critics began to see in his Preface a "conclusive summing up by a strong, wise, and impartial mind". Other critics found value in more specific aspects of Johnson's work. T.S. Eliot praised his lucidity in identifying Shakespeare's genre: "The distinction between the tragic and the comic is an account of the way in which we try to live; when we get below it, as in *King Lear*, we have an account of the way in which we do live" (Eliot 296). Eliot shared Johnson's distaste for the superficial distinctions through which Shakespeare's plays had been labeled tragic, comic, and historic. Rather, he saw that, in the interchange tragic and comic scenes, Shakespeare produces literature that is true to life. Indeed, Charles Warren points out that "Eliot in his susceptibilities sounds a little like Dr. Johnson," whom he praised in various ways . Arthur Sherbo, editor of *Johnson on*

Shakespeare, saw that, despite its weaknesses, the Preface is still worthy of study: Where Johnson deviated from the traditional criticism of various aspects of Shakespeare's art he was often wrong...But this does not detract from the merited fame of the Preface as a magnificent restatement of the eighteenth century's thinking on Shakespeare. (Sherbo 60)

Such a view of Johnson is best described as qualified praise; he acknowledges its weaknesses without ignoring its strengths. Donald Green echoes Sherbo's praises, stressing that Johnson gave the eighteenth century's critics "their first really effective and memorable expression" (Greene, *Samuel Johnson* 185). More recently, also, Johnson has earned the recognition of modern critics. In his analysis of Shakespeare's depictions of reality, for example, A.D. Nuttall commends Johnson's approach to the Bard as poet of nature. Johnson, he says, "finds in Shakespeare's adherence to nature a profound and ordered uniformity" . Indeed, in many ways, the importance that Nuttall prescribes to realism is similar to that of Johnson. In his conclusion, he points out their mutual dislike for "the pastoral convention," in favour of forms less "insulated from this varying world" (185, 193). Nuttall embraces Shakespeare's version of reality, which he sees as an unconscious challenge to transcendentalism.

Edward Tomarken, too, defends the Preface. Never denying that it is a "largely derivative work," Tomarken argues that it directly links the criticism of the eighteenth century to that of today. He points out that it "speaks directly to us, raising new questions and presenting new resolutions for modern Shakespereans, theoreticians, and literary critics in general". Today's critics have generally looked beyond the origins of the work to its original methodological contributions, where they have found much value. More than any other modern critic, however, Harold Bloom has fully embraced Johnson's approach to Shakespeare. Arguably today's preeminent scholar of Shakespeare, Bloom singles out Johnson as "the foremost of interpreters" and "first among all Western literary critics" (Bloom 2). Such praise for Johnson, particularly in reference to his edition of Shakespeare, is almost unprecedented. He sees Johnson's contribution to both literary criticism generally and Shakespearean criticism specifically as indispensable. He defines "Johnson's vitality as a critic" by noting that he is "always sufficiently *inside* Shakespeare's plays to judge them as he judges human life, without ever forgetting that Shakespeare's function is to bring life to mind" . Bloom's tribute to Johnsonian criticism is not mere lip service, however; he integrates Johnson's principles into his own approach to Shakespeare's works.

Bloom echoes Johnson's focus on creativity, stressed not only in the Preface to Shakespeare, but also in the Lives of the Poets, where Johnson points out that Milton's work "is not the greatest of heroic poems, only because it is not the first". For Bloom, Shakespeare's ingenuity is of prime importance, and his invention was not only literary, but linguistic: "Early modern English was shaped by Shakespeare: the *Oxford English Dictionary* is made in his image" (Bloom 10). Bloom also incorporates Johnson's notion of Shakespeare as the poet of nature into his own work, calling Hamlet "art's tribute to nature" . Bloom's focus in examining Shakespeare is, in fact, his "originality in the representation of character". On the whole, Bloom is simultaneously a distinctly modern and distinctly Johnsonian critic.

Johnson was among the first of the Bard's editors. His Preface, however, betrays his reliance on his few predecessors. Nevertheless, his edition has affected the study of Shakespeare since its publication in 1765. Whether praised or censured, critics have garnished Johnson's edition—its Preface, in particular—with much attention. Johnson did not begin the study of Shakespeare, nor did he set an unchallenged precedent in the field. Still, Johnson's approach to the poet of nature has survived until the present. Certainly, Johnson's Preface does not enjoy the same popular appeal as Shakespeare's works. As long as scholars continue to examine Shakespeare, however, Johnson's work will remain important. Truly, Shakespeare endures. So does Johnson.

Chapter 18

Critical Essays

Preface to Shakespeare

That praises are without reason lavished on the dead, and that the honours due only to excellence are paid to antiquity, is a complaint likely to be always continued by those, who, being able to add nothing to truth, hope for eminence from the heresies of paradox; or those, who, being forced by disappointment upon consolatory expedients, are willing to hope from posterity what the present age refuses, and flatter themselves that the regard which is yet denied by envy, will be at last bestowed by time.

Antiquity, like every other quality that attracts the notice of mankind, has undoubtedly votaries that reverence it, not from reason, but from prejudice. Some seem to admire indiscriminately whatever has been long preserved, without considering that time has sometimes co-operated with chance; all perhaps are more willing to honour past than present excellence; and the mind contemplates genius through the shades of age, as the eye surveys the sun through artificial opacity. The great contention of criticism is to find the faults of the moderns, and the beauties of the ancients. While an authour is yet living we estimate his powers by his worst performance, and when he is dead we rate them by his best.

To works, however, of which the excellence is not absolute and definite, but gradual and comparative; to works not raised upon principles demonstrative and scientifick, but appealing wholly to observation and experience, no other test can be applied than length of duration and continuance of esteem.

What mankind have long possessed they have often examined and compared, and if they persist to value the possession, it is because frequent comparisons have confirmed opinion in its favour. As among the works of nature no man can properly call a river deep or a mountain high, without the knowledge of many mountains and many rivers; so in the productions of genius, nothing can be stiled excellent till it has been compared with other works of the same kind. Demonstration immediately displays its power, and has nothing to hope or fear from the flux of years; but works tentative and experimental must be estimated by their proportion to the general and collective ability of man, as it is discovered in a long succession of endeavours. Of the first building that was raised, it might be with certainty determined that it was round or square, but whether it was spacious or lofty must have been referred to time. The Pythagorean scale of numbers was at once discovered to be perfect; but the poems of Homer we yet know not to transcend the common limits of human intelligence, but by remarking, that nation after nation, and century after century, has been able to do little more than transpose his incidents, new name his characters, and paraphrase his sentiments.

The reverence due to writings that have long subsisted arises therefore not from any credulous confidence in the superior wisdom of past ages, or gloomy persuasion of the degeneracy of mankind, but is the consequence of acknowledged and indubitable positions, that what has been longest known has been most considered, and what is most considered is best understood.

The Poet, of whose works I have undertaken the revision, may now begin to assume the dignity of an ancient, and claim the privilege of established fame and prescriptive veneration. He has long outlived his century, the term commonly fixed as the test of literary merit. Whatever advantages he might once derive from personal allusions, local customs, or temporary opinions, have for many years been lost; and every topick of merriment or motive of sorrow, which the modes of artificial life afforded him, now only obscure the scenes which they once illuminated. The effects of favour and competition are at an end; the tradition of his friendships and his enmities has perished; his works support no opinion with arguments, nor supply any faction with invectives; they can neither indulge vanity nor gratify malignity, but are read without any other reason than the desire of pleasure, and are therefore praised only as pleasure is obtained; yet, thus unassisted by interest or passion, they have past through variations of taste and changes of manners, and, as they devolved from one generation to another, have received new honours at every transmission.

But because human judgment, though it be gradually gaining upon certainty, never becomes infallible; and approbation, though long continued, may yet be only the approbation of prejudice or fashion; it is proper to inquire, by what peculiarities of excellence Shakespeare has gained and kept the favour of his countrymen.

Nothing can please many, and please long, but just representations of general nature. Particular manners can be known to few, and therefore few only can judge how nearly they are copied. The irregular combinations of fanciful invention may delight a-while, by that novelty of which the common satiety of life sends us all in quest; but the pleasures of sudden wonder are soon exhausted, and the mind can only repose on the stability of truth.

Shakespeare is above all writers, at least above all modern writers, the poet of nature; the poet that holds up to his readers a faithful mirrour of manners and of life. His characters are not modified by the customs of particular places, unpractised by the rest of the world; by the peculiarities of studies or professions, which can operate but upon small numbers; or by the accidents of transient fashions or temporary opinions: they are the genuine progeny of common humanity, such as the world will always supply, and observation will always find. His persons act and speak by the influence of those general passions and principles by which all minds are agitated, and the whole system of life is continued in motion. In the writings of other poets a character is too often an individual; in those of Shakespeare it is commonly a species. It is from this wide extension of design that so much instruction is derived. It is this which fills the plays of Shakespeare with practical axioms and domestick wisdom.

It was said of Euripides, that every verse was a precept and it may be said of Shakespeare, that from his works may be collected a system of civil and oeconomical prudence. Yet his real power is not shown in the splendour of particular passages, but by the progress of his fable, and the tenour of his dialogue; and he that tries to recommend him by select quotations, will succeed like the pedant in Hierocles, who, when he offered his house to sale, carried a brick in his pocket as a specimen.

It will not easily be imagined how much Shakespeare excells in accommodating his sentiments to real life, but by comparing him with other authours. It was observed of the ancient schools of declamation, that the more diligently they were frequented, the more was the student disqualified for the world, because he found nothing there which he should ever meet in any other place. The same remark may be applied to every stage but that of Shakespeare. The theatre, when it is under any other direction, is peopled by such characters as were never seen, conversing in a language which was never heard, upon topicks which will never arise in the commerce of mankind. But the dialogue of this authour is often so evidently determined by the incident which produces it, and is pursued with so much ease and simplicity, that it seems scarcely to claim the merit of fiction, but to have been gleaned by diligent selection out of common conversation, and common occurrences.

Upon every other stage the universal agent is love, by whose power all good and evil is distributed, and every action quickened or retarded. To bring a lover, a lady and a rival into the fable; to entangle them in contradictory obligations, perplex them with oppositions of interest, and harrass them with violence of desires inconsistent with each other; to make them meet in rapture and part in agony; to fill their mouths with hyperbolical joy and outrageous sorrow; to distress them as nothing human ever was distressed; to deliver them as nothing human ever was delivered, is the business of a modern dramatist. For this probability is violated, life is misrepresented, and language is depraved. But love is only one of many passions, and as it has no great influence upon the sum of life, it has little operation in the dramas of a poet, who caught his ideas from the living world, and exhibited only what he saw before him. He knew, that any other passion, as it was regular or exorbitant, was a cause of happiness or calamity.

Characters thus ample and general were not easily discriminated and preserved, yet perhaps no poet ever kept his personages more distinct from each other. I will not say with Pope, that every speech may be assigned to the proper speaker, because many speeches there are which have nothing characteristical; but, perhaps, though some may be equally adapted to every person, it will be difficult to find, any that can be properly transferred from the present possessor to another claimant. The choice is right, when there is reason for choice.

Other dramatists can only gain attention by hyperbolical or aggravated characters, by fabulous and unexampled excellence or depravity, as the writers of barbarous romances invigorated the reader by a giant and a dwarf; and he that should form his expectations of human affairs from the play, or from the tale, would be equally deceived. Shakespeare has no heroes; his scenes are occupied only by men, who act and speak as the reader thinks that he should himself have spoken or acted on the same occasion:Even where the agency is supernatural the dialogue is level with life. Other writers disguise the most natural passions and most frequent incidents: so that he who contemplates them in the book will not know them in the world: Shakespeare approximates the remote, and familiarizes the wonderful; the event which he represents will not happen, but if it were possible, its effects would be probably such as he has assigned; and it may be said, that he has not only shewn human nature as it acts in real exigences, but as it would be found in trials, to which it cannot be exposed. This therefore is the praise of Shakespeare, that his drama is the mirrour of life; that he who has mazed his imagination, in following the phantoms which other writers raise up before him, may here be cured of his delirious extasies, by reading human sentiments in human language; by scenes from which a hermit may estimate the transactions of the world, and a confessor predict the progress of the passions.

His adherence to general nature has exposed him to the censure of criticks, who form their judgments upon narrower principles. Dennis and Rhymer think his Romans not sufficiently Roman; and Voltaire censures his kings as not completely royal. Dennis is offended, that Menenius, a senator of Rome, should play the buffoon; and Voltaire perhaps thinks decency violated when the Danish Usurper is represented as a drunkard. But Shakespeare always makes nature predominate over accident; and if he preserves the essential character, is not very careful of distinctions superinduced and adventitious. His story requires Romans or kings, but he thinks only on men. He knew that Rome, like every other city, had men of all dispositions; and wanting a buffoon, he went into the senate-house for that which the senate-house would certainly have afforded him. He was inclined to shew an usurper and a murderer not only odious but despicable, he therefore added drunkenness to his other qualities, knowing that kings love wine like other men, and that wine exerts its natural power upon kings. These are the petty cavils of petty minds; a poet overlooks the casual distinction of country and condition, as a painter, satisfied with the figure, neglects the drapery.

The censure which he has incurred by mixing comick and tragick scenes, as it extends to all his works, deserves more consideration. Let the fact be first stated, and then examined.

Shakespeare's plays are not in the rigorous and critical sense either tragedies or comedies, but compositions of a distinct kind; exhibiting the real state of sublunary nature, which partakes of good and evil, joy and sorrow, mingled with endless variety of proportion and innumerable modes of combination; and expressing the course of the world, in which the loss of one is the gain of another; in which, at the same time, the reveller is hasting to his wine, and the mourner burying his friend; in which the malignity of one is sometimes defeated by the frolick of another; and many mischiefs and many benefits are done and hindered without design.

Out of this chaos of mingled purposes and casualties the ancient poets, according to the laws which custom had prescribed, selected some the crimes of men, and some their absurdities; some the momentous vicissitudes of life, and some the lighter occurrences; some the terrours of distress, and some the gayeties of prosperity. Thus rose the two modes of imitation, known by the names of tragedy and comedy, compositions intended to promote different ends by contrary means, and considered as so little allied, that I do not recollect among the Greeks or Romans a single writer who attempted both.

Shakespeare has united the powers of exciting laughter and sorrow not only in one mind, but in one composition. Almost all his plays are divided between serious and ludicrous characters, and, in the successive evolutions of the design, sometimes produce seriousness and sorrow, and sometimes levity and laughter.

That this is a practice contrary to the rules of criticism will be readily allowed; but there is always an appeal open from criticism to nature. The end of writing is to instruct; the end of poetry is to instruct by pleasing. That the mingled drama may convey all the instruction of tragedy or comedy cannot be denied, because it includes both in its alterations of exhibition, and approaches nearer than either to the appearance of life, by shewing how great machinations and slender designs may promote or obviate one another, and the high and the low co-operate in the general system by unavoidable concatenation.

It is objected, that by this change of scenes the passions are interrupted in their progression, and that the principal event, being not advanced by a due gradation of preparatory incidents, wants at last the power to move, which constitutes the perfection of dramatick poetry. This reasoning is so specious, that it is received as true even by those who in daily experience feel it to be false. The interchanges of mingled scenes seldom fail to produce the intended vicissitudes of passion. Fiction cannot move so much, but that the attention may be easily transferred; and though it must be allowed that pleasing melancholy be sometimes interrupted by unwelcome levity, yet let it be considered likewise, that melancholy is often not pleasing, and that the disturbance of one man may be the relief of another; that different auditors have different habitudes; and that, upon the whole, all pleasure consists in variety.

The players, who in their edition divided our authour's works into comedies, histories, and tragedies, seem not to have distinguished the three kinds, by any very exact or definite ideas.

An action which ended happily to the principal persons, however serious or distressful through its intermediate incidents, in their opinion constituted a comedy. This idea of a comedy continued long amongst us, and plays were written, which, by changing the catastrophe, were tragedies to-day and comedies to-morrow.

Tragedy was not in those times a poem of more general dignity or elevation than comedy; it required only a calamitous conclusion, with which the common criticism of that age was satisfied, whatever lighter pleasure it afforded in its progress.

History was a series of actions, with no other than chronological succession, independent of each other, and without any tendency to introduce or regulate the conclusion. It is not always very nicely distinguished from tragedy. There is not much nearer approach to unity of action in the tragedy of "Antony and Cleopatra", than in the history of "Richard the Second". But a history might be continued through many plays; as it had no plan, it had no limits.

Through all these denominations of the drama, Shakespeare's mode of composition is the same; an interchange of seriousness and merriment, by which the mind is softened at one time, and exhilarated at another. But whatever be his purpose, whether to gladden or depress, or to conduct the story, without vehemence or emotion, through tracts of easy and familiar dialogue, he never fails to attain his purpose; as he commands us, we laugh or mourn, or sit silent with quiet expectation, in tranquillity without indifference.

When Shakespeare's plan is understood, most of the criticisms of Rhymer and Voltaire vanish away. The play of "Hamlet" is opened, without impropriety, by two sentinels; Iago bellows at Brabantio's window, without injury to the scheme of the play, though in terms which a modern audience would not easily endure; the character of Polonius is seasonable and useful; and the Grave-diggers themselves may be heard with applause.

Shakespeare engaged in dramatick poetry with the world open before him; the rules of the ancients were yet known to few; the publick judgment was unformed; he had no example of such fame as might force him upon imitation, nor criticks of such authority as might restrain his extravagance: He therefore indulged his natural disposition, and his disposition, as Rhymer has remarked, led him to comedy. In tragedy he often writes with great appearance of toil and study, what is written at last with little felicity; but in his comick scenes, he seems to produce without labour, what no labour can improve. In tragedy he is always struggling after some occasion to be comick, but in comedy he seems to repose, or to luxuriate, as in a mode of thinking congenial to his nature. In his tragick scenes there is always something wanting, but his comedy often surpasses expectation or desire. His comedy pleases by the thoughts and the language, and his tragedy for the greater part by incident and action. His tragedy seems to be skill, his comedy to be instinct.

The force of his comick scenes has suffered little diminution from the changes made by a century and a half, in manners or in words. As his personages act upon principles arising from genuine passion, very little modified by particular forms, their pleasures and vexations are communicable to all times and to all places; they are natural, and therefore durable; the adventitious peculiarities of personal habits, are only superficial dies, bright and pleasing for a little while, yet soon fading to a dim tinct, without any remains of former lustre;

but the discriminations of true passion are the colours of nature; they pervade the whole mass, and can only perish with the body that exhibits them. The accidental compositions of heterogeneous modes are dissolved by the chance which combined them; but the uniform simplicity of primitive qualities neither admits increase, nor suffers decay. The sand heaped by one flood is scattered by another, but the rock always continues in its place. The stream of time, which is continually washing the dissoluble fabricks of other poets, passes without injury by the adamant of Shakespeare.

If there be, what I believe there is, in every nation, a stile which never becomes obsolete, a certain mode of phraseology so consonant and congenial to the analogy and principles of its respective language as to remain settled and unaltered; this stile is probably to be sought in the common intercourse of life, among those who speak only to be understood, without ambition of elegance. The polite are always catching modish innovations, and the learned depart from established forms of speech, in hope of finding or making better; those who wish for distinction forsake the vulgar, when the vulgar is right; but there is a conversation above grossness and below refinement, where propriety resides, and where this poet seems to have gathered his comick dialogue. He is therefore more agreeable to the ears of the present age than any other authour equally remote, and among his other excellencies deserves to be studied as one of the original masters of our language.

These observations are to be considered not as unexceptionably constant, but as containing general and predominant truth. Shakespeare's familiar dialogue is affirmed to be smooth and clear, yet not wholly without ruggedness or difficulty; as a country may be eminently fruitful, though it has spots unfit for cultivation: His characters are praised as natural, though their sentiments are sometimes forced, and their actions improbable; as the earth upon the whole is spherical, though its surface is varied with protuberances and cavities.

Shakespeare with his excellencies has likewise faults, and

faults sufficient to obscure and overwhelm any other merit. I shall shew them in the proportion in which they appear to me, without envious malignity or superstitious veneration. No question can be more innocently discussed than a dead poet's pretensions to renown; and little regard is due to that bigotry which sets candour higher than truth.

His first defect is that to which may be imputed most of the evil in books or in men. He sacrifices virtue to convenience, and is so much more careful to please than to instruct, that he seems to write without any moral purpose. From his writings indeed a system of social duty may be selected, for he that thinks reasonably must think morally; but his precepts and axioms drop casually from him; he makes no just distribution of good or evil, nor is always careful to shew in the virtuous a disapprobation of the wicked; he carries his persons indifferently through right and wrong, and at the close dismisses them without further care, and leaves their examples to operate by chance. This fault the barbarity of his age cannot extenuate; for it is always a writer's duty to make the world better, and justice is a virtue independant on time or place.

The plots are often so loosely formed, that a very slight consideration may improve them, and so carelessly pursued, that he seems not always fully to comprehend his own design. He omits opportunities of instructing or delighting which the train of his story seems to force upon him, and apparently rejects those exhibitions which would be more affecting, for the sake of those which are more easy.

It may be observed, that in many of his plays the latter part is evidently neglected. When he found himself near the end of his work, and, in view of his reward, he shortened the labour, to snatch the profit. He therefore remits his efforts where he should most vigorously exert them, and his catastrophe is improbably produced or imperfectly represented.

He had no regard to distinction of time or place, but gives to one age or nation, without scruple, the customs, institutions, and opinions of another, at the expence not only of likelihood, but of possibility. These faults Pope has endeavoured, with more zeal than judgment, to transfer to his imagined interpolators. We need not wonder to find Hector quoting Aristotle, when we see the loves of Theseus and Hippolyta combined with the Gothic mythology of fairies. Shakespeare, indeed, was not the only violator of chronology, for in the same age Sidney, who wanted not the advantages of learning, has, in his "Arcadia", confounded the pastoral with the feudal times, the days of innocence, quiet and security, with those of turbulence, violence and adventure.

In his comick scenes he is seldom very successful, when he engages his characters in reciprocations of smartness and contest of sarcasm; their jests are commonly gross, and their pleasantry licentious; neither his gentlemen nor his ladies have much delicacy, nor are sufficiently distinguished from his clowns by any appearance of refined manners. Whether he represented the real conversation of his time is not easy to determine; the reign of Elizabeth is commonly supposed to have been a time of stateliness, formality and reserve, yet perhaps the relaxations of that severity were not very elegant. There must, however, have been always some modes of gayety preferable to others, and a writer ought to chuse the best.

In tragedy his performance seems constantly to be worse, as his labour is more. The effusions of passion which exigence forces out are for the most part striking and energetick; but whenever he solicits his invention, or strains his faculties, the offspring of his throes is tumour, meanness, tediousness, and obscurity.

In narration he affects a disproportionate pomp of diction and a wearisome train of circumlocution, and tells the incident imperfectly in many words, which might have been more plainly delivered in few. Narration in dramatick poetry is, naturally tedious, as it is unanimated and inactive, and obstructs the progress of the action; it should therefore always be rapid, and enlivened by frequent interruption. Shakespeare found it an encumbrance, and instead of lightening it by brevity, endeavoured to recommend it by dignity and splendour.

His declamations or set speeches are commonly cold and

weak, for his power was the power of nature; when he endeavoured, like other tragick writers, to catch opportunities of amplification, and instead of inquiring what the occasion demanded, to show how much his stores of knowledge could supply, he seldom escapes without the pity or resentment of his reader.

It is incident to him to be now and then entangled with an unwieldy sentiment, which he cannot well express, and will not reject; he struggles with it a while, and if it continues stubborn, comprises it in words such as occur, and leaves it to be disentangled and evolved by those who have more leisure to bestow upon it.

Not that always where the language is intricate the thought is subtle, or the image always great where the line is bulky; the equality of words to things is very often neglected, and trivial sentiments and vulgar ideas disappoint the attention, to which they are recommended by sonorous epithets and swelling figures.

But the admirers of this great poet have never less reason to indulge their hopes of supreme excellence, than when he seems fully resolved to sink them in dejection, and mollify them with tender emotions by the fall of greatness, the danger of innocence, or the crosses of love. He is not long soft and pathetick without some idle conceit, or contemptible equivocation. He no sooner begins to move, than he counteracts himself; and terrour and pity, as they are rising in the mind, are checked and blasted by sudden frigidity.

A quibble is to Shakespeare, what luminous vapours are to the traveller; he follows it at all adventures, it is sure to lead him out of his way, and sure to engulf him in the mire. It has some malignant power over his mind, and its fascinations are irresistible. Whatever be the dignity or profundity of his disquisition, whether he be enlarging knowledge or exalting affection, whether he be amusing attention with incidents, or enchaining it in suspense, let but a quibble spring up before him, and he leaves his work unfinished. A quibble is the golden apple for which he will always turn aside from his career, or stoop from his elevation. A quibble poor and barren as it is, gave him such delight, that he was content to purchase it, by the sacrifice of reason, propriety and truth. A quibble was to him the fatal Cleopatra for which he lost the world, and was content to lose it.

It will be thought strange, that, in enumerating the defects of this writer, I have not yet mentioned his neglect of the unities; his violation of those laws which have been instituted and established by the joint authority of poets and of criticks.

For his other deviations from the art of writing, I resign him to critical justice, without making any other demand in his favour, than that which must be indulged to all human excellence; that his virtues be rated with his failings: But, from the censure which this irregularity may bring upon him, I shall, with due reverence to that learning which I must oppose, adventure to try how I can defend him.

His histories, being neither tragedies nor comedies, are not subject to any of their laws; nothing more is necessary to all the praise which they expect, than that the changes of action be so prepared as to be understood, that the incidents be various and affecting, and the characters consistent, natural and distinct. No other unity is intended, and therefore none is to be sought.

In his other works he has well enough preserved the unity of action. He has not, indeed, an intrigue regularly perplexed and regularly unravelled; he does not endeavour to hide his design only to discover it, for this is seldom the order of real events, and Shakespeare is the poet of nature: But his plan has commonly what Aristotle requires, a beginning, a middle, and an end; one event is concatenated with another, and the conclusion follows by easy consequence. There are perhaps some incidents that might be spared, as in other poets there is much talk that only fills up time upon the stage; but the general system makes gradual advances, and the end of the play is the end of expectation.

To the unities of time and place he has shewn no regard, and perhaps a nearer view of the principles on which they stand will diminish their value, and withdraw from them the veneration which, from the time of Corneille, they have very generally received by discovering that they have given more trouble to the poet, than pleasure to the auditor.

The necessity of observing the unities of time and place arises from the supposed necessity of making the drama credible. The criticks hold it impossible, that an action of months or years can be possibly believed to pass in three hours; or that the spectator can suppose himself to sit in the theatre, while ambassadors go and return between distant kings, while armies are levied and towns besieged, while an exile wanders and returns, or till he whom they saw courting his mistress, shall lament the untimely fall of his son. The mind revolts from evident falsehood, and fiction loses its force when it departs from the resemblance of reality.

From the narrow limitation of time necessarily arises the contraction of place. The spectator, who knows that he saw the first act at Alexandria, cannot suppose that he sees the next at Rome, at a distance to which not the dragons of Medea could, in so short a time, have transported him; he knows with certainty that he has not changed his place; and he knows that place cannot change itself; that what was a house cannot become a plain; that what was Thebes can never be Persepolis.

Such is the triumphant language with which a critick exults over the misery of an irregular poet, and exults commonly without resistance or reply. It is time therefore to tell him, by the authority of Shakespeare, that he assumes, as an unquestionable principle, a position, which, while his breath is forming it into words, his understanding pronounces to be false. It is false, that any representation is mistaken for reality; that any dramatick fable in its materiality was ever credible, or, for a single moment, was ever credited.

The objection arising from the impossibility of passing the first hour at Alexandria, and the next at Rome, supposes, that when the play opens the spectator really imagines himself at Alexandria, and believes that his walk to the theatre has been a voyage to Egypt, and that he lives in the days of Antony and Cleopatra. Surely he that imagines this, may imagine more. He that can take the stage at one time for the palace of the Ptolemies, may take it in half an hour for the promontory of Actium. Delusion, if delusion be admitted, has no certain limitation; if the spectator can be once persuaded, that his old acquaintance are Alexander and Caesar, that a room illuminated with candles is the plain of Pharsalia, or the bank of Granicus, he is in a state of elevation above the reach of reason, or of truth, and from the heights of empyrean poetry, may despise the circumscriptions of terrestrial nature. There is no reason why a mind thus wandering in extasy should count the clock, or why an hour should not be a century in that calenture of the brains that can make the stage a field.

The truth is, that the spectators are always in their senses, and know, from the first act to the last, that the stage is only a stage, and that the players are only players. They come to hear a certain number of lines recited with just gesture and elegant modulation. The lines relate to some action, and an action must be in some place; but the different actions that compleat a story may be in places very remote from each other; and where is the absurdity of allowing that space to represent first Athens, and then Sicily, which was always known to be neither Sicily nor Athens, but a modern theatre?

By supposition, as place is introduced, time may be extended; the time required by the fable elapses for the most part between the acts; for, of so much of the action as is represented, the real and poetical duration is the same.

If, in the first act, preparations for war against Mithridates are represented to be made in Rome, the event of the war may, without absurdity, be represented, in the catastrophe, as happening in Pontus; we know that there is neither war, nor preparation for war; we know that we are neither in Rome nor Pontus; that neither Mithridates nor Lucullus are before us.

The drama exhibits successive imitations of successive actions, and why may not the second imitation represent an action that happened years after the first; if it be so connected with it, that nothing but time can be supposed to intervene? Time is, of all modes of existence, most obsequious to the imagination; a lapse of years is as easily conceived as a passage of hours. In contemplation we easily contract the time of real actions, and therefore willingly permit it to be contracted when we only see their imitation. It will be asked, how the drama moves, if it is not credited. It is credited with all the credit due to a drama. It is credited, whenever it moves, as a just picture of a real original; as representing to the auditor what he would himself feel, if he were to do or suffer what is there feigned to be suffered or to be done. The reflection that strikes the heart is not, that the evils before us are real evils, but that they are evils to which we ourselves may be exposed. If there be any fallacy, it is not that we fancy the players, but that we fancy ourselves unhappy for a moment; but we rather lament the possibility than suppose the presence of misery, as a mother weeps over her babe, when she remembers that death may take it from her. The delight of tragedy proceeds from our consciousness of fiction; if we thought murders and treasons real, they would please no more.

Imitations produce pain or pleasure, not because they are mistaken for realities, but because they bring realities to mind. When the imagination is recreated by a painted landscape, the trees are not supposed capable to give us shade, or the fountains coolness; but we consider, how we should be pleased with such fountains playing beside us, and such woods waving over us. We are agitated in reading the history of "Henry the Fifth", yet no man takes his book for the field of Agencourt. A dramatick exhibition is a book recited with concomitants that encrease or diminish its effect. Familiar comedy is often more powerful on the theatre, than in the page; imperial tragedy is always less. The humour of Petruchio may be heightened by grimace; but what voice or what gesture can hope to add dignity or force to the soliloquy of Cato.

A play read, affects the mind like a play acted. It is therefore evident, that the action is not supposed to be real, and it follows that between the acts a longer or shorter time may be allowed to pass, and that no more account of space or duration is to be taken by the auditor of a drama, than by the reader of a narrative, before whom may pass in an hour the life of a hero, or the revolutions of an empire.

Whether Shakespeare knew the unities, and rejected them by design, or deviated from them by happy ignorance, it is, I think, impossible to decide, and useless to inquire. We may reasonably suppose, that, when he rose to notice, he did not want the counsels and admonitions of scholars and criticks, and that he at last deliberately persisted in a practice, which he might have begun by chance. As nothing is essential to the fable, but unity of action, and as the unities of time and place arise evidently from false assumptions, and, by circumscribing the extent of the drama, lessen its variety, I cannot think it much to be lamented, that they were not known by him, or not observed: Nor, if such another poet could arise, should I very vehemently reproach him, that his first act passed at Venice, and his next in Cyprus. Such violations of rules merely positive, become the comprehensive genius of Shakespeare, and such censures are suitable to the minute and slender criticism of Voltaire:

Non usque adeo permiscuit imis
Longus summa dies, ut non, si voce Metelli
Serventur leges, malint a Caesare tolli.

Yet when I speak thus slightly of dramatick rules, I cannot but recollect how much wit and learning may be produced against me; before such authorities I am afraid to stand, not that I think the present question one of those that are to be decided by mere authority, but because it is to be suspected, that these precepts have not been so easily received but for better reasons than I have yet been able to find. The result of my enquiries, in which it would be ludicrous to boast of impartiality, is, that the unities of time and place are not essential to a just drama, that though they may sometimes conduce to pleasure, they are always to be sacrificed to the nobler beauties of variety and instruction; and that a play, written with nice observation of critical rules, is to be contemplated as an elaborate curiosity, as the product of superfluous and ostentatious art, by which is shewn, rather what is possible, than what is necessary.

He that, without diminution of any other excellence, shall preserve all the unities unbroken, deserves the like applause with the architect, who shall display all the orders of architecture in a citadel, without any deduction from its strength; but the principal beauty of a citadel is to exclude the enemy; and the greatest graces of a play, are to copy nature and instruct life.

Perhaps, what I have here not dogmatically but deliberately written, may recal the principles of the drama to a new examination. I am almost frighted at my own temerity; and when I estimate the fame and the strength of those that maintain the contrary opinion, am ready to sink down in reverential silence; as Aeneas withdrew from the defence of Troy, when he saw Neptune shaking the wall, and Juno heading the besiegers.

Those whom my arguments cannot persuade to give their approbation to the judgment of Shakespeare, will easily, if they consider the condition of his life, make some allowance for his ignorance.

Every man's performances, to be rightly estimated, must be compared with the state of the age in which he lived, and with his own particular opportunities; and though to the reader a book be not worse or better for the circumstances of the authour, yet as there is always a silent reference of human works to human abilities, and as the enquiry, how far man may extend his designs, or how high he may rate his native force, is of far greater dignity than in what rank we shall place any particular performance, curiosity is always busy to discover the instruments, as well as to survey the workmanship, to know how much is to be ascribed to original powers, and how much to casual and adventitious help. The palaces of Peru or Mexico were certainly mean and incommodious habitations, if compared to the houses of European monarchs; yet who could forbear to view them with astonishment, who remembered that they were built without the use of iron?

The English nation, in the time of Shakespeare, was yet struggling to emerge from barbarity. The philology of Italy had been transplanted hither in the reign of Henry the Eighth; and the learned languages had been successfully cultivated by Lilly and More; by Pole, Cheke, and Gardiner; and afterwards by Smith, Clerk, Haddon, and Ascham. Greek was now taught to boys in the principal schools; and those who united elegance with learning, read, with great diligence, the Italian and Spanish poets. But literature was yet confined to professed scholars, or to men and women of high rank. The publick was gross and dark; and to be able to read and write, was an accomplishment still valued for its rarity.

Nations, like individuals, have their infancy. A people newly awakened to literary curiosity, being yet unacquainted with the true state of things, knows not how to judge of that which is proposed as its resemblance. Whatever is remote from common appearances is always welcome to vulgar, as to childish credulity; and of a country unenlightened by learning, the whole people is the vulgar. The study of those who then aspired to plebeian learning was laid out upon adventures, giants, dragons, and enchantments. The Death of Arthur was the favourite volume. The mind, which has feasted on the luxurious wonders of fiction, has no taste of the insipidity of truth. A play which imitated only the common occurrences of the world, would, upon the admirers of Palmerin and Guy of Warwick, have made little impression; he that wrote for such an audience was under the necessity of looking round for strange events and fabulous transactions, and that incredibility, by which maturer knowledge is offended, was the chief recommendation of writings, to unskilful curiosity.

Our authour's plots are generally borrowed from novels, and it is reasonable to suppose, that he chose the most popular, such as were read by many, and related by more; for his audience could not have followed him through the intricacies of the drama, had they not held the thread of the story in their hands.

The stories, which we now find only in remoter authours, were in his time accessible and familliar. The fable of "As You Like It", which is supposed to be copied from Chaucer's Gamelyn, was a little pamphlet of those times; and old Mr. Cibber remembered the tale of Hamlet in plain English prose, which the criticks have now to seek in Saxo Grammaticus.

His English histories he took from English chronicles and English ballads; and as the ancient writers were made known to his countrymen by versions, they supplied him with new subjects; he dilated some of Plutarch's lives into plays, when they had been translated by North.

His plots, whether historical or fabulous, are always crouded with incidents, by which the attention of a rude people was more easily caught than by sentiment or argumentation; and such is the power of the marvellous even over those who despise it, that every man finds his mind more strongly seized by the tragedies of Shakespeare than of any other writer; others please us by particular speeches, but he always makes us anxious for the event, and has perhaps excelled all but Homer in securing the first purpose of a writer, by exciting restless and unquenchable curiosity, and compelling him that reads his work to read it through.

The shows and bustle with which his plays abound have the same original. As knowledge advances, pleasure passes from the eye to the ear, but returns, as it declines, from the ear to the eye. Those to whom our authour's labours were exhibited had more skill in pomps or processions than in poetical language, and perhaps wanted some visible and discriminated events, as comments on the dialogue. He knew how he should most please; and whether his practice is more agreeable to nature, or whether his example has prejudiced the nation, we still find that on our stage something must be done as well as said, and inactive declamation is very coldly heard, however musical or elegant, passionate or sublime.

Voltaire expresses his wonder, that our authour's extravagancies are endured by a nation, which has seen the tragedy of Cato. Let him be answered, that Addison speaks the language of poets, and Shakespeare, of men. We find in Cato innumerable beauties which enamour us of its authour, but we see nothing that acquaints us with human sentiments or human actions; we place it with the fairest and the noblest progeny which judgment propagates by conjunction with learning, but "Othello" is the vigorous and vivacious offspring of observation impregnated by genius. Cato affords a splendid exhibition of artificial and fictitious manners, and delivers just and noble sentiments, in diction easy, elevated and harmonious, but its hopes and fears communicate no vibration to the heart; the composition refers us only to the writer; we pronounce the name of Cato, but we think on Addison.

The work of a correct and regular writer is a garden accurately formed and diligently planted, varied with shades, and scented with flowers; the composition of Shakespeare is a forest, in which oaks extend their branches, and pines tower in the air, interspersed sometimes with weeds and brambles, and sometimes giving shelter to myrtles and to roses; filling the eye with awful pomp, and gratifying the mind with endless diversity. Other poets display cabinets of precious rarities, minutely finished, wrought into shape, and polished unto brightness. Shakespeare opens a mine which contains gold and diamonds in unexhaustible plenty, though clouded by incrustations, debased by impurities, and mingled with a mass of meaner minerals.

It has been much disputed, whether Shakespeare owed his excellence to his own native force, or whether he had the common helps of scholastick education, the precepts of critical science, and the examples of ancient authours.

There has always prevailed a tradition, that Shakespeare wanted learning, that he had no regular education, nor much skill in the dead languages. Johnson, his friend, affirms, that "He had small Latin and no Greek."; who, besides that he had no imaginable temptation to falsehood, wrote at a time when the character and acquisitions of Shakespeare were known to multitudes. His evidence ought therefore to decide the controversy, unless some testimony of equal force could be opposed.

Some have imagined, that they have discovered deep learning in many imitations of old writers; but the examples which I have known urged, were drawn from books translated in his time; or were such easy coincidencies of thought, as will happen to all who consider the same subjects; or such remarks on life or axioms of morality as float in conversation, and are transmitted through the world in proverbial sentences.

I have found it remarked, that, in this important sentence, "Go before, I'll follow," we read a translation of, I prae, sequar.

I have been told, that when Caliban, after a pleasing dream, says, "I cry'd to sleep again," the authour imitates Anacreon, who had, like every other man, the same wish on the same occasion.

There are a few passages which may pass for imitations, but so few, that the exception only confirms the rule; he obtained them from accidental quotations, or by oral communication, and as he used what he had, would have used more if he had obtained it.

The "Comedy of Errors" is confessedly taken from the Menaechmi of Plautus; from the only play of Plautus which was then in English. What can be more probable, than that he who copied that, would have copied more; but that those which were not translated were inaccessible?

Whether he knew the modern languages is uncertain. That his plays have some French scenes proves but little; he might easily procure them to be written, and probably, even though he had known the language in the common degree, he could not have written it without assistance. In the story of "Romeo and Juliet" he is observed to have followed the English translation, where it deviates from the Italian; but this on the other part proves nothing against his knowledge of the original. He was to copy, not what he knew himself, but what was known to his audience.

It is most likely that he had learned Latin sufficiently to make him acquainted with construction, but that he never advanced to an easy perusal of the Roman authours. Concerning his skill in modern languages, I can find no sufficient ground of determination; but as no imitations of French or Italian authours have been discovered, though the Italian poetry was then high in esteem, I am inclined to believe, that he read little more than English, and chose for his fables only such tales as he found translated.

That much knowledge is scattered over his works is very justly observed by Pope, but it is often such knowledge as books did not supply. He that will understand Shakespeare, must not be content to study him in the closet, he must look for his meaning sometimes among the sports of the field, and sometimes among the manufactures of the shop. There is however proof enough that he was a very diligent reader, nor was our language then so indigent of books, but that he might very liberally indulge his curiosity without excursion into foreign literature. Many of the Roman authours were translated, and some of the Greek; the reformation had filled the kingdom with theological learning; most of the topicks of human disquisition had found English writers; and poetry had been cultivated, not only with diligence, but success. This was a stock of knowledge sufficient for a mind so capable of appropriating and improving it.

But the greater part of his excellence was the product of his own genius. He found the English stage in a state of the utmost rudeness; no essays either in tragedy or comedy had appeared, from which it could be discovered to what degree of delight either one or other might be carried. Neither character nor dialogue were yet understood. Shakespeare may be truly said to have introduced them both amongst us, and in some of his happier scenes to have carried them both to the utmost height.

By what gradations of improvement he proceeded, is not easily known; for the chronology of his works is yet unsettled. Rowe is of opinion, that "perhaps we are not to look for his beginning, like those of other writers, in his least perfect works; art had so little, and nature so large a share in what he did, that for ought I know," says he, "the performances of his youth, as they were the most vigorous, were the best." But the power of nature is only the power of using to any certain purpose the materials which diligence procures, or opportunity supplies. Nature gives no man knowledge, and when images are collected by study and experience, can only assist in combining or applying them.

Shakespeare, however favoured by nature, could impart only what he had learned; and as he must increase his ideas, like other mortals, by gradual acquisition, he, like them, grew wiser as he grew older, could display life better, as he knew it more, and instruct with more efficacy, as he was himself more amply instructed.

There is a vigilance of observation and accuracy of distinction which books and precepts cannot confer; from this almost all original and native excellence proceeds. Shakespeare must have looked upon mankind with perspicacity, in the highest degree curious and attentive. Other writers borrow their characters from preceding writers, and diversify them only by the accidental appendages of present manners; the dress is a little varied, but the body is the same. Our authour had both matter and form to provide; for except the characters of Chaucer, to whom I think he is not much indebted, there were no writers in English, and perhaps not many in other modern languages, which shewed life in its native colours.

The contest about the original benevolence or malignity of man had not yet commenced. Speculation had not yet attempted to analyse the mind, to trace the passions to their sources, to unfold the seminal principles of vice and virtue, or sound the depths of the heart for the motives of action. All those enquiries, which from that time that human nature became the fashionable study, have been made sometimes with nice discernment, but often with idle subtilty, were yet unattempted. The tales, with which the infancy of learning was satisfied, exhibited only the superficial appearances of action, related the events but omitted the causes, and were formed for such as delighted in wonders rather than in truth. Mankind was not then to be studied in the closet; he that would know the world, was under the necessity of gleaning his own remarks, by mingling as he could in its business and amusements.

Boyle congratulated himself upon his high birth, because it favoured his curiosity, by facilitating his access. Shakespeare had no such advantage; he came to London a needy adventurer, and lived for a time by very mean employments. Many works of genius and learning have been performed in states of life, that appear very little favourable to thought or to enquiry; so many, that he who considers them is inclined to think that he sees enterprise and perseverance predominating over all external agency, and bidding help and hindrance vanish before them. The genius of Shakespeare was not to be depressed by the weight of poverty, nor limited by the narrow conversation to which men in want are inevitably condemned; the incumbrances of his fortune were shaken from his mind, "as dewdrops from a lion's mane."

Though he had so many difficulties to encounter, and so little assistance to surmount them, he has been able to obtain an exact knowledge of many modes of life, and many casts of native dispositions; to vary them with great multiplicity; to mark them by nice distinctions; and to shew them in full view by proper combinations. In this part of his performances He had none to imitate, but has himself been imitated by all succeeding writers; and it may be doubted, whether from all his successors more maxims of theoretical knowledge, or more rules of practical prudence, can be collected, than he alone has given to his country.

Nor was his attention confined to the actions of men; he was an exact surveyor of the inanimate world; his descriptions have always some peculiarities, gathered by contemplating things as they really exist. It may be observed, that the oldest poets of many nations preserve their reputation, and that the following generations of wit, after a short celebrity, sink into oblivion. The first, whoever they be, must take their sentiments and descriptions immediately from knowledge; the resemblance is therefore just, their descriptions are verified by every eye, and their sentiments acknowledged by every breast. Those whom their fame invites to the same studies, copy partly them, and partly nature, till the books of one age gain such authority, as to stand in the place of nature to another, and imitation, always deviating a little, becomes at last capricious and casual. Shakespeare, whether life or nature be his subject, shews plainly, that he has seen with his own eyes; he gives the image which he receives, not weakened or distorted by the intervention of any other mind; the ignorant feel his representations to be just, and the learned see that they are compleat.

Perhaps it would not be easy to find any authour, except Homer, who invented so much as Shakespeare, who so much advanced the studies which he cultivated, or effused so much novelty upon his age or country. The form, the characters, the language, and the shows of the English drama are his. "He seems," says Dennis, "to have been the very original of our English tragical harmony, that is, the harmony of blank verse, diversified often by dissyllable and trissyllable terminations. For the diversity distinguishes it from heroick harmony, and by bringing it nearer to common use makes it more proper to gain attention, and more fit for action and dialogue. Such verse we make when we are writing prose; we make such verse in common conversation."

I know not whether this praise is rigorously just. The dissyllable termination, which the critick rightly appropriates to the drama, is to be found, though, I think, not in Gorboduc which is confessedly before our authour; yet in Hieronnymo, of which the date is not certain, but which there is reason to believe at least as old as his earliest plays. This however is certain, that he is the first who taught either tragedy or comedy to please, there being no theatrical piece of any older writer, of which the name is known, except to antiquaries and collectors of books, which are sought because they are scarce, and would not have been scarce, had they been much esteemed.

To him we must ascribe the praise, unless Spenser may divide it with him, of having first discovered to how much smoothness and harmony the English language could be softened. He has speeches, perhaps sometimes scenes, which have all the delicacy of Rowe, without his effeminacy. He endeavours indeed commonly to strike by the force and vigour of his dialogue, but he never executes his purpose better, than when he tries to sooth by softness.

Yet it must be at last confessed, that as we owe every thing to him, he owes something to us; that, if much of his praise is paid by perception and judgement, much is likewise given by custom and veneration. We fix our eyes upon his graces, and turn them from his deformities, and endure in him what we should in another loath or despise. If we endured without praising, respect for the father of our drama might excuse us; but I have seen, in the book of some modern critick, a collection of anomalies which shew that he has corrupted language by every mode of depravation, but which his admirer has accumulated as a monument of honour.

He has scenes of undoubted and perpetual excellence, but perhaps not one play, which, if it were now exhibited as the work of a contemporary writer, would be heard to the conclusion. I am indeed far from thinking, that his works were wrought to his own ideas of perfection; when they were such as would satisfy the audience, they satisfied the writer. It is seldom that authours, though more studious of fame than Shakespeare, rise much above the standard of their own age; to add a little of what is best will always be sufficient for present praise, and those who find themselves exalted into fame, are willing to credit their encomiasts, and to spare the labour of contending with themselves.

It does not appear, that Shakespeare thought his works worthy of posterity, that he levied any ideal tribute upon future times, or had any further prospect, than of present popularity and present profit. When his plays had been acted, his hope was at an end; he solicited no addition of honour from the reader. He therefore made no scruple to repeat the same jests in many dialogues, or to entangle different plots by the same knot of perplexity, which may be at least forgiven him, by those who recollect, that of Congreve's four comedies, two are concluded by a marriage in a mask, by a deception, which perhaps never happened, and which, whether likely or not, he did not invent.

So careless was this great poet of future fame, that, though he retired to ease and plenty, while he was yet little "declined into the vale of years," before he could be disgusted with fatigue, or disabled by infirmity, he made no collection of his works, nor desired to rescue those that had been already published from the depravations that obscured them, or secure to the rest a better destiny, by giving them to the world in their genuine state.

Of the plays which bear the name of Shakespeare in the late editions, the greater part were not published till about seven years after his death, and the few which appeared in his life are apparently thrust into the world without the care of the authour, and therefore probably without his knowledge.

Of all the publishers, clandestine or professed, their negligence and unskilfulness has by the late revisers been sufficiently shown. The faults of all are indeed numerous and gross, and have not only corrupted many passages perhaps beyond recovery, but have brought others into suspicion, which are only obscured by obsolete phraseology, or by the writer's unskilfulness and affectation. To alter is more easy than to explain, and temerity is a more common quality than diligence. Those who saw that they must employ conjecture to a certain degree, were willing to indulge it a little further. Had the authour published his own works, we should have sat quietly down to disentangle his intricacies, and clear his obscurities; but now we tear what we cannot loose, and eject what we happen not to understand.

The faults are more than could have happened without the concurrence of many causes. The stile of Shakespeare was in itself ungrammatical, perplexed and obscure; his works were transcribed for the players by those who may be supposed to have seldom understood them; they were transmitted by copiers equally unskilful, who still multiplied errours; they were perhaps sometimes mutilated by the actors, for the sake of shortening the speeches; and were at last printed without correction of the press.

In this state they remained, not as Dr. Warburton supposes, because they were unregarded, but because the editor's art was not yet applied to modern languages, and our ancestors were accustomed to so much negligence of English printers, that they could very patiently endure it. At last an edition was undertaken by Rowe; not because a poet was to be published by a poet, for Rowe seems to have thought very little on correction or explanation, but that our authour's works might appear like those of his fraternity, with the appendages of a life and recommendatory preface. Rowe has been clamorously blamed for not performing what he did not undertake, and it is time that justice be done him, by confessing, that though he seems to have had no thought of corruption beyond the printer's errours, yet he has made many emendations, if they were not made before, which his successors have received without acknowledgment, and which, if they had produced them, would have filled pages and pages with censures of the stupidity by which the faults were committed, with displays of the absurdities which they involved, with ostentatious exposition of the new reading, and self congratulations on the happiness of discovering it.

Of Rowe, as of all the editors, I have preserved the preface and have likewise retained the authour's life, though not written with much elegance or spirit; it relates however what is now to be known, and therefore deserves to pass through all succeeding publications.

The nation had been for many years content enough with Mr. Rowe's performance, when Mr. Pope made them acquainted with the true state of Shakespeare's text, shewed that it was extremely corrupt, and gave reason to hope that there were means of reforming it. He collated the old copies, which none had thought to examine before, and restored many lines to their integrity; but, by a very compendious criticism, he rejected whatever he disliked, and thought more of amputation than of cure.

I know not why he is commended by Dr. Warburton for distinguishing the genuine from the spurious plays. In this choice he exerted no judgement of his own; the plays which he received, were given by Hemings and Condel, the first editors; and those which he rejected, though, according to the licentiousness of the press in those times, they were printed during Shakespeare's life, with his name, had been omitted by his friends, and were never added to his works before the edition of 1664, from which they were copied by the later printers. This was a work which Pope seems to have thought unworthy of his abilities, being not able to suppress his contempt of "the dull duty of an editor". He understood but half his undertaking. The duty of a collator is indeed dull, yet, like other tedious tasks, is very necessary; but an emendatory critick would ill discharge his duty, without qualities very different from dulness. In perusing a corrupted piece, he must have before him all possibilities of meaning, with all possibilities of expression.

Such must be his comprehension of thought, and such his copiousness of language. Out of many readings possible, he must be able to select that which best suits with the state, opinions, and modes of language prevailing in every age, and with his authour's particular cast of thought, and turn of expression. Such must be his knowledge, and such his taste. Conjectural criticism demands more than humanity possesses, and he that exercises it with most praise has very frequent need of indulgence. Let us now be told no more of the dull duty of an editor.

Confidence is the common consequence of success. They whose excellence of any kind has been loudly celebrated, are ready to conclude, that their powers are universal. Pope's edition fell below his own expectations, and he was so much offended, when he was found to have left any thing for others to do, that he past the latter part of his life in a state of hostility with verbal criticism.

I have retained all his notes, that no fragment of so great a writer may be lost; his preface, valuable alike for elegance of composition and justness of remark, and containing a general criticism on his authour, so extensive that little can be added, and so exact, that little can be disputed, every editor has an interest to suppress, but that every reader would demand its insertion.

Pope was succeeded by Theobald, a man of narrow comprehension and small acquisitions, with no native and intrinsick splendour of genius, with little of the artificial light of learning, but zealous for minute accuracy, and not negligent in pursuing it. He collated the ancient copies, and rectified many errors. A man so anxiously scrupulous might have been expected to do more, but what little he did was commonly right. In his report of copies and editions he is not to be trusted, without examination. He speaks sometimes indefinitely of copies, when he has only one. In his enumeration of editions, he mentions the two first folios as of high, and the third folio as of middle authority; but the truth is, that the first is equivalent to all others, and that the rest only deviate from it by the printer's negligence. Whoever has any of the folios has all, excepting those diversities which mere reiteration of editions will produce. I collated them all at the beginning, but afterwards used only the first.

Of his notes I have generally retained those which he retained himself in his second edition, except when they were confuted by subsequent annotators, or were too minute to merit preservation. I have sometimes adopted his restoration of a comma, without inserting the panegyrick in which he celebrated himself for his achievement. The exuberant excrescence of diction I have often lopped, his triumphant exultations over Pope and Rowe I have sometimes suppressed, and his contemptible ostentation I have frequently concealed; but I have in some places shewn him, as he would have shewn himself, for the reader's diversion, that the inflated emptiness of some notes may justify or excuse the contraction of the rest.

Theobald, thus weak and ignorant, thus mean and faithless, thus petulant and ostentatious, by the good luck of having Pope for his enemy, has escaped, and escaped alone, with reputation, from this undertaking. So willingly does the world support those who solicite favour, against those who command reverence; and so easily is he praised, whom no man can envy.

Our authour fell then into the hands of Sir Thomas Hanmer, the Oxford editor, a man, in my opinion, eminently qualified by nature for such studies. He had, what is the first requisite to emendatory criticism, that intuition by which the poet's intention is immediately discovered, and that dexterity of intellect which dispatches its work by the easiest means. He had undoubtedly read much; his acquaintance with customs, opinions, and traditions, seems to have been large; and he is often learned without shew. He seldom passes what he does not understand, without an attempt to find or to make a meaning, and sometimes hastily makes what a little more attention would have found. He is solicitous to reduce to grammar, what he could not be sure that his authour intended to be grammatical. Shakespeare regarded more the series of ideas, than of words; and his language, not being designed for the reader's desk, was all that he desired it to be, if it conveyed his meaning to the audience.

Hanmer's care of the metre has been too violently censured. He found the measures reformed in so many passages, by the silent labours of some editors, with the silent acquiescence of the rest, that he thought himself allowed to extend a little further the license, which had already been carried so far without reprehension; and of his corrections in general, it must be confessed, that they are often just, and made commonly with the least possible violation of the text.

But, by inserting his emendations, whether invented or borrowed, into the page, without any notice of varying copies, he has appropriated the labour of his predecessors, and made his own edition of little authority. His confidence indeed, both in himself and others, was too great; he supposes all to be right that was done by Pope and Theobald; he seems not to suspect a critick of fallibility, and it was but reasonable that he should claim what he so liberally granted.

As he never writes without careful enquiry and diligent consideration, I have received all his notes, and believe that every reader will wish for more.

Of the last editor it is more difficult to speak. Respect is due to high place, tenderness to living reputation, and veneration to genius and learning; but he cannot be justly offended at that liberty of which he has himself so frequently given an example, nor very solicitous what is thought of notes, which he ought never to have considered as part of his serious employments, and which, I suppose, since the ardour of composition is remitted, he no longer numbers among his happy effusions.

The original and predominant errour of his commentary, is acquiescence in his first thoughts; that precipitation which is produced by consciousness of quick discernment; and that confidence which presumes to do, by surveying the surface, what labour only can perform, by penetrating the bottom. His notes exhibit sometimes perverse interpretations, and sometimes improbable conjectures; he at one time gives the authour more profundity of meaning than the sentence admits, and at another discovers absurdities, where the sense is plain to every other reader. But his emendations are likewise often happy and just; and his interpretation of obscure passages learned and sagacious.

Of his notes, I have commonly rejected those, against which the general voice of the publick has exclaimed, or which their own incongruity immediately condemns, and which, I suppose, the authour himself would desire to be forgotten. Of the rest, to part I have given the highest approbation, by inserting the offered reading in the text; part I have left to the judgment of the reader, as doubtful, though specious; and part I have censured without reserve, but I am sure without bitterness of malice, and, I hope, without wantonness of insult.

It is no pleasure to me, in revising my volumes, to observe how much paper is wasted in confutation. Whoever considers the revolutions of learning, and the various questions of greater or less importance, upon which wit and reason have exercised their powers, must lament the unsuccessfulness of enquiry, and the slow advances of truth, when he reflects, that great part of the labour of every writer is only the destruction of those that went before him. The first care of the builder of a new system, is to demolish the fabricks which are standing. The chief desire of him that comments an authour, is to shew how much other commentators have corrupted and obscured him. The opinions prevalent in one age, as truths above the reach of controversy, are confuted and rejected in another, and rise again to reception in remoter times. Thus the human mind is kept in motion without progress. Thus sometimes truth and errour, and sometimes contrarieties of errour, take each other's place by reciprocal invasion. The tide of seeming knowledge which is poured over one generation, retires and leaves another naked and barren; the sudden meteors of intelligence which for a while appear to shoot their beams into the regions of obscurity, on a sudden withdraw their lustre, and leave mortals again to grope their way.

These elevations and depressions of renown, and the contradictions to which all improvers of knowledge must for ever be exposed, since they are not escaped by the highest and brightest of mankind, may surely be endured with patience by criticks and annotators, who can rank themselves but as the satellites of their authours. How canst thou beg for life, says Achilles to his captive, when thou knowest that thou art now to suffer only what must another day be suffered by Achilles?

Dr. Warburton had a name sufficient to confer celebrity on those who could exalt themselves into antagonists, and his notes have raised a clamour too loud to be distinct. His chief assailants are the authours of the Canons of Criticism and of the Review of Shakespeare's Text; of whom one ridicules his errours with airy petulance, suitable enough to the levity of the controversy; the other attacks them with gloomy malignity, as if he were dragging to justice an assassin or incendiary. The one stings like a fly, sucks a little blood, takes a gay flutter, and returns for more; the other bites like a viper, and would be glad to leave inflammations and gangrene behind him. When I think on one, with his confederates, I remember the danger of Coriolanus, who was afraid that "girls with spits, and boys with stones, should slay him in puny battle;" when the other crosses my imagination, I remember the prodigy in "Macbeth",

An eagle tow'ring in his pride of place,
was by a mousing owl hawk'd at and kill'd.

Let me however do them justice. One is a wit, and one a scholar. They have both shewn acuteness sufficient in the discovery of faults, and have both advanced some probable interpretations of obscure passages; but when they aspire to conjecture and emendation, it appears how falsely we all estimate our own abilities, and the little which they have been able to perform might have taught them more candour to the endeavours of others.

Before Dr. Warburton's edition, "Critical Observations on Shakespeare" had been published by Mr. Upton, a man skilled in languages, and acquainted with books, but who seems to have had no great vigour of genius or nicety of taste. Many of his explanations are curious and useful, but he likewise, though he professed to oppose the licentious confidence of editors, and adhere to the old copies, is unable to restrain the rage of emendation, though his ardour is ill seconded by his skill. Every cold empirick, when his heart is expanded by a successful experiment, swells into a theorist, and the laborious collator some unlucky moment frolicks in conjecture.

"Critical, historical and explanatory notes" have been likewise published upon Shakespeare by Dr. Grey, whose diligent perusal of the old English writers has enabled him to make some useful observations. What he undertook he has well enough performed, but as he neither attempts judicial nor emendatory criticism, he employs rather his memory than his sagacity. It were to be wished that all would endeavour to imitate his modesty who have not been able to surpass his knowledge.

I can say with great sincerity of all my predecessors, what I hope will hereafter be said of me, that not one has left Shakespeare without improvement, nor is there one to whom I have not been indebted for assistance and information. Whatever I have taken from them it was my intention to refer to its original authour, and it is certain, that what I have not given to another, I believed when I wrote it to be my own. In some perhaps I have been anticipated; but if I am ever found to encroach upon the remarks of any other commentator, I am willing that the honour, be it more or less, should be transferred to the first claimant, for his right, and his alone, stands above dispute; the second can prove his pretensions only to himself, nor can himself always distinguish invention, with sufficient certainty, from recollection.

They have all been treated by me with candour, which they have not been careful of observing to one another. It is not easy to discover from what cause the acrimony of a scholiast can naturally proceed. The subjects to be discussed by him are of very small importance; they involve neither property nor liberty; nor favour the interest of sect or party. The various readings of copies, and different interpretations of a passage, seem to be questions that might exercise the wit, without engaging the passions. But, whether it be, that "small things make mean men proud," and vanity catches small occasions; or that all contrariety of opinion, even in those that can defend it no longer, makes proud men angry; there is often found in commentaries a spontaneous strain of invective and contempt, more eager and venomous than is vented by the most furious controvertist in politicks against those whom he is hired to defame.

Perhaps the lightness of the matter may conduce to the vehemence of the agency; when the truth to be investigated is so near to inexistence, as to escape attention, its bulk is to be enlarged by rage and exclamation: That to which all would be indifferent in its original state, may attract notice when the fate of a name is appended to it. A commentator has indeed great temptations to supply by turbulence what he wants of dignity, to beat his little gold to a spacious surface, to work that to foam which no art or diligence can exalt to spirit.

The notes which I have borrowed or written are either illustrative, by which difficulties are explained; or judicial, by which faults and beauties are remarked; or emendatory, by which depravations are corrected.

The explanations transcribed from others, if I do not subjoin any other interpretation, I suppose commonly to be right, at least I intend by acquiescence to confess, that I have nothing better to propose.

After the labours of all the editors, I found many passages which appeared to me likely to obstruct the greater number of readers, and thought it my duty to facilitate their passage. It is impossible for an expositor not to write too little for some, and too much for others. He can only judge what is necessary by his own experience; and how long soever he may deliberate, will at last explain many lines which the learned will think impossible to be mistaken, and omit many for which the ignorant will want his help. These are censures merely relative and must be quietly endured.

I have endeavoured to be neither superfluously copious, nor scrupulously reserved, and hope that I have made my authour's meaning accessible to many who before were frighted from perusing him, and contributed something to the publick, by diffusing innocent and rational pleasure. The compleat explanation of an authour not systematick and consequential, but desultory and vagrant, abounding in casual allusions and light hints, is not to be expected from any single scholiast. All personal reflections, when names are suppressed, must be in a few years irrecoverably obliterated; and customs, too minute to attract the notice of law, such as mode of dress, formalities of conversation, rules of visits, disposition of furniture, and practices of ceremony, which naturally find places in familiar dialogue, are so fugitive and unsubstantial that they are not easily retained or recovered.

What can be known, will be collected by chance, from the recesses of obscure and obsolete papers, perused commonly with some other view. Of this knowledge every man has some, and none has much; but when an authour has engaged the publick attention, those who can add any thing to his illustration, communicate their discoveries, and time produces what had eluded diligence.

To time I have been obliged to resign many passages, which, though I did not understand them, will perhaps hereafter be explained, having, I hope, illustrated some, which others have neglected or mistaken, sometimes by short remarks or marginal directions, such as every editor has added at his will, and often by comments more laborious than the matter will seem to deserve; but that which is most difficult is not always most important, and to an editor nothing is a trifle by which his authour is obscured.

The poetical beauties or defects I have not been very diligent to observe. Some plays have more, and some fewer judicial observations, not in proportion to their difference of merit, but because I gave this part of my design to chance and to caprice. The reader, I believe, is seldom pleased to find his opinion anticipated; it is natural to delight more in what we find or make, than in what we receive. Judgement, like other faculties, is improved by practice, and its advancement is hindered by submission to dictatorial decisions, as the memory grows torpid by the use of a table book. Some initiation is however necessary; of all skill, part is infused by precept, and part is obtained by habit; I have therefore shewn so much as may enable the candidate of criticism to discover the rest.

To the end of most plays, I have added short strictures, containing a general censure of faults, or praise of excellence; in which I know not how much I have concurred with the current opinion; but I have not, by any affectation of singularity, deviated from it. Nothing is minutely and particularly examined, and therefore it is to be supposed, that in the plays which are condemned there is much to be praised, and in these which are praised much to be condemned.

The part of criticism in which the whole succession of editors has laboured with the greatest diligence, which has occasioned the most arrogant ostentation, and excited the keenest acrimony, is the emendation of corrupted passages, to which the publick attention having been first drawn by the violence of contention between Pope and Theobald, has been continued by the persecution, which, with a kind of conspiracy, has been since raised against all the publishers of Shakespeare.

That many passages have passed in a state of depravation through all the editions is indubitably certain; of these the restoration is only to be attempted by collation of copies or sagacity of conjecture. The collator's province is safe and easy, the conjecturer's perilous and difficult. Yet as the greater part of the plays are extant only in one copy, the peril must not be avoided, nor the difficulty refused.

Of the readings which this emulation of amendment has hitherto produced, some from the labours of every publisher have advanced into the text; those are to be considered as in my opinion sufficiently supported; some I have rejected without mention, as evidently erroneous; some I have left in the notes without censure or approbation, as resting in equipoise between objection and defence; and some, which seemed specious but not right, I have inserted with a subsequent animadversion.

Having classed the observations of others, I was at last to try what I could substitute for their mistakes, and how I could supply their omissions. I collated such copies as I could procure, and wished for more, but have not found the collectors of these rarities very communicative. Of the editions which chance or kindness put into my hands I have given an enumeration, that I may not be blamed for neglecting what I had not the power to do.

By examining the old copies, I soon found that the late publishers, with all their boasts of diligence, suffered many passages; to stand unauthorised, and contented themselves with Rowe's regulation of the text, even where they knew it to be arbitrary, and with a little consideration might have found it to be wrong. Some of these alterations are only the ejection of a word for one that appeared to him more elegant or more intelligible. These corruptions I have often silently rectified; for the history of our language, and the true force of our words, can only be preserved, by keeping the text of authours free from adulteration. Others, and those very frequent, smoothed the cadence, or regulated the measure; on these I have not exercised the same rigour; if only a word was transposed, or a particle inserted or omitted, I have sometimes suffered the line to stand; for the inconstancy of the copies is such, as that some liberties may be easily permitted. But this practice I have not suffered to proceed far, having restored the primitive diction wherever it could for any reason be preferred.

The emendations, which comparison of copies supplied, I have inserted in the text; sometimes where the improvement was slight, without notice, and sometimes with an account of the reasons of the change.

Conjecture, though it be sometimes unavoidable, I have not wantonly nor licentiously indulged. It has been my settled principle, that the reading of the ancient books is probably true, and therefore is not to be disturbed for the sake of elegance, perspicuity, or mere improvement of the sense. For though much credit is not due to the fidelity, nor any to the judgement of the first publishers, yet they who had the copy before their eyes were more likely to read it right, than we who only read it by imagination.

But it is evident that they have often made strange mistakes by ignorance or negligence, and that therefore something may be properly attempted by criticism, keeping the middle way between presumption and timidity. Such criticism I have attempted to practise, and where any passage appeared inextricably perplexed, have endeavoured to discover how it may be recalled to sense, with least violence. But my first labour is, always to turn the old text on every side, and try if there be any interstice, through which light can find its way; nor would Huetius himself condemn me, as refusing the trouble of research, for the ambition of alteration. In this modest industry I have not been unsuccessful. I have rescued many lines from the violations of temerity, and secured many scenes from the inroads of correction. I have adopted the Roman sentiment, that it is more honourable to save a citizen, than to kill an enemy, and have been more careful to protect than to attack.

I have preserved the common distribution of the plays into acts, though I believe it to be in almost all the plays void of authority. Some of those which are divided in the later editions have no division in the first folio, and some that are divided in the folio have no division in the preceding copies. The settled mode of the theatre requires four intervals in the play, but few, if any, of our authour's compositions can be properly distributed in that manner. An act is so much of the drama as passes without intervention of time or change of place. A pause makes a new act. In every real, and therefore in every imitative action, the intervals may be more or fewer, the restriction of five acts being accidental and arbitrary. This Shakespeare knew, and this he practised; his plays were written, and at first printed in one unbroken continuity, and ought now to be exhibited with short pauses, interposed as often as the scene is changed, or any considerable time is required to pass. This method would at once quell a thousand absurdities.

In restoring the authour's works to their integrity, I have considered the punctuation as wholly in my power; for what could be their care of colons and commas, who corrupted words and sentences. Whatever could be done by adjusting points is therefore silently performed, in some plays with much diligence, in others with less; it is hard to keep a busy eye steadily fixed upon evanescent atoms, or a discursive mind upon evanescent truth.

The same liberty has been taken with a few particles, or other words of slight effect. I have sometimes inserted or omitted them without notice. I have done that sometimes, which the other editors have done always, and which indeed the state of the text may sufficiently justify. The greater part of readers, instead of blaming us for passing trifles, will wonder that on mere trifles so much labour is expended, with such importance of debate, and such solemnity of diction. To these I answer with confidence, that they are judging of an art which they do not understand; yet cannot much reproach them with their ignorance, nor promise that they would become in general, by learning criticism, more useful, happier or wiser.

As I practised conjecture more, I learned to trust it less; and after I had printed a few plays, resolved to insert none of my own readings in the text. Upon this caution I now congratulate myself, for every day encreases my doubt of my emendations. Since I have confined my imagination to the margin, it must not be considered as very reprehensible, if I have suffered it to play some freaks in its own dominion. There is no danger in conjecture, if it be proposed as conjecture; and while the text remains uninjured, those changes may be safely offered, which are not considered even by him that offers them as necessary or safe.

If my readings are of little value, they have not been ostentatiously displayed or importunately obtruded. I could have written longer notes, for the art of writing notes is not of difficult attainment.

The work is performed, first by railing at the stupidity, negligence, ignorance, and asinine tastelessness of the former editors, and shewing, from all that goes before and all that follows, the inelegance and absurdity of the old reading; then by proposing something, which to superficial readers would seem specious, but which the editor rejects with indignation; then by producing the true reading, with a long paraphrase, and concluding with loud acclamations on the discovery, and a sober wish for the advancement and prosperity of genuine criticism.

All this may be done, and perhaps done sometimes without impropriety. But I have always suspected that the reading is right, which requires many words to prove it wrong; and the emendation wrong, that cannot without so much labour appear to be right. The justness of a happy restoration strikes at once, and the moral precept may be well applied to criticism, quod dubitas ne feceris.

To dread the shore which he sees spread with wrecks, is natural to the sailor. I had before my eye, so many critical adventures ended in miscarriage, that caution was forced upon me. I encountered in every page Wit struggling with its own sophistry, and Learning confused by the multiplicity of its views. I was forced to censure those whom I admired, and could not but reflect, while I was dispossessing their emenations, how soon the same fate might happen to my own, and how many of the readings which I have corrected may be some other editor defended and established.

Criticks, I saw, that other's names efface,
And fix their own, with labour, in the place;
Their own, like others, soon their place resign'd,
Or disappear'd, and left the first behind.—Pope.

That a conjectural critick should often be mistaken, cannot be wonderful, either to others or himself, if it be considered that in his art there is no system, no principal and axiomatical truth that regulates subordinate positions. His chance of errour is renewed at every attempt; an oblique view of the passage a slight misapprehension of a phrase, a casual inattention to the parts connected, is sufficient to make him not only fail but fail ridiculously; and when he succeeds best, he produces perhaps but one reading of many probable, and he that suggests another will always be able to dispute his claims.

It is an unhappy state, in which danger is hid under pleasure. The allurements of emendation are scarcely resistible. Conjecture has all the joy and all the pride of invention, and he that has once started a happy change, is too much delighted to consider what objections may rise against it.

Yet conjectural criticism has been of great use in the

learned world; nor is it my intention to depreciate a study, that has exercised so many mighty minds, from the revival of learning to our own age, from the Bishop of Aleria to English Bentley. The criticks on ancient authours have, in the exercise of their sagacity, many assistances, which the editor of Shakespeare is condemned to want. They are employed upon grammatical and settled languages, whose construction contributes so much to perspicuity, that Homer has fewer passages unintelligible than Chaucer.

The words have not only a known regimen, but invariable quantities, which direct and confine the choice. There are commonly more manuscripts than one; and. they do not often conspire in the same mistakes. Yet Scaliger could confess to Salmasius how little satisfaction his emendations gave him. Illudunt nobis conjecturae nostrae, quarum nos pudet, posteaquam in meliores cofices incidimus. And Lipsius could complain, that criticks were making faults, by trying to remove them, Ut olim vitiis, ita nunc remediis laboratur. And indeed, where mere conjecture is to be used, the emendations of Scaliger and Lipsius, notwithstanding their wonderful sagacity and erudition, are often vague and disputable, like mine or Theobald's.

Perhaps I may not be more censured for doing wrong, than for doing little; for raising in the publick expectations, which at last I have not answered. The expectation of ignorance is indefinite, and that of knowledge is often tyrannical. It is hard to satisfy those who know not what to demand, or those who demand by design what they think impossible to be done. I have indeed disappointed no opinion more than my own; yet I have endeavoured to perform my task with no slight solicitude. Not a single passage in the whole work has appeared to me corrupt, which I have not attempted to restore; or obscure, which I have not endeavoured to illustrate. In many I have failed like others; and from many, after all my efforts, I have retreated, and confessed the repulse. I have not passed over, with affected superiority, what is equally difficult to the reader and to myself, but where I could not instruct him, have owned my ignorance. I might easily have accumulated a mass of seeming learning upon easy scenes; but it ought not to be imputed to negligence, that, where nothing was necessary, nothing has been done, or that, where others have said enough, I have said no more.

Notes are often necessary, but they are necessary evils. Let him, that is yet unacquainted with the powers of Shakespeare, and who desires to feel the highest pleasure that the drama can give, read every play from the first scene to the last, with utter negligence of all his commentators. When his fancy is once on the wing, let it not stoop at correction or explanation. When his attention is strongly engaged, let it disdain alike to turn aside to the name of Theobald and Pope. Let him read on through brightness and obscurity, through integrity and corruption; let him preserve his comprehension of the dialogue and his interest in the fable. And when the pleasures of novelty have ceased, let him attempt exactness; and read the commentators.

Particular passages are cleared by notes, but the general effect of the work is weakened. The mind is refrigerated by interruption; the thoughts are diverted from the principal subject; the reader is weary, he suspects not why; and at last throws away the book, which he has too diligently studied.

Parts are not to be examined till the whole has been surveyed; there is a kind of intellectual remoteness necessary for the comprehension of any great work in its full design and its true proportions; a close approach shews the smaller niceties, but the beauty of the whole is discerned no longer.

It is not very grateful to consider how little the succession of editors has added to this authour's power of pleasing. He was read, admired, studied, and imitated, while he was yet deformed with all the improprieties which ignorance and neglect could accumulate upon him; while the reading was yet not rectified, nor his allusions understood; yet then did Dryden pronounce "that Shakespeare was the man, who, of all modern and perhaps ancient poets, had the largest and most comprehensive soul. All the images of nature were still present to him, and he drew them not laboriously, but luckily: When he describes any thing, you more than see it, you feel it too.

Those who accuse him to have wanted learning, give him the greater commendation: he was naturally learned: he needed not the spectacles of books to read nature; he looked inwards, and found her there. I cannot say he is every where alike; were he so, I should do him injury to compare him with the greatest of mankind. He is many times flat and insipid; his comick wit degenerating into clenches, his serious swelling into bombast. But he is always great, when some great occasion is presented to him: No man can say, he ever had a fit subject for his wit, and did not then raise himself as high above the rest of poets,

"Quantum lenta solent inter viburna cupressi."

It is to be lamented, that such a writer should want a commentary; that his language should become obsolete, or his sentiments obscure. But it is vain to carry wishes beyond the condition of human things; that which must happen to all, has happened to Shakespeare, by accident and time; and more than has been suffered by any other writer since the use of types, has been suffered by him through his own negligence of fame, or perhaps by that superiority of mind, which despised its own performances, when it compared them with its powers, and judged those works unworthy to be preserved, which the criticks of following ages were to contend for the fame of restoring and explaining.

Among these candidates of inferiour fame, I am now to stand the judgment of the publick; and wish that I could confidently produce my commentary as equal to the encouragement which I have had the honour of receiving. Every work of this kind is by its nature deficient, and I should feel little solicitude about the sentence, were it to be pronounced only by the skilful and the learned.

The Augustan Reprint Society

Lewis Theobald's edition of Shakespeare (1734) is one cornerstone of modern Shakespearian scholarship and hence of English literary scholarship in general. It is the first edition of an English writer in which a man with a professional breadth and concentration of reading in the writer's period tried to bring all relevant, ascertainable fact to bear on the establishment of the author's text and the explication of his obscurities. For Theobald was the first editor of Shakespeare who displayed a well grounded knowledge of Shakespeare's language and metrical practice and that of his contemporaries, the sources and chronology of his plays, and the broad range of Elizabethan-Jacobean drama as a means of illuminating the work of the master writer. Thus both in the edition itself and in his Preface, which stands as the first significant statement of a scholar's editorial duties and methods in handling an English classic, Theobald takes his place as an important progenitor of modern English studies.

It is regrettable, though it was perhaps historically inevitable, that this pioneer of English literary scholarship should have been tagged "piddling Theobald" by Pope and crowned the first king of The Dunciad. Pope's edition of Shakespeare was completed by 1725, and in the following year Theobald made the poet his implacable enemy when he issued his Shakespeare Restored, which demolished Pope's pretensions as an editor by offering some two hundred corrections. But the conflict was not merely strife between two writers: it was a clash between two kinds of criticism in which the weight of tradition and polite taste were all on the side of Pope. What Theobald had done, in modern terms, was to open the rift between criticism and scholarship or, in eighteenth-century terms, to proclaim himself a "literal critic" and to insist upon the need for "literal criticism" in the understanding and just appreciation of an older writer.

The new concept, which Theobald owed largely to Richard Bentley as primate of the classical scholars, was of course the 2 narrower one—implicit in it was the idea of specialization—and Theobald's opponents among the literati were quick to assail him as a mere "Word-catcher".

His own edition of Shakespeare, therefore, was the work of a man and a method on trial. At first Theobald had proposed simply to write further commentary on Shakespeare's plays, but by 1729 he determined to issue a new edition and in October of that year signed a contract with Tonson. From the first Theobald found warm support for his project among booksellers, incipient patrons, and men of learning. His work went forward steadily; subscribers, including members of the Royal Family, were readily forthcoming; and by late 1731 Theobald felt that his labors were virtually complete. But vexing delays occurred in the printing so that the edition, though dated 1733, did not appear until early in 1734, New Style. When it did appear, it was plain to all that Theobald's vindication of himself and his method was complete. Judicious critics like the anonymous author of Some Remarks on the Tragedy of Hamlet (1736) were quick to applaud Theobald's achievement, and even Pope himself was silenced.

Ultimately of course Theobald came under severe attack by succeeding editors of Shakespeare, notably Warburton and Johnson, yet both men were guilty of unwarranted abuse of their predecessor, whose edition was nine times issued in the course of the century and was still in current use by the time of Coleridge (cf. Wm. Jaggard, Shakespeare Bibliography, 1911, pp. 499-504). Warburton and Johnson's abuse, coupled with that of Pope, obscured Theobald's real achievements for more than a century until J.C. Collins did much to rehabilitate his reputation by an essay celebrating him as "The Porson of Shakespearian Criticism" (Essays and Studies, 1895, pp. 263-315). Collins's emotional defence was largely substantiated by T.R. Lounsbury's meticulous The Text of Shakespeare (1906), R.F. Jones's Lewis Theobald (1919), which brought much new material to light, and most recently by R.B. McKerrow's dispassionate appraisal, "The Treatment of Shakespeare's Text by his Earlier 3 Editors, 1709-1768" (Proceedings of the British Academy, XIX, 1933, 23-27). As a result, so complete has been Theobald's vindication that even in a student's handbook he is hailed as "the great pioneer of serious Shakespeare scholarship" and as "the first giant" in the field (A Companion to Shakespeare Studies, 1934, ed. H. Granville Barker and G. B. Harrison, pp. 306-07).

Theobald's Preface occupied his attention for over a year and gave him much trouble in the writing. Its originality was, and still is, a matter of sharp dispute. The first we hear of it is in a letter of 12 November 1731 from Theobald to his coadjutor

Warburton, who had expressed some concern about what Theobald planned to prefix to his edition. Theobald announced a major change in plan when he replied that "The affair of the Prolegomena I have determined to soften into a Preface." He then proceeded to make a strange request:

But, dear Sir, will you, at your leisure hours, think over for me upon the contents, topics, orders, &c. of this branch of my labour? You have a comprehensive memory, and a happiness of digesting the matter joined to it, which my head is often too much embarrassed to perform.... But how unreasonable is it to expect this labour, when it is the only part in which I shall not be able to be just to my friends: for, to confess assistance in a Preface will, I am afraid, make me appear too naked (John Nichols, Illustrations of the Literary History of the Eighteenth Century, 1817, II, 621-22).

His next letter, which contains the list of acknowledgements substantially as printed, thanks Warburton for consenting to give the requested help, announces that he is himself busy about "the Contents... wch. I am Endeavouring to modell in my Head, in Order to communicate them to you, for your Directions & 4 refinement," indicates that he has "already rough-hewn the Exordium & Conclusion," and asserts that "What I shall send you from Time to Time, I look upon only as Materials: wch I hope may grow into a fine Building, under your judicious Management".

Warburton apparently misunderstood or overlooked Theobald's remarks about materials, for in his next letter Theobald was obliged to return, somewhat ambiguously, to the same point:

I make no Question of my being wrong in the disjointed Parts of my Preface, but my Intention was, (after I had given you the Conclusion, & the Manner in wch. I meant to start) to give you a List of all the other general Heads design'd to be handled, then to transmit to you, at proper Leisure, my rough Working off of each respective Head, that you might have the Trouble only of refining & embellishing wth: additional Inrichments: of the general Arrangement, wch. you should think best for the whole; & of making the proper Transitions from Subject to Subject, wch. I account no inconsiderable Beauty (Ibid., pp. 289-90). Finally on January 10, 1733, Theobald wrote Warburton: "I promise myself now shortly to sit down upon ye fine Synopsis, wch. you so modestly call the Skeleton of Preface"

It is clear from the foregoing that Theobald wrote most of the Preface topic by topic, and probably followed the plan for the general structure as submitted by Warburton. Yet it is equally clear that certain parts of the Preface, such as the contrast between Julius Caesar and Addison's Cato, which Warburton later claimed as his and which Theobald omitted from his second edition, were furnished Theobald as "additional Inrichments" (D.N. Smith, Eighteenth Century Essays on Shakespeare, 1903, pp. xlviii-ix). When later a break did occur between the two men, 5 neither was free from blame. Theobald had asked and got so much help with the Preface that he should have acknowledged the debt, no matter how naked it might have made him seem.

Warburton, on the other hand, had had honest warning that acknowledgement would not be made for this part of his help; and if his synopsis were followed, as seems likely, his condemnation of the Preface as "Theobald's heap of disjointed stuff" was disingenuous, to say the least. Far less defensible was his assertion in the same letter to Thomas Birch that, apart from the section on Greek texts, virtually the entire Preface was stitched together from notes which he had supplied (Nichols, Illustrations, II, 81).

Three further points concerning the Preface demand mention. First, the section on Shakespeare's life is often dismissed as a simple recension of Rowe's Life (1709). Actually, however, the expansion itself is a characteristic example of Theobald's habit of exploring original sources. To take only a single instance, Rowe says that Shakespeare's "Family, as appears by the Register and Publick Writings relating to that Town, were of good Figure and Fashion there, and are mention'd as Gentlemen" (ed. S.H. Monk, Augustan Society Reprints, 1949, p. ii). To this statement Theobald adds plentiful detail drawn from the same Stratford records, from tombs in the Stratford Church, and from documents in the Heralds' Office connected with the coat of arms obtained for the playwright's father. Such typical expansions were the result of conscientious research.

Second, all critics have agreed to condemn the digression in which Theobald advertised his ability to emend Greek texts. Theobald himself was hesitant about including it lest he be indicted for pedantry, but was encouraged to do so by Warburton, who later scoffed at what he had originally admired. This much may be said in Theobald's behalf. Such a digression would not have seemed irrelevant in an age which took its classical scholarship seriously; and such digressions, arising naturally out of context and strategically placed before the conclusion, were not 6 only allowed but actually encouraged by classical rhetoricians like Cicero and Quintilian, whose teachings were still standard in the English schools.

.Finally, the Preface exists in two forms. The later and shorter form was that designed for Theobald's second edition (1740), which omits all passages presumably contributed by Warburton and more besides, the section on Greek texts, and the list of acknowledgements to contemporary Shakespearian enthusiasts. This abridged form has been frequently reprinted. From a copy in the University of Michigan Library the original Preface is here reproduced for the first time.

Preface: The subject of this thesis is Alexander Pope's edition of Shakespeare: *The Works of Shakespear in Six Volumes, Collated and Corrected by Mr Pope, (Jacob Tonson, London: 1725).* My aim is to examine the nature of the editorial and critical decisions which informed it.

This will, I hope, fill a critical gap. Pope's edition of Shakespeare has been rarely discussed. Where it has been discussed it has been treated without sympathy. Consequently, the story of Pope's work is incomplete and distorted. It is a secondary contention that a study of Pope's edition can help us directly or obliquely to a better understanding of Shakespeare, of Pope, and of the requirements and difficulties of editing Shakespeare's plays.

I have tried to take every question from the most basic

level, and have made few assumptions about either Shakespeare, Pope or editorial procedure and tradition. Accordingly when particular scenes in Shakespeare's plays are examined in detail, some context is given, and where scenes and speeches are referred to, some or all of their content is quoted. It is an inevitable consequence of studying an edition that some considerations are at, or even below, the level of the single word.

On the other hand my study is partial to Pope in that I attempt to adopt his priorities as a prerequisite for study; I hope only to grapple with his decisions after trying to understand them. A result of this partiality is that the critical issues examined are those that seem to have concerned Pope, which are not necessarily those that have concerned later editors. Pope's complaint about the talentless in his *Epistle to Dr. Arbuthnot*, that

Comma's and points they set exactly right,
And 'twere a sin to rob them of their Mite.
Yet ne'r one sprig of laurel grac'd these ribalds,
From slashing Bentley down to pidling Tibalds.

suggests a set of priorities which I hope to follow, concentrating rather more on Pope and Shakespeare's rights to their 'laurel' than on their points and commas. Pope's emphasis on poetic sensibility is not the same as the rigorous requirements for accuracy faced by every modern editor, or even for editors following Pope such as '*Tibald*' (Lewis Theobald). Indeed, while studying Pope's edition, many errors have become apparent in it: misprints, mis-spellings, misplaced punctuation. I have largely ignored the peppering of such errors that continues throughout the volumes, partly in deference to what I imagine Pope's priorities were, partly because such errors can be easily and mechanically sought by anybody minded to seek them, and partly because such an examination is unlikely to provide a significant contribution to knowledge.

At a larger level too the questions I ask have been dictated by what I assume to have been Pope's own anxieties and interests as he undertook his edition. These, as I hope to show, centre on Pope's worries over Shakespeare's creative powers and the authenticity of much of the text that had any claim to be by Shakespeare.

The method employed by this thesis varies from simple factual presentation to attempts at qualitative judgement, what used to be called 'literary criticism'. Since Pope put extremely few notes, fewer still explaining why he had taken a particular decision, the explanation for his decisions must draw on evidence from elsewhere in his edition and elsewhere in his life and work. Therefore no matter how much evidence accumulates, the means of moving towards an explanation for Pope's edition remains essentially conjectural. I am unable to say at any point that a situation was *certainly* so, and have to remain in that uneasy realm where one possibility vies with another.

I have not attempted an account of every play in Pope's edition, nor to cover every editorial issue in the plays I do discuss. The thesis concentrates on five works: *The Life and Death of King John, The Taming of the Shrew, The Life and Death of Richard the Second, Romeo and Juliet,* and *The Life and Death of King Lear*. I have chosen these plays to demonstrate how wide-ranging were Pope's editorial and critical decisions. Since the quality and extent of Pope's poetical taste are the issues over which debate has ranged, the chosen plays are of different kinds, and represent his histories, tragedies and comedies. Variety, however, was not the only consideration. Some of the texts in Pope's edition differ only trivially from their originals and from later editions. Such plays (for example *The Merry Wives of Windsor*) do not further our understanding of Pope's edition. Other plays, which are the focus of particular modern editorial and critical interest, such as *Hamlet*, present in Pope's edition comparatively few critical challenges. The chosen plays offer a range of difficulties and show a broad sample of Pope's responses. However, since it is eventually my contention that Pope's editorial procedure is not a describable *process*, but a creative *activity*, it is impossible to represent the whole by examining parts, and this thesis can be no more than an introduction to Pope's work which displays some of the problems Pope faced and suggests part of the way in which he dealt with them.

Throughout the thesis, parallel texts (bound separately) are used to illustrate the difference between Pope's edition and the texts he was editing. These attempt to align on the page points of interest and to indicate where there are gaps or additions at a glance. Each text extract is labelled x.y where x is the chapter number and y is the ordinal of the parallel text in that chapter. For example, Chapter IV on *Richard II* has three parallel texts numbered 4.1, 4.2 and 4.3. Within each parallel text features which are referred to in the main body of the thesis are indicated by a thin vertical line to the right of the text. Each vertical line is numbered, for example:

Ben. I pray thee good Mercutio lets retire,The day is hot, the Capulets abroad:And if we meet, we shal not scape a brawle, for now thesehot dayes, is the mad blood stirring. *Mer.* Thou are like one of these fellowes, that when heenters the confines of a Taverne, claps me his Sword uponthe Table, and sayes, God send thee no need of thee: and bythe operation of the second cup, drawes him on the Drawer,when indeed there is no need. *Ben.* Am I like such a Fellow?

Here Benvolio's speech is numbered '1' and may be referred to as 'the speech marked 1' in the body of the thesis. To save the reader having to cross-refer between two texts continually, the relevant quotation is sometimes included in the thesis itself.

Choosing which editions to use for these parallel texts has not always been easy. It seems from the evidence of Pope's correspondence that he took as the basis of his editing, Rowe's edition of Shakespeare. However, this does not imply that Rowe was a 'copy text' with the importance that term implies today. It is clear from a number of notes throughout Pope's edition and in his Preface, that he saw his text as differentiated from the 'common books'. These I take to mean the folios, including also Rowe's edition which is, on the whole, a folio text reprinted in modern type with scene divisions and stage directions. It is in an attempt to be sympathetic to Pope that I have allowed the distinctions between folio texts and Rowe to dissolve except where a particular example demands attention. It seems that Pope was able to float between the 'common books' disregarding slight differences of spelling and the odd differing word: these, I shall argue, were not of primary importance to his project. Since Pope had access to the 1623 Folio, and since this text represents fairly, on the whole, the contents of the other folios and Rowe, I have taken this F1 text in all of the parallel texts to represent 'unedited Shakespeare', or what Pope termed 'the common books'.

One means of defining Pope's editorial position is to contrast it with others. Pope, in the Preface, and in notes throughout the text of the plays, often implicitly sets himself up for comparison with the editors of the folio texts. But these contrasts are not the only ones which enable us to see Pope's sometimes unique editorial stance. The controversy immediately following the publication of Pope's edition, and particularly the quarrel with the next editor of Shakespeare, Lewis Theobald, provide material with which to understand Pope's editorial aspirations. The final chapter of the thesis discusses the immediate legacy of Pope's edition, and in particular suggests that *The Dunciad* offers an opportunity for further insight into Pope's beliefs about his edition of Shakespeare.

Throughout the thesis, Pope's edition is contrasted with other editions as a means of helping to understand what Pope might have been doing, or what he might have been avoiding doing. Johnson's edition is frequently cited, since points of activity in Pope often correspond to points where Johnson puts a note, sometimes referring directly to Pope's edition. Although Johnson does not, as he promises in his Preface, reproduce all of Pope's notes in his edition, he seems frequently to have made similar deductions about Pope's editorial decisions to those suggested in this thesis: Johnson seems to have made an effort to guess at Pope's procedures and the reasoning behind them.

As a representative modern 'Shakespeare' text, I have generally selected the editions in the Arden series. Although each presents its own particular problems, I have generally taken the Arden texts to represent the result of the editorial tradition which looks to Theobald as its progenitor< – the tradition which emphasises attention to the printed texts, advocates non-intervention on purely critical grounds, and tends to combine Shakespearean texts. (*King Lear*, an extreme example, which I discuss in chapter VII, is in the Arden edition a conflation, or inclusive combination, of the quarto and folio texts of the play, very different from Pope's partial and selective combination.)

Over the last twenty years or so, a new approach to editing has been gaining academic support in the field. It is frequently argued that where 'original Shakespearean texts' vary, they are entirely different 'versions' of a play, and are printed accordingly.

The essays in *The Division of the Kingdoms*, for example, generally expound a belief that there are two distinct plays, the *Tragedy* and the *History* of King Lear. I have not entered into discussion with this body of opinion since Pope's practice is only obliquely relevant. The overwhelming consensus for the last two centuries or so has been that Pope's Shakespeare is valueless.

Anyone attempting to suggest otherwise is bound to feel as Johnson felt in his Preface to Shakespeare when denying the universal applicability of the Unities of Time and Place: 'I cannot but recollect how much wit and learning may be produced against me. I am almost frighted at my own temerity; and when I estimate the fame and strength of those that maintain the contrary opinion, am ready to sink down in reverential silence; as Æneas withdraw from the defence of Troy when he saw Neptune shaking the wall, and Juno heading the besiegers.' Brian Vickers, for example, in the second volume of his monumental collection of criticism of Shakespeare claims that Pope's method as an editor was 'the quite arbitrary workings of his own taste'. Vickers charges Pope with rejecting 'what he called "trash" such as puns and word-play' and complains that 'over 1,500 lines of Shakespeare suffered this ignominy'. The case sounds devastating:

I never cease to be surprised by the arrogance with which

Pope treats Shakespeare – despite his effusive panegyrics – and rejects lines or whole scenes that offend him. Sometimes he attempts to minimise the criticism by holding the players – those vulgar, unlearned, irresponsible people (nowhere is Pope's superiority more misplaced) – to blame for corrupting the text.

It is the contention of the thesis that Vickers' use of the word 'Shakespeare' embodies a critical, not a factual, premise. (Not even the ultra-conservative editors of the New Oxford edition assume that all the words, all the lines, in all the early texts, were written by Shakespeare.) I am offering a picture of Pope in the process of attempting to answer the question with which he was inevitably faced.

Which or these plays, which of these words, which of these lines – were truly Shakespeare? Painting this picture inevitably involves supposition. In an attempt to resist Vickers' notions of Pope's 'taste' and 'arrogance' I have drawn attention to what seem violently contrasting critical positions. Further, I have drawn attention to the differences of opinion between Pope and some of his contemporaries and immediate successors. Comparisons between Pope and Johnson, for example, as frequently distinguish these poets' opinions and beliefs, as they confirm their similarities. I have occasionally drawn on Pope's other critical writings (such as *An Essay on Criticism* and his Preface to his translation of Homer) in an attempt to ascertain his general critical principles. It is however part of my case that editing Shakespeare presented Pope with critical problems which he had not foreseen, that Pope might, in the end, have taken the point of Johnson's reproof of Pope for calling the duty of an editor 'dull': An emendatory critic would ill discharge his duty, without qualities very different from dullness. In perusing a corrupted piece, he must have before him all possibilities of meaning, with all possibilities of expression. Such must be his comprehension of thought, and such his copiousness of language. Such must be his knowledge, and such his taste. Conjectural criticism demands more than humanity possesses, and he that exercises it with most praise, has very frequent need of indulgence.

Critical Essay Hawthorne's Preface

When Hawthorne defined his purpose as a writer of "romances," his first care was to distinguish the romance from the novel. After we finish reading his definition of a *novel,* as opposed to a *romance,* we get the feeling that Hawthorne was groping toward a conception of fiction that was more unique than he realized. Others before him, from Henry Fielding on, had wondered where to place fiction among the several kinds of literature, but Hawthorne's emphasis on fiction as an *art* form, his insistence that it be tested by laws appropriate to its mode of existence rather than to its accuracy as a document, clearly establishes a sound critical principle for distinguishing the novel from a romance. Other critics such as Henry James, who wrote a critical book on Hawthorne, elaborates upon the distinction, but, here, Hawthorne's choice of an analogy is particularly relevant to his argument. But most important of all to Hawthorne's distinction between a romance and a novel is his life-long insistence that the kind of truth which he wanted to portray was the "truth of the human heart," and that the best way to portray this was by using the strategy of indirection. The "truth" which he hoped to conceive is of a different order from the truth conveyed by ordinary didactic fiction, by philosophy, or by the symbolism of the exact sciences. It is a truth that can be expressed only in the images of the imagination, and as Hawthorne himself thought, this truth cannot be "grasped" except in such images. The most striking way in which Hawthorne's work foreshadows all modern fiction lies in the mythic and poetic aspects of his novel. When, in the Preface to *The House of the Seven Gables,* Hawthorne made his now famous distinction between the novel and the romance, he was not at all intending to assign "truth" to the novel and mere "fantasy," or escapist dreaming, to the romance. He was distinguishing between "fact" (which the novel deals with) and "truth" (which is the traditional province of the romance), and at the same time he was suggesting an orientation in which "fact" is external and "truth" internal. So far as he was defending, implicitly, the validity of his own practice as a romancer, he was implying the word "mere" before the word "fact." (He was ambivalent about this, as he so often was on other matters, to be sure. He thought that Emerson was too idealistic, and he greatly admired the "beef and ale" realism of Anthony Trollope.)

The romantic artist creates, Hawthorne thought, by transforming fact into symbol—that is, by transforming it into *meaningful* fact. Facts which he cannot see as meaningful may be discarded. He is at liberty to manipulate his materials, to shape them freely into meaningful patterns, so long as he does *not* violate the "truth of the human heart." Hawthorne felt that he himself could best pursue his desired truth by looking within and exercising a kind of imaginative sympathy in both his subject and his method. In a very suggestive metaphor in another of his prefaces—that to *The Snow-Image and Other Twice-Told Tales* in 1851—he defined his role as an artist as that of a person who has been burrowing into the depths of human nature by the light of *observation*.

In addition to his theory of fiction, Hawthorne also tells us the subject of *The House of the Seven Gables*; that theme, he says, is that wrong and retribution, as well as sin and suffering, will be carried on through generations. He further announces that he will observe how the wrongdoing of one generation lives into successive generations until it finally becomes a "pure and uncontrollable mischief." In an even more serious tone, he adds that he hopes that this work might warn mankind against accumulating "ill-gotten gold, or real estate," and bequeathing them to later, innocent generations. The *romance* provides, then, in Hawthorne's view of the matter, *texts for sermons* on the sins of pride and avarice and on the fact of mutability.

The *novel*, on the other hand, presents us with the "legendary mist" of the distant past, intermingling with the memories of the recent past, especially in the minds of the House of the Seven Gable's inhabitants. Hawthorne combines his conviction about the continuum of history and about the interdependence of person and place into a complex idea of a self extended in time, in space, and through its own layered awareness. Within that self, the past intrudes on the present as the subconscious intrudes on the conscious. In this sense, the novel presents the old Pyncheon house, haunted by the *guilt* of the founder and the *ghost* of his victim.

Hawthorne knows that what he wants to say cannot be said wholly in the Preface; thus, here he comments more freely on his intentions in the work than was customary with him, and then he tells us to read the novel *attentively* if we would know its meaning.

Maturity and Recognition

The pension Johnson had received in 1762 had freed him from the necessity of writing for a living, but it had not released him from his obligation to complete the Shakespeare edition, for which he had taken money from subscribers. His long delay in bringing that project to fruition provoked some satiric notice from the poet Charles Churchill:

He for subscribers baits his hook,
And takes their cash—but where's the book?

The edition finally appeared in eight volumes in 1765. Johnson edited and annotated the text and wrote a preface, which is his greatest work of literary criticism. As editor and annotator he sought to establish the text, freed from later corruptions, and to explain diction that by then had become obsolete and obscure. Johnson's approach was to immerse himself in the books Shakespeare had read—his extensive reading for his Dictionary eased this task—and to examine the early editions as well as those of his 18th-century predecessors. His annotations are often shrewd, though his admiration reveals at times different concerns from those of some of his contemporaries and of later scholars.

In his Preface Johnson addressed several critical issues. For one, he vigorously defends Shakespeare against charges of failing to adhere to the Neoclassical doctrine of the dramatic unities of time, place, and action. Johnson alertly observes that time and place are subservient to the mind: since the audience does not confound stage action with reality, it has no trouble with a shift in scene from Rome to Alexandria. Some critics had made similar points before, but Johnson's defence was decisive. He also questions the need for purity of dramatic genre. In defending Shakespearian tragicomedy against detractors, he asserts that "there is always an appeal open from criticism to nature." Echoing Hamlet, Johnson claims that Shakespeare merits praise, above all, as "the poet of nature; the poet that holds up to his readers a faithful mirror of manners and of life." He goes on to say that "in the writings of other poets a character is too often an individual: in those of Shakespeare it is commonly a species" and that "Shakespeare has no heroes; his scenes are occupied only by men." These comments inveigh against the rigid notions of decorum upheld by critics, such as Voltaire, who would not allow kings to be drunkards or senators to be buffoons. Johnson's concern for "general nature" means that he is not much interested in accidental traits of a character, such as the "Roman ness" of Julius Caesar or Brutus, but in traits that are common to all humanity.

Shakespeare and Branagh Deliver Aural Pleasure

In Shakespeare's Much Ado About Nothing, the play's preoccupation with women's chastity is central to the plot. Many critics have dealt at length with the reactions expressed in the comedy to Hero's supposed betrayal of Claudio. Some critics have considered the implication of the remarkable number of cuckold jokes; Michael Mangan notes that the play is more obsessed with this idea than any other of its period. But Shakespeare also is concerned in this play with male chastity or fidelity, and while this motif is subtler than that of female fidelity, it nevertheless runs through the whole play and has its most obvious manifestation in the song, "Sigh no more ladies," sung by Balthasar at the very heart of the play before the double gulling scene.

The lyrics of the song serve to remind the audience (if at all necessary) that relationships between men and women are fraught with difficulties. They suggest that men and women are very different in their attitudes about love. The song portrays men as inconstant, with one foot in the sea and one on shore, whereas, by implication, women are naturally monogamous. (Beatrice, however, appears to be the inconstant men's equal in believing herself as incapable of fidelity in marriage as they are. God will only send no horns if he sends her no husband, she jokes [2.1.24].)

In his 1993 film of the play, Kenneth Branagh makes the song central to his interpretation, privileging it even more than the play does. Virgil Thomson notes, in "Music for Much Ado About Nothing," that Shakespeare's use of music generally takes "no time at all out of the play's dramatic pacing" (qtd. in Stevens 89). Yet Branagh breaks cinematic convention by delaying the start of the action with the song's recital at the beginning and interrupting the narrative in the middle of the film for the song to be heard again.

The song performed in the film is longer than it would have been in a typical theatrical production, without the lush scenery to captivate the audience. Branagh obviously thought the lyrics important enough to risk tampering with Shakespeare's magical pacing. He even uses the song's melody as a recurring motif. Branagh then concludes the film with a leisurely pan out, with all the characters dancing to a rousing choral rendition of the same song. I would argue that the song, "Sigh no more ladies," is the only significant representative of the play's darker commentary on heterosexual relationships that is left intact in the film. Branagh's decision to use the song as the primary critical subtext to the romantic comedy is problematic for two reasons. First, audiences tend to ignore song lyrics, and second, his own jolly treatment of the sons obscures the lyrics' bitter taste.

Much of the play's original subtext contrasts sharply with the jubilant focus on romantic love in the text. Shakespeare achieves this through references, mostly in the form of humorous banter, to the difficulty men and women have in remaining chaste. Yet Branagh cuts many of these references. The motif of men's fickle nature is introduced very early in Shakespeare's play when Beatrice refers to Benedick as Signor Mountanto (1.1.30), perhaps with a bawdy quibble on the idea of his mounting women, and then compares him to Cupid's challenger, setting up his bills in Messina (1.1.37).

This is the first of many references in the play to Benedick as a ladies' man, an aspect of his character that Branagh completely does away with in his movie. While he keeps the reference to Mountanto, which is obscure enough for a modern audience that it will not besmirch Benedick's reputation, Branagh cuts the references to Cupid. Benedick, in Shakespeare's script, is not a celibate bachelor-his anxiety is about marriage, not sex.

There are at least eight references in the play to Benedick's reputation as a Casanova of sorts (1.1.37, 1.1.52, 1.1.102, 1.1.119, 1.1.237, 3.2.9-10, 5.2.1-23, 5.3.113), and Branagh does away with six of these (1.1.37, 1.1.102, 1.1.237, 3.2.9-10, 5.2.1-23, 5.3.113). In addition, there are at least seven references to his generally inconstant and changeable nature (1.1.66-83, 2.1.258-63, 2.3.222-35, 4.1.275-79, 5.1.163-66, 5.2.1-23, 5.4.106), two of which Branagh omits in the film (5.1.163-66, 5.2.1-23). The most significant and obvious of these edited references comes at the end of the play, when Beatrice and Benedick are about to be married. Claudio comments that Benedick will "out of question" prove a "double dealer" to Beatrice unless she looks "exceeding narrowly" to him (5.4.113-15). The double standard that existed at the time is obvious.

It is acceptable for Claudio to warn Beatrice on her wedding day that Benedick will be unfaithful to her unless she keeps a sharp watch. This is supposed to be humorous and agrees with the "hey nonny nonny" stoicism urged on women by the song. But the idea of Hero being unfaithful to Claudio certainly is not considered funny by anyone. Why does Branagh cut Claudio's line? He keeps the song, which deals in general terms with men's infidelity to women, but he cuts six out of the eight references to Benedick's philandering tendencies. Is it because a modern audience would no longer accept Benedick as the hero of a romantic comedy if he were shown to be a philanderer? Does it darken the end of the comedy too much to have this warning that Beatrice's future happiness may well be in jeopardy, especially if the film is, as Celestino Deleyto in his article "Men in Leather" suggests, told primarily from Beatrice's point of view ? To what extent are these cuts a result of Branagh conforming to the Hollywood romantic comedy formula, or are they as much a result of mere economy-cutting those jokes that neither further the plot nor are easily comprehended by a modern audience?

The theme of female chastity emerges obsessively in the proliferation of cuckold jokes in the play. Of at least eleven cuckold jests in the play (1.1.187, 1.1.226, 1.1.247, 1.1.251, 2.1.20, 2.1.39, 2.3.59, 3.4.41-45, 3.4.61, 5.2.36, 5.4.122) Branagh omitted eight (1.1.187, 1.1.226, 1.1.247, 2.1.20, 2.1.39, 3.4.41-45, 3.4.61, 5.4.122). Some are quite arcane, of course, but what effect do these omissions have on our understanding of the play? Certainly, their absence decreases the atmosphere of paranoia in Messina, thus centering all male insecurity in the figure of Claudio, and to some extent exonerating the other men. In Shakespeare's play, all the men seem anxious about the prospect of their future wives' infidelity, particularly Benedick. Yet in Branagh's film, only Claudio comes across as jealous-first of Don Pedro, wooing on his behalf, then of the man who enters Hero's bed chamber.

I contend that the cuts to the script make Claudio (Robert Sean Leonard) less sympathetic than in the play. In Shakespeare's Messina, it is no wonder that Claudio is quick to think Hero has deceived him. The banter he exchanges with his male companions is dominated by cuckold jokes. In Messina, as Michael Mangan observes, "to be married is to be cuckolded already". Joseph Westlund in "The Temptation to Isolate" concurs, describing Messina as "a troubling world in which everyone readily suspects everyone else". The atmosphere of paranoia, like the arms race before a war, leads inexorably to an accusation-Hero's undoing in the church is the release of all the men's pent-up anxiety.

In Branagh's film, the paranoia about women's chastity, and the inconstancy by which men are characterized in the song, rest almost entirely with Claudio. As in the play, first he doubts his best friend, then his fiancé. His love for Hero fluctuates dramatically with his state of mind. He only likes her when he must set out for war, but loves her in peacetime when he knows that she is Leonato's sole heir. He scarcely registers her death when he thinks she was unfaithful and then mourns it exceedingly when he hears she was innocent. When, at the end of the film, Benedick defends his own switch from committed bachelordom to committed husband with "man is a giddy thing", it does not seem to apply to his character as much as to his friend's.

It is Claudio who has been "to one thing constant never." Indeed, the camera focuses on Robert Sean Leonard's face at this moment. But what of the women's anxiety, expressed indirectly in the song and in Beatrice's admission that Benedick played for her heart with false dice? In a way, by removing so many of the cuckold jokes and stressing the song, Branagh evens out the balance between female anxiety over male infidelity and male anxiety over female infidelity in a way that reveals modern attitudes to the subject. In Elizabethan England, because of the law of primogeniture, a woman's chastity within marriage was the only guarantee that a man did not leave his estate, name, everything to another man's son. The male anxiety over female infidelity was thus mostly caused by material concerns-who would inherit all the stuff-your own son, or a bastard? Women's anxiety over men's infidelity was centered more on emotions-a fear of being hurt-or on survival-being cast off penniless.

Today, the anxiety over infidelity for both sexes is more often the same-it is caused by the fear of being emotionally hurt; inheritance is no longer a key issue. Branagh seems to have aimed for this modern equality in anxiety in the film. He emphasizes Beatrice's pain over the past deception practiced on her by Benedick by zooming in on Emma Thompson's face as she talks about it wistfully. Branagh also shows that for Claudio, Hero's supposed betrayal is personally hurtful more than offensive to his honor by casting a young American with an informal accent in the role. Robert Sean Leonard's young Claudio does not give the impression of deeply considering his family's honor. As a result of these cuts to the dialogue, much rests in the film on the lyrics of the song. They have to suggest, almost single-handedly, the rich consideration of the challenges facing couples that makes Much Ado About

Nothing such a complex play. Branagh was very conscious of this. In his introduction to the screenplay, Branagh explains that he views the song as an articulation of the play's moral-"a hard-won confirmation of a certain reality in the relationships between men and women" (xiv). This is vague, but it suggests that Branagh holds the view of men and women expressed in the song to be accurate-men are deceivers, and since it is their nature, women had better just accept it, consoling themselves by not taking it too seriously (an opinion, as Harry Berger, Jr. argues, that he shares with Don Pedro). Branagh very consciously decided to have the lyrics sung three times in the film, and wanted the words themselves up on screen so that the audience would tune in to the language and, he writes, "understand the simplicity, gravity and beauty of the song lyrics" (xvi). "Gravity" is the right word for some of the lyrics, and yet this quality is not well served by their presentation in the film, with Beatrice delivering the words wryly, and her on-screen audience laughing uproariously at her conclusion.

The film opens with the words of the song appearing one by one, karaoke style, in white on a black screen as Emma Thompson's Beatrice reads them slowly and dryly. Deleyto astutely observes that this technique seems to prompt "the spectator to sing, or at least recite, along and thus identify with the content of what is being said and with the speaking voice. Even before the importance of the message sinks in, the film is, therefore, demanding total identification with Beatrice". The many close-ups of Emma Thompson throughout the film would seem to support Deleyto's theory. If his supposition is correct, then the song becomes her recommendation to her own sex not to take men or their infidelities to heart, but rather to adopt her own blithe and independent stance. Whereas, in the original play, when sung by Balthasar, "it suggests" in Sheldon Zitner's words, "the self-servins nature of male counsel: that women reconcile themselves to playing in an unfair game". Branagh seems to sit on the fence between these two readings of the song: he sees it both as full of "gravity" (xiv) and as creating a mood of "high romanticism" and "deep tranquillity". Perhaps he is just responding to the mixture of the serious and the merry in the play. John F. Cox recognizes this tonal dichotomy in Branagh's use of the song as a key to his film: "The 'fraud of men' was underscored in the Hero-Claudio-Don John story, but the advice to 'sigh not so, but let them go' was ironically countered by the film's powerful emphasis on the sexuality that impels women and men together".

The film's lighthearted renditions of the song's lyrics reinforce not only the conventions of romantic comedy, but also the Elizabethan double standards inherent in the play-when men betray women, women are to let them go and be blithe about it; but when women betray men, men are permitted to ruin their reputations in the most painful and public manner, making a travesty of their wedding day, as Claudio and Don Pedro do to Hero. Claudio, so far from singing "Hey nonny nonny," throws Hero back to her father as "a rotten orange". In this scene, Branagh renders Claudio less sympathetic than in Shakespeare's script by directing him to be physically violent with Hero. Yet, through editing, Branagh has diminished the motif of men betraying women, except with his inconsistent emphasis on the song.

The song also may not be the best vehicle to convey what Branagh views as "the moral" of the play. In reviewing the reactions of critics, students, scholars (and even characters) to the song, both in the text and in performance, what emerges is that it is generally given less attention than it deserves. Critical commentary on the song tends to be slight. The lyrics treat a major theme of the play, which is betrayal in love, and they offer what Zitner almost uniquely identifies as "hardly reassuring counsel" to women who have suffered from men's deceit. Critics and editors alike most often dismiss the song with a remark about it "softening the mood, and preparing for talk of love". Wey writes, "Balthasar is then brought on stage [lines 44-92] to help in the plot which will eventually unite Benedick and Beatrice in love and matrimony". He also notes the conjunction of music in the play with "harmony and happiness and love among the principal characters". Even

Branagh, in the screenplay, writes that the song appeals to Claudio's high romanticism in the garden. In what way would a song about men deceiving women and women letting them go put the audience or Claudio in a romantic mood? W. H. Auden's answer is that Claudio is not paying attention to the lyrics: "Claudio is in a dreamy, lovesick state he will not notice that the mood and words of the song are in complete contrast to his daydream".

So why is it that many critics, who, one assumes, are not similarly infatuated, write about the song's romantic qualities? Is it that the critics, editors, and reviewers are lulled by the music of the song to such an extent that, like Claudio, they ignore the lyrics? Certainly, the commentary in most editions concentrates on the settings and the instruments that may have been used, but there is rarely a word about the way in which the song expands on a central theme of the play and re-examines it from the woman's point of view. Or is it because the song deals only with female sexual insecurity that many male critics can find it romantic and even "soothing?". To what degree do audiences generally register song lyrics? I asked all the students in my two Shakespeare Comedy and Film classes at University College Dublin, after they had seen and taken notes on Branagh's film, why they thought he had opened the film with the words of the song, and they had no answer. I asked them what they thought the song was about, and the lyrics had made no impression on them. It was only when I had them read the song in their texts that they recognized the lyrics' significance.

I asked my students what their practice was when they encountered a song in Shakespeare's plays, and some admitted that they tended to skip over the lyrics. I report this, not to shame them, but to supply proof for my theory that most spectators, watching a film or play, may remember the tune of a song that breaks up the narrative, but will make no particular note of the lyrics, if indeed, they even can hear them clearly. Adrienne L. McLean in Cinema Journal contends that songs in nonmusical films are apt to be disregarded as sections in which nothing significant occurs. Even published critics are not exempt from this tendency to ignore lyrics. Douglas Brode, who wrote Shakespeare in the Movies, published by Oxford University Press, did not register the name (and refrain) of the song correctly and referred to it as "Cry no more ladies". What Brecht perceived about the emotional impact of theatre diminishing its intellectual clout seems to be particularly true of songs, even though Brecht himself used them to contribute to his alienation effect. Audiences watching Balthasar sing "Sigh no more" in that lovely Tuscan garden in Branagh's film are enjoying the melody and the scenery; they are not thinking about the words.

Thomson confirms this primacy of the visual over the musical: "Stylistically speaking, music for a spoken play must always be subservient to the visual element". Even Branagh's attempt to make the audience aware of the lyrics by putting them up on screen at the beginning seems to have backfired. Perhaps it takes the audience those opening minutes to adjust to the Elizabethan language, and therefore, it is not an ideal place for significant lines to be recited. It is especially surprising that the lyrics of the song are ignored in this particular play as it draws our attention to words and to an assessment of their worth more than many of Shakespeare's others: it is "language, which this play-with the self-conscious verbal wit of Beatrice and Benedick and the malapropisms of Dogberry-keeps uppermost in its audience's attention perhaps more than any other of the comedies." This concentrated focus on the way people speak should throw emphasis on the lyrics of the songs in the play, but if my students, who were studying the film after reading the play, paid no attention to the lyrics, what chance has the general public? We make the same mistake that so many of the characters do in not noting words the way we should. Perhaps it is a function of the fact that we now are unused to reading anything but credits on a film screen, and so words on the screen, especially at the beginning or end of a film, tend to be viewed as details included only for passionate film buffs, who actually care about the identity of the best boy, etc. We assume now, in contrast to silent film audiences, that the real information in a film is conveyed in images-the words are mere footnotes. Therefore, if we accept that modern audiences, even modern readers, pay little attention to the lyrics of the song, how important can the lyrics of Shakespeare's songs be? Was Shakespeare, a consummate man of the theatre, aware that his audience might miss the lyrics, or were their ears better able than ours to assimilate both melodic and verbal information? Thomson contends that Shakespeare was "wary of all music's disruptive dangers and ever so careful lest musicians, a powerful and privileged group in [his...] England, steal the show from poetry". At the same time, we know that theatregoers went to "hear" a play rather than "see" one-the arts of rhetoric being at least as important, if not more so, than the visual effects.

It seems to me that Shakespeare took great care over the songs in his plays; they were not just random entertainments to break up the narrative. Not only are the lyrics pertinent to the themes and plots of the plays, but also they are aimed particularly at the group of characters on stage who hear them. This is obvious in Twelfth Night, in which Feste sings a carpe diem song, "O Mistress Mine," to Toby and Andrew, a couple of aging bachelors who are wasting their lives away on drink and immature hijinks instead of getting down to the serious business of comedy-finding a mate. At first, "Sigh no more ladies" seems an odd choice for Balthasar to sing. In fact, John Stevens in his introduction to Shakespeare in Music comments: "Baithasar's song, charming though it is, looks rather stuck on to the play.

The fusing power of Shakespeare's imagination does not appear, in this play, to have comprehended music; there are no effects that any other Elizabethan playwright could not have contrived". The song certainly seems an odd choice to sing to a group of men. The lyrics directly address women, and seem neither to suit the newly betrothed Claudio, who would rather think about nuptial bliss than betrayal, nor the conspirators, who plot to convince the commitment-phobic Benedick to trust love again. At the same time, the lyrics also are very appropriate for this group of men. They each will make ladies sigh from woe. Benedick has in the past, we learn from Beatrice, played for Beatrice's heart with false dice. Claudio and Don Pedro will betray and deceive Hero, bringing her to church when they know they are to rupture the wedding and ruin her reputation.

Leonato will betray Hero, believing the words of foreign men over his own daughter's confirmation of her innocence. If these men had noted the words to the song, perhaps they would have acted differently. A. R. Humphreys in his commentary in the Arden edition believes Shakespeare is directing the song to the audience, reminding them of the "fraud of men" set in motion against Hero in the previous scene. Holger Klein in his edition, in contrast, thinks the song functions to "tune Benedick in to what will follow" and to prepare him for the image the conspirators present of "Beatrice's supposed languishing". Alexander Leggatt voices one plausible theory for the on- and off-stage audience's lack of attention to these lyrics, so contrary to the spirit of romantic comedy. Leggatt comments on the fact that Benedick complains about Balthasar's voice, and that Don Pedro answers Balthasar's self-deprecatory remarks about his singing with no more than politeness.

He sees these lines as having inspired the stage tradition of burlesquing the song. If the song is burlesqued, it cuts through any facile romanticism. Furthermore, the audience's attention will be focused on the singer's technique (or lack thereof). In such a case, if the lyrics are noted at all, they will not be taken seriously, but seen as merely one more droll aspect of an absurd performance. However, as Deleyto observes, this is not the route taken by Branagh. The only trace of this tradition appears when Beatrice recites the words ironically to open the film and her on-screen audience guffaws "in a way," as Independent reviewer Adam Mars-Jones wrote, "that makes us think we must be missing something". When the song is sung in its original place in the play, however, Patrick Doyle as Balthasar renders it beautifully. His voice does not draw our attention away from the lyrics and their edgy message, but the location does. Branagh's script gives details on the mood the director was hoping to create: The camera tracks around the circular fountain as BALTHASAR sings and the lounging nobles breathe an image of deep tranquillity. The camera movement is slow. The music is beautiful, melodic, dancing on the late afternoon air. In the background we can see our household servants. Beyond them the vines, the olive groves, the lush countryside.

Not only is the setting distracting, but so too are the gentle movements of all the characters. Once again, the song is seen as creating a romantic mood-in complete contradiction to the lyrics that aim to console women for the heartbreak and turmoil in their emotional lives. Branagh indeed seems to be guilty of what J. Hoberman of The Village Voice described as "blandly ignoring the play's disturbing undercurrents-the sexual paranoia and the patriarchal cruelty of the social order". Of course, in more immediate terms, Balthasar's song seems to anticipate Leonato and Claudio's descriptions in the same scene of Beatrice's anguish over Benedick. While she appears blithe and bonny in society, they claim that in private, not only does she sigh for Benedick, but "weeps, sobs, beats her heart, tears her hair, prays [and] curses". If anyone needs the song's words of consolation, it is this absurd, fictional Beatrice, created by the old man and the naïve boy, neither of whom know anything about a young woman in love. However, Auden noticed the song's parallels with Shakespeare's characterization of Beatrice: The song is actually about the irresponsibility of men and folly of women taking them seriously, and recommends as an antidote good humour and common sense. If one imagines these sentiments being the expression of a character, the only character they suit is Beatrice. Wey, in a footnote, reveals that he sees the song as an extension of the men's plot, carefully chosen to support their description of Beatrice:

This song, like the remaining two songs in Much Ado, is admirably suited to the dramatic context. It is a love lament from the woman's point of view in which women deceived by men's inconstancy and indifference are advised to forget the man and be merry. This is good psychological softening of Benedick for it helps convince him that what he overhears his friends saying is true-that Beatrice's gay exterior is evidence that she inwardly sighs for him. In fact, Don Pedro's account in a later scene of Beatrice's state of mind closely echoes the sentiments suggested for the woman in the song. This is a compelling idea, and while Balthasar gives no indication of being in on the plot, Don Pedro has heard the song before and so would have had a chance to recognize its suitability.

It seems that Shakespeare also provides the song to contrast the way men behave when women are unfaithful with the way women are expected to behave when men are unfaithful. We see Claudio and Leonato behave very badly indeed in the church scene. Shakespeare, I am convinced, did not mean us to sympathize with them in this scene. Leonato's speech about the ruined Hero with its emphasis on the word "mine" is a study in self-absorption. The fact that Beatrice is shocked by the public nature of Claudio's rejection is also significant. As F. H. Mares points out in the Cambridge introduction to the play, none of the Claudio figures in the sources reject the Hero figure in such a humiliatingly public way. Shakespeare made this change to render Claudio less sympathetic.

Similarly, Shakespeare has changed the Hero character so that she appears younger and more vulnerable than in the sources. At a time when the ideal woman had a voice that was "ever soft / Gentle and low", Hero's silence when Claudio rejects her must have been viewed as virtuous by her original audience. She is barely allowed to speak in the accusation scene, and then, she must retreat and pretend to be dead. At the end of the play, she must accept the man who hurt her so dreadfully with good grace, with "hey nonny nonny."

Did Shakespeare accept the double standard? In King Lear, he has his mad king rail brilliantly against two kinds of justice, one for the rich and one for the poor, but was he prepared to accept that women had to be chaste while men could be wayward? In Much Ado About Nothing, Shakespeare does not appear to recommend any revolutionary tactics for women. But there is a definite sense of melancholy in the song that seems to suggest, along with the darkening of the Claudio figure and the increased victimization of the Hero figure, that he recognized the unfairness of the system, even while not knowing how it could be altered.

This is typical of his comedies. Cesario and Orsino in Twelfth Night have a long conversation on the way in which men and women are different in love, with Orsino contradicting himself in his passion. Once again, Shakespeare seems to promote the idea that women are more constant than men and more stoical in their suffering. And he seems to pity them for this. Far from beating their hearts and tearing their hair as Claudio imagines Beatrice doing (really more a reflection of men's license in showing their outrage at female infidelity) women sit "like patience on a monument, / Smiling at grief. Shakespeare's Much Ado About Nothing is a tremendously complex comedy.

Critics who dismiss the play as an "all fun light as air" romantic comedy are seriously underestimating it. The play is really about the challenges of monogamy. Instead of delivering a conventional happy-ever-after ending, Shakespeare shows us two couples who are about to embark on their married lives with considerable emotional baggage in tow. Hero and Beatrice both have been hurt by their spouses in the past, and if we read the banter carefully, the forecast is for more of the same. The only way these marriages will survive is if the women exercise the stoicism and tolerance urged upon them by the song. Branagh picks up on this in his screenplay, but downplays the double standard: he writes, "Much Ado About Nothing speaks loudly and gloriously about love the cruelty of it, the joy of it. The question of tolerance in love and the danger of judging others".

But in Shakespeare's day, it was only dangerous for women to judge men, not the other way around. Beatrice's harsh judgment of men prepares her for nothing but celibacy until her cousin points out her pride. Meanwhile, Benedick, similarly harsh in his judgment of women, presumably enjoys the freedom of sowing his wild oats at the brothels he mentions. Claudio and Leonato are forgiven their harsh judgment of Hero, so much so that she is not given even a line of reproach when she welcomes back her former fiancé. Is "hey nonny nonny" enough to console her?

Shakespeare does give women one other option in the song besides stoicism in the face of male inconstancy; the song also urges women to let men go. This is an ambiguous line of course. It could mean that the women should let their husbands go to their mistresses, and thus supports the double standard. Or it could be a more radical piece of advice, urging the women to let any man who is inconstant depart their lives, and choose rather the independent celibacy that Beatrice makes so blithe.

That is why the song fits so well in the middle of the play, before Beatrice and Benedick have rejected their single lives, and why it seems odd placed at the end of the play, as in the Branagh film, when the couples dance to celebrate their upcoming nuptials. Beatrice and Hero emphatically are not letting their men go at the end; they are taking them on permanently, despite the past hurt.

They must do this to fulfill the demands of the comic genre that ultimately supports marriage as the basis for a harmonious society. In the film, the song is misplaced at the end because the lyrics urge passive stoicism, and what the end of comedy demands is active commitment. The live-and-let-live attitude of the song is replaced by Claudio's warning to Beatrice to live a life of vigilance to keep her husband constant. Meanwhile, Benedick jokingly seizes on a future of cuckoldry; he quips, "no staff so reverend as one tipped with horn". He has assumed a measure of that stoic tolerance the song urged on the ladies. At the end of the comedy, Beatrice, Benedick, and Hero seem to accept suffering in love as part of their lot, which they will lighten with dance, songs, and jokes, as throughout the course of the play. I am not alone in thinking the song misplaced at the conclusion. Penny Gay remembers the Bill Alexander Royal Shakespeare Company production in 1990, which I too was fortunate enough to see:

The final dance was performed to a lusty choral reprise of "Sigh no more, ladies": it was an imposition of communal harmony which Susan Fleetwood [who played Beatrice] thought inappropriate-the song "says that men will always be unfaithful, and it completely negates what's gone before." Whether it was a deliberate irony on Alexander's part or an unthinking attempt to provide the traditional up-beat ending to a comedy, it failed finally to convince: the play itself, in this embodiment, was about a society's loss of faith in the conventions it had created and lived by for so long. The "hey nonny nonny" of the song refers us back to the title of the play, Much Ado About Nothing. Both title and song seem to urge us not to repeat Claudio's mistake in succumbing to paranoia, or to love only our own wit, like Benedick and Beatrice, whose sins of intellectual pride shut out the possibility of love. Rather, like that same couple reformed, the play urges its audience to accept the trials of marriage with good humour, and to trust and tolerate our partners despite human fickleness.

Foundations Study Guide: Literary Theory

Literary theory attempts to establish principles for interpreting and evaluating literary texts. Two of the most important issues in literary theory are authorial intention and interpretive objectivity. Is the author's intention responsible for the meanings of a text? Can readers arrive at an objective understanding of those meanings? Currently fashionable theory answers no to both questions. It suggests that meanings are created and recreated by influences beyond the control of either writers or readers. This view is diametrically opposed to the classical tradition in literary theory.

Aristotelian Theory: Aristotle originated the kind of literary theory that emphasizes the objective features of texts and the authorial intentions that those features reveal. He sought to explain and evaluate literature as a product of human design. His *Poetics* analyzes the objective features of Greek epics and dramas as means that are more or less appropriate to the full realization of various literary intentions.

In Aristotelian analysis, text-making intentions are understood as distinct from social influences and psychological motives. Aristotle appreciated the fact that Greek playwrights derived their themes and stories from the commonly held attitudes and commonly recounted myths of Greek society. He also knew that playwrights might be motivated largely by the desire to win prizes and other forms of public recognition. A psychologist or sociologist might perform an interesting analysis of these background influences on a play—without even beginning to explain and access the choices that its author made to produce the specific *artistic* effects that he intended. That, however, is the task to which Aristotle addresses himself as a literary theorist.

A classical example of Aristotle's analytical method is his treatment of the tragic protagonist. As Aristotle suggests, an author who intends to arouse the tragic emotions of "pity and fear" must choose his means of doing so, and the available means can be rationally estimated. The author can choose a central character who is perfectly bad, perfectly good, or somewhere in the middle. The downfall of a perfectly bad character would be comic, not tragic; the downfall of a perfectly good character would be merely hateful. The choice of an "intermediate" character is therefore the appropriate means of producing the tragic effect. The downfall of such a character can arouse pity for the defeat of good qualities and fear for the results of bad ones.

Aristotle's concern with the rational adaptation of literary means to literary ends includes concern with the unity of literary works. He assumes that an author's various purposes should be consistent with one another and that every element of a work—plot, character, style, and so forth— should contribute to those purposes, not frustrate or divert attention from them.

One interesting thing about Aristotle's literary theory is that it is not culture-bound. Although the Aristotelian standard of unity (for instance) is exemplified in certain works of the Greeks, it is not applicable merely to Greek or even Western Art. The Aztec lyric is governed by different intentions from those of Greek tragedy, but it can be rationally assessed in regard to its consistency and efficiency in fulfilling those intentions.

Aristotelianism after Aristotle: In the hands of later

practitioners, especially those of the Renaissance, "Aristotelian" theory often degenerated into a system of rules that were far from universally applicable. But essentially Aristotelian assumptions were likely to come into play whenever critics of any school made a serious effort to assess works or authors according to their ability to accomplish their literary intentions.

For example, during the Enlightenment, the first great age of English criticism, leading critics informed themselves as best they could about the distinctive intentions of the authors they studied and analyzed the degree of skill that those authors showed in choosing literary means appropriate to their ends. Two of the most impressive works of that age, Alexander Pope's *An Essay on Criticism* and Samuel Johnson's *Preface to Shakespeare,* are attempts by cultivated readers to recover the principles by which great authors practiced their craft.

During the Romantic period of the late eighteenth and early nineteenth centuries, literary theory often based itself on psychological or social speculation rather than objective analysis of artistic strategies. Nevertheless, the best of this Romantic theory is significant for its emphasis on the individual mind as creator of meaning and organic unity in literary works. Shelley's *A Defence of Poetry* depicts poets not simply as creatures of social circumstances but as "the unacknowledged legislators of the World." Coleridge's *Biographia Literaria* argues that real poetry displays a unity of "the general, with the concrete; the idea, with the image," and that this unity is imposed by the individual creative imagination.

In the twentieth century, Ayn Rand produced a unique combination of Romantic and Aristotelian approaches to literary theory. The essays collected in her Romantic Manifesto advocate a literature produced by rational selection, in the Aristotelian manner, and marked by imaginative unification or "integration," in the Romanitc manner. Rand's definition of art as "a selective re-creation of reality according to an artist's metaphysical value-judgments" is widely applicable. It identifies the process of choice by which artists convert their contexts—"reality," as they understand it—into specific literary texts.

Current Controversies: It cannot be said that the late twentieth century is the golden age of either Romantic or Aristotelian theory. Currently fashionable theory is animated by the assumptions of Marx, Freud, and such contemporary continental thinkers as Michel Foucault. It is preoccupied with the ways in which political or psychosocial phenomena affect the processes of writing and reading. Its crucial assumption is that literature is "constructed" not by authors but by environmental influences, and that neither authors nor readers can "transcend" such influences.

One of the weaknesses of such theory is its inability to account for the ways in which very individual texts emerge from general contexts. Shakespeare's *Macbeth* is about (among other subjects) the political problems of a hierarchical society. The play's political context is a necessary condition for its existence—but not a sufficient condition. If context were sufficient to "construct" the salient features of the play, then the political environment of Elizabethan England would have produced thousands of *Macbeth*s.

Readers as well as writers exist in political contexts, but if they could not transcend those contexts and arrive at a comprehension of works produced in environments very different from their own, then *Macbeth* would have run out of readers long ago. The same logic applies to theories of psychosocial construction. Many people have had miserable relationships with their fathers, but there is only one *Brothers Karamazov,* and the novel can be read and understood even by orphans.

The effects of current theories are not all bad. They have led critics who instinctively oppose them to refine their own ideas and account for what went wrong with those of other people. Some of the most valuable critiques of current theories, especially those descended from Marx and Freud, can be found in Frederick Crew's book *Skeptical Engagements.* Gerald Graff, in *Literature Against Itself,* provides a well-argued account of the mistaken assumptions that underlie postmodern theory.

(Unfortunately, little can be learned from Graff's later work, which is an abject concession to the fallacies of academic political correctness.)

Politics by Other Means, by David Bromwich, is a many-sided defence of individualism in literary study. Bromwich offers cogent reasons for believing that even literary tradition is not simply a "social" artifact but is actively created by the choices of writers and readers. Papers by Stephen Cox criticize current academic tendencies on the basis of classical-liberal assumptions about the agency of the individual and the importance of rational procedures in analysis and theory.

The "Chicago School" of Criticism: The foundations of current theories had, in fact, been undermined long before the theories themselves appeared. The so-called Chicago Critics, who flourished in the 1950s, constructed defenses of authorial intention and critical objectivity that continue to repay close study. Chief among the Chicago Critics were R.S. Crane and Elder Olson, both powerful advocates of Aristotelian theory.

To a great degree, Crane and Olso defined themselves by opposition to the "New Criticism," a tendency that once dominated academic theory and that still exerts and influence on practical criticism. The New Critics justly opposed people's perennial inclination to reduce the meaning of literature to a paraphrasable "message." What was important to the New Critics was the richness of the literary text itself, not the circumstances in which was written or the moral or political causes in which it might be enlisted.

But the New Critics often proceeded as if the text could be understood apart from any consideration of authorial intentions. They neglected the author's ability to impose structure by using objectively ascertainable textual markers to include certain meanings and exclude others. As a result, they sometimes discovered as many "meanings" in a text as their own ingenuity could possibly supply. "Meanings" that flatly contradicted either one another or any conceivable authorial intention were construed as "ironies" and "tensions" that "enriched" the over interpreted text. This defect of the New Criticism was exposed with devastating effect by Olson and Crane, who tried to revive interest in the author's power to unify and control the text.

Crane developed some of the best evidence for this power in his studies of the great unifying device of plot. Crane and Olson also demonstrated the importance of understanding ways in which authors work with specific literary forms to accomplish their intentions. Olson's *The Theory of Comedy*, which illuminates a form that is notoriously resistant to analysis, is particularly worthy of notice.

The Chicago Critics' investigation of major literary forms and effects was pursued by Wayne Booth in two important books: *The Rhetoric of Fiction*, a learned analysis of the novel form, and *A Rhetoric of Irony*, a provocative attempt to explain the ways in which authors communicate certain meanings by pretending to communicate others. E.D. Hirsch, Jr., continued and advanced the Chicago Critics' work on authorial intentions. His *Validity in Interpretation* and *The Aims of Interpretation* are the most distinguished books on the subject. Hirsch attempts to vindicate a literary theory that gives full weight to authors' intended meanings. Do authors really know their own intentions? Doesn't the meaning of a text change over time? How can we be sure that the meaning we find in a text is the same one that the author intended? Hirsch's answers to these and other questions provide a persuasive defence of intentionalist theory as a basis of literary interpretation. Hirsch also provides sound arguments for regarding theory and interpretation as rational and objective processes.

Hirsch's discussion of the determinacy of authorial meanings is especially important to consider at a time when many prominent theorists assert that the meaning of a text necessarily varies with the race, class, and gender of its audience. Hirsch makes a useful distinction between *meaning* and *significance*: various readers may regard a text as significant to them in various ways, but they are responding, still, to the same text, a text with particular meanings, established by a particular author.

The Implications of Theory: The fashionable claim that the meaning of a text is "constructed" by the various contexts in which it is read should remind of us what is at stake in literary theory. Debates about theory are concerned with something more important than rival approaches to obscure poems. Ultimately, literary theory is about the human mind and its processes of communication. It is about our ability to understand what people say, write, and mean. Literary theory is a ferociously contested field because it has crucial implications for every other field that is based on the interpretation of words. What we know about the world, especially the world of the past, comes largely form written documents. Our confidence in our ability to understand the world depends on our possession of sound working theories about the way in which texts communicate ideas across formidable barriers of time and cultural difference. Those "multiculturalists" who deny the validity of general and objective statements about the human condition are frequently inspired by literary theories that induce skepticism about people's ability to communicate their meanings across cultural and temporal barriers. Influential schools of legal thought that subject Constitutional rights to endless reinterpretation "in the light of current circumstances" depend on theories that posit the unknowability or irrelevance of the Founding Fathers' literary intentions. To these intellectual and political problems, the solution is not less concern with literary theory but a better understanding of its principles and possibilities.

A Critical Analysis of Shakespeare's Hamlet

Hamlet. Is he an insane madman or a revengeful, scheming, genius? There are many conflicting ideas and theories on this subject, and hopefully this paper may be of some assistance in clearing up the confusion. The paper is divided into three separate analytic sections beginning with the beginning of Hamlet's so called madness, and why it may have occurred. Next, is an analysis of why Hamlet delays revenging his father's death. To conclude the paper, Hamlet's incestuous acts towards his mother are discussed, in William Shakespeare's Hamlet. In the first act Hamlet seems to be in a perfectly sane state of mind throughout all five scenes. It is in the second scene where the audience begins to see a change in his character. Ophelia meets with Polonius and recalls the meeting she had previously with Hamlet. She tells her father that Hamlet came to her disheveled and in a shaken state of mind, speaking of "horrors.". Her father immediately believes that he is "Mad for thy love?".

Ophelia answers a question posed by Polonius by which she replied that she had told Hamlet that she could not see or communicate with him any more. Her father makes reference to Hamlet's madness once again by proclaiming that what his daughter said, "... hath made him (Hamlet) mad." The argument of whether Hamlet is insane because of his love for Ophelia is often debated, but a more confusing and complex situation is the struggle within Hamlet's mind. His personal struggle is revealed to the audience in scene one of the third act. In this scene Hamlet recites his famous "To be or not to be-that is the question:" speech. Here the audience truly realizes that Hamlet is torn two ways in his life.

To be or not to be, essentially is Hamlet debating on whether he should toil the pains of living in such a harsh world and fight to avenge his father's murder or take his own life. Hamlet is confused as to whether he should avenge his father's death when he himself, as Sigmund Freud's "Oedipus Rex Complex" suggests, wished to murder his father to gain all of his mother's attention. But, in the back of Hamlet's mind, which keeps him in constant turmoil, is his loyalty to his family and moreover his father.

Hamlet, in act four scene two, meets with Rosencrantz and Guildenstern and he seems to be breaking down into insanity. Hamlet had just killed Polonius, and his two friends were questioning him as to where he placed the body of the dead man. The strange thing about this scene is that Hamlet seems to play with Rosencrantz and Guildenstern and does not give them a straight answer. Hamlet has practically transformed into a different person and doesn't seem to be completely sane.

Next is another situation that cannot be totally explained. The situation being Hamlet's delays in avenging his father's death. The first that Hamlet learns of his father's death is in act one scene five, where he follows the ghost. Hamlet is told, by the ghost, that he (the ghost) is the soul of Hamlet's father, and that he was murdered by Claudius.

This all took place at the beginning of the play and Hamlet waited until the end of the play to get revenge for his father's murder. Then again there are different perspectives as to whether Hamlet waited until the end to actually gain revenge. For within the play there are many insinuations that Hamlet tortured Claudius all the way up until he killed the king. Two instances are particularly evident.

First, the play within a play confirms that Claudius was the murderer of Hamlet's father. Hamlet stages the Murder of Gonzago in which the actor who is playing the part of the king is murdered in the same manner that Claudius killed Hamlet's father. At the moment that the actor playing the part of the king is killed Claudius leaps from his seat and rushes out of the theater infuriated.

This violent action by the king over joys Hamlet for now he knows that it was Claudius who murdered his father. More than the fact that he knows that Claudius is the murderer, Hamlet is slowly and painfully gaining his revenge of his fathers death. The other instance where Hamlet could have killed Claudius was in act three scene three.

In this particular scene Hamlet comes upon Claudius while he is knelt in prayer. Hamlet draws his sword and intends to kill Claudius there in prayer but then decides to wait. Hamlet comes to the conclusion that he should wait until Claudius is commuting a sin so he will go to hell, as opposed to killing him in prayer where he would then go to heaven. This is another example as to why Hamlet procrastinates revenging his father's death. The obvious reason Hamlet waits is to bring more than just the pain of his sword to Claudius and torture him until the end.

Finally, Hamlet's sexual attraction towards his mother is to be discussed. In act three scene four, Hamlet enters his mothers bedroom at her wish and first kills Polonius, then proceeds to make love to his mother. This action is called the "Oedipus Rex Complex", which was invented by Sigmund

Freud on the basis of Oedipus the epic poem by Sophocles. This theory states that all young men wish to destroy their fathers so that their mother's attention will be guided on them solely. Also the fact that Hamlet thought that Polonius was Claudius adds to the evidence that Hamlet had the "Oedipus Complex". Hamlet was obsessed with his mother but before the situation in the bedroom escalated his father, the ghost, appeared and reminded him of the plight which he was supposed to be accomplishing.

Hamlet's madness at times is justified and at other times is pure insanity. At first Hamlet seems to be going mad over the fact that he is not allowed to see Ophelia. Then it seems that the fact that he is overwhelmed with his father's death, and begins to fight with himself over the thought of suicide. He is then determined to gain revenge for his father and goes about torturing Claudius in a systematic and genius manner. Finally, Hamlet is caught up in his love for his mother which brings him back to the point of insanity. In conclusion Hamlet is torn between two worlds, that of the sane and well and that of the crazed and insane.

Othello

Different people have different opinions of the motives of Iago, in the play "Othello," by one William Shakespeare. Colerige famously said that Iago acted with a "motiveless malignity," or a pure hate of Othello and everything that he did. Others have disagreed with the author of perhaps the most famous critical analysis of Othello. They have suggested that he acted out of pure sexual jealousy, out of a envy of Othello's rank and class, or out of pure racism.

Perhaps the most arguable case against Coleridge is the idea that Iago was a blatant racist. Right from the get-go Iago cries to Brabantio that Othello is "an old black ram" "tupping" his "white ewe." We have not even learned the name of this black ram yet, and someone unfamiliar with the story would be purposely led to believe that Othello was somewhat of a predator, or that he could even be raping Desdemona. The first half of Act 1 Scene 1 comprises of Iago and Roderigo, who we are introduced to immediately, speaking of Othello in a derogatory way. Iago alleges to Brabantio that Othello is "the devil" on line, and warns Brabantio that he has lost "half his soul" because of the two races involved in the marriage. Roderigo, in all his wisdom, even chips in when he yells to Brabantio that he will have "his nephews neigh to him." Iago refers to his as "thick lips" on line 67, and continuously calls him just "him" or "he", or "the moor." Straight away we understand Iago's main motive in his manipulation and degradation of Othello.

The Exploration of Literature

An English degree is about self development and education through the exploration of literature. A student who chooses English will never be expected to learn information by rote, or recycle the views of academics. Developing a unique creativity in relation to the course is the apotheosis of literary study. A degree in English encourages the challenge of critical views, and a communication of new opinions. Students are given freedom to construct a degree programme based on personal interests and strengths.

The structure of any individual degree course is likely to centre around the benefits of personal academic choice. A host university will provide support and resources to enable effective tuition, but the significance of the award rests with the enthusiasm and motivation of a student. Tutors and lecturers can supply expert guidance in the themes and ideas which might appeal to individual academic acumen, but ultimately the degree is a personal achievement. An English degree is the production of the student, not the teacher. Lecture programmes are constructed to offer useful background knowledge, and will often allow fascinating scope for expert opinion. Students are given the opportunity to work with the most current literary views, delivered by the country's foremost academics. However, individual research of selective material is just as valid — if not more so. Students will become adept at mapping a path through critical theories and ideas.

No one English student is like another, and even students

from the same university will refine their approaches to be radically individual. An English degree will encourage the discussion of academic interests with other students — refining areas of investigation by discussion and debate. Teaching oneself is a fascinating and liberating practice. Similarly, the construction is a two way process. As students piece together, and assemble ideas and literature of personal interest, so the aspects to which they are drawn will construct them as critics. English students are engaging in a dynamic process of assimilation. They learn to refine and engage in discussions which interest them.

Students will learn to formulate their own ideas, invent their own theories, and apply them to the texts they study. Questioning accepted notions is positively encouraged. The skill enmeshed with this creative focus is an effective communication of fresh ideas. In English it is the student who teaches others their ideas.

Twelfth Night Characters Analysis

This is justly considered as one of the most delightful of Shakespeare's comedies. It is full of sweetness and pleasantry. It is perhaps too good-natured for comedy. It has little satire, and no spleen. It aims at the ludicrous rather than the ridiculous. It makes us laugh at the follies of mankind, not despise them, and still less bear any ill-will towards them. Shakespeare's comic genius resembles the bee rather in its power of extracting sweets from weeds or poisons, than in leaving a sting behind it.

He gives the most amusing exaggeration of the prevailing foibles of his characters, but in a way that they themselves, instead of being offended at, would almost join in to humour; he rather contrives opportunities for them to shew themselves off in the happiest lights, than renders them contemptible in the perverse construction of the wit or malice of others.-There is a certain stage of society in which people become conscious of their peculiarities and absurdities, affect to disguise what they are, and set up pretensions to what they are not.

This gives rise to a corresponding style of comedy, the

object of which is to detect the disguises of self-love, and to make reprisals on these preposterous assumptions of vanity, by marking the contrast between the real and the affected character as severely as possible, and denying to those, who would impose on us for what they are not, even the merit which they have. This is the comedy of artificial life, of wit and satire, such as we see it in Congreve, Wycherley, Vanburgh, etc.

To this succeeds a state of society from which the same sort of affectation and pretence are banished by a greater knowledge of the world or by their successful exposure on the stage; and which by neutralizing the materials of comic character, both natural and artificial, leaves no comedy at all—but the sentimental.

Such is our modern comedy. There is a period in the progress of manners anterior to both these, in which the foibles and follies of individuals are of nature's planting, not the growth of art or study; in which they are therefore unconscious of them themselves, or care not who knows them, if they can but have their whim out; and in which, as there is no attempt at imposition, the spectators rather receive pleasure from humouring the inclinations of the persons they laugh at, than wish to give them pain by exposing their absurdity.

This may be called the comedy of nature, and it is the comedy which we generally find in Shakespeare.—Whether the analysis here given be just or not, the spirit of his comedies is evidently quite distinct from that of the authors above mentioned, as it is in its essence the same with that of Cervantes, and also very frequently of Molière, though he was more systematic in his extravagance than Shakespeare. Shakespeare's comedy is of a pastoral and poetical cast. Folly is indigenous to the soil, and shoots out with native, happy, unchecked luxuriance.

Absurdity has every encouragement afforded it; and nonsense has room to flourish in. Nothing is stunted by the churlish, icy hand of indifference or severity. The poet runs riot in a conceit, and idolises a quibble. His whole object is to turn the meanest or rudest objects to a pleasurable account.

The relish which he has of a pun, or of the quaint humour of a low character, does not interfere with the delight with which he describes a beautiful image, or the most refined love.

The Clown's forced jests do not spoil the sweetness of the character of Viola; the same house is big enough to hold Malvolio, the Countess, Maria, Sir Toby, and Sir Andrew Aguecheek. For instance, nothing can fall much lower than this last character in intellect or morals: yet how are his weaknesses nursed and dandled by Sir Toby into something "high fantastical," when on Sir Andrew's commendation of himself for dancing and fencing, Sir Toby answers—"Wherefore are these things hid? Wherefore have these gifts a curtain before them? Are they like to take dust like mistress Moll's picture? Why dost thou not go to church in a galliard, and come home in a coranto? My very walk should be a jig! I would not so much as make water but in a cinque-pace. What dost thou mean? Is this a world to hide virtues in? I did think by the excellent constitution of thy leg, it was framed under the star of a galliard!"

How Sir Toby, Sir Andrew, and the Clown afterwards chirp over their cups, how they "rouse the night-owl in a catch, able to draw three souls out of one weaver!" What can be better than Sir Toby's unanswerable answer to Malvolio, "Dost thou think, because thou art virtuous, there shall be no more cakes and ale?"—In a word, the best turn is given to everything, instead of the worst.

There is a constant infusion of the romantic and enthusiastic, in proportion as the characters are natural and sincere: whereas, in the more artificial style of comedy, everything gives way to ridicule and indifference, there being nothing left but affectation on one side, and incredulity on the other.—Much as we like Shakespeare's comedies, we cannot agree with Dr. Johnson that they are better than his tragedies; nor do we like them half so well. If his inclination to comedy sometimes led him to trifle with the seriousness of tragedy, the poetical and impassioned passages are the best parts of his comedies. The great and secret charm of TWELFTH NIGHT is the character of Viola.

Much as we like catches and cakes and ale, there is something that we like better. We have a friendship for Sir Toby; we patronize Sir Andrew; we have an understanding with the Clown, a sneaking kindness for Maria and her rogueries; we feel a regard for Malvolio, and sympathize with his gravity, his smiles, his cross garters, his yellow stockings, and imprison-ment in the stocks. But there is something that excites in us a stronger feeling than all this-it is Viola's confession of her love.

"Duke. What's her history?
Viola. A blank, my lord, she never told her love:
She let concealment, like a worm i' th' bud,
Feed on her damask cheek; she pin'd in thought,
And with a green and yellow melancholy,
She sat like Patience on a monument
Smiling at grief. Was not this love indeed!
We men may say more, swear more, but indeed,
Our shews are more than will, for still we prove
Much in our vows, but little in our love.
Duke. But died thy sister of her love, my boy?
Viola. I am all the daughters of my father's house,
And all the brothers too;—and yet I know not"—
Shakespeare alone could describe the effect
of his own poetry.
"Oh, it came o'er the ear like the sweet south
That breathes upon a bank of violets,
Stealing and giving odour."

What we so much admire here is not the image of Patience on a monument, which has been generally quoted, but the lines before and after it. "They give a very echo to the seat where love is throned." How long ago it is since we first learnt to repeat them; and still, still they vibrate on the heart, like the sounds which the passing wind draws from the trembling strings of a harp left on some desert shore! There are other passages of not less impassioned sweetness. Such is Olivia's address to Sebastian, whom she supposes to have already deceived her in a promise of marriage.

"Blame not this haste of mine; if you mean well,

Now go with me and with this holy man
Into the chantry by: there before him,
And underneath that consecrated roof,
Plight me the full assurance of your faith,
That my most jealous and too doubtful soul
May live at peace"
We have already said something of
Shakespeare's songs. One of the most
beautiful of them occurs in this play, with
a preface of his own to it.
"Duke. O fellow, come, the song we had last night
Mark it, Cesario, it is old and plain;
The spinsters and the knitters in the sun,
And the free maids that weave their thread with bones,
Do use to chaunt it: it is silly sooth,
And dallies with the innocence of love,
Like the old age.
SONG.
Come away, come away, death,
And in sad cypress let me be laid;
Fly away, fly away, breath;
I am slain by a fair cruel maid.
My shroud of white, stuck all with yew,
O prepare it;
My part of death no one so true
Did share it.
Not a flower, not a flower sweet,
On my black coffin let there be strown;
Not a friend, not a friend greet
My poor corse, where my bones shall be thrown:
A thousand thousand sighs to save,
Lay me, O, where
Sad true lover never find my grave,
To weep there!"

Who after this will say that Shakespear's genius was only fitted for comedy? Yet after reading other parts of this play, and particularly the garden-scene where Malvolio picks up the letter, if we were to say that his genius for comedy was less than his genius for tragedy, it would perhaps only prove that our own taste in such matters is more saturnine than mercurial.

"Enter MARIA.

Sir Toby. Here comes the little villain:—How now, my nettle of India?

Maria. Get ye all three into the box-tree: Malvolio's coming down this walk: he has been yonder i' the sun, practising behaviour to his own shadow this half hour: observe him, for the love of mockery; for I know this letter will make a contemplative idiot of him.

Close, in the name of jesting! Lie thou there; for here comes the trout that must be caught with tickling.They hide themselves. Maria throws down a letter, and Exit.

Enter MALVOLIO.

Malvolio. 'Tis but fortune; all is fortune. Maria once told me, she did affect me; and I have heard herself come thus near, that, should she fancy, it should be one of my complexion. Besides, she uses me with a more exalted respect than any one else that follows her. What should I think on't?

Sir Toby. Here's an over-weening rogue!

Fabian. O, peace! Contemplation makes a rare turkey-cock of him; how he jets under his advanced plumes!

Sir Andrew. 'Slight, I could so beat the rogue:—

Sir Toby. Peace, I say.

Malvolio. To be count Malvolio;—

Sir Toby. Ah, rogue!

Sir Andrew. Pistol him, pistol him.

Sir Toby. Peace, peace!

Malvolio. There is example for't; the lady of the Strachy married the yeoman of the wardrobe.

Sir Andrew. Fie on him, Jezebel!

Fabian. O, peace! now he's deeply in; look, how imagination blows him.

Malvolio. Having been three months married to her, sitting in my chair of state,—

Sir Toby. O for a stone bow, to hit him in the eye!

Malvolio. Calling my officers about me, in my branch'd velvet gown; having come from a day-bed, where I have left Olivia sleeping.

Sir Toby. Fire and brimstone!
Fabian. O, peace, peace!
Malvolio. And then to have the humour
of state: and after a demure travel of regard,—
telling them, I know my place, as I would
they should do theirs,—to ask for my kins-
man Toby.—
Sir Toby. Bolts and shackles!
Fabian. O, peace, peace, peace! now, now.
Malvolio. Seven of my people, with an obedient start,
make out for him; I frown the while; and, perchance,
wind up my watch, or play with some rich
jewel. Toby approaches; curtsies there to me.
Sir Toby. Shall this fellow live?
Fabian. Though our silence be drawn from us with cares,
yet peace.
Malvolio. I extend my hand to him thus, quenching my
familiar smile with an austere regard to controul.
Sir Toby. And does not Toby take you a blow o' the lips
then?
Malvolio. Saying—Cousin Toby, my fortunes having
cast me on your niece, give me this prerogative of
speech,—
Sir Toby. What, what?
Malvolio. You must amend your drunkenness.
Fabian. Nay, patience, or we break the sinews of our
plot.
Malvolio. Besides, you waste the treasure of your time with
a foolish knight—
Sir Andrew. That's me, I warrant you.
Malvolio. One Sir Andrew—
Sir Andrew. I knew, 'twas I; for many do call me fool.
Malvolio. What employment have we here?
Taking up the letter."

The letter and his comments on it are equally good. If poor Malvolio's treatment afterwards is a little hard, poetical justice is done in the uneasiness, which Olivia suffers on account of her mistaken attachment to Cesario, as her insensibility to the violence of the Duke's passion is atoned for by the discovery of Viola's concealed love of him.

Bibliography

Alabama. Conecuh County. 1830 U.S. Federal Census. Micropublication M19, roll 3. 1840 U.S. Federal Census. Micropublication M704, roll 2. Washington: National Archives.

American Baptist Historical Society, letter. 25 July 1973, from Edward C. Starr, Curator, 1106 South Goodman Street, Rochester, New York 14620 to Mr. Ronald Stratton, Pittsfield, Massachusetts. Photocopy held in 2003 by Debbie Parker Wayne (Cushing, Texas).

Florida. Escambia County. 1860 U.S. Federal Census, population schedule. Micropublication M653, roll 106. Washington: National Archives.

Florida. Santa Rosa County. 1870 U.S. Federal Census. Micropublication M593, roll 133. Washington: National Archives.

Georgia. Crawford County. 1850 U.S. Federal Census, population schedule. Micropublication T6, roll 55. Washington: National Archives.

Johnson, Peter Lazarus, letter. 20 June 1904, from Woods, Panola County, Texas, to Sally Chunn. Photocopy held in 2003 by Debbie Parker Wayne (Cushing, Texas).

Johnson, Samuel C., Sr., Family Bible Records. Unknown publication data or original location. Photocopy of family birth, marriage and death pages held in 2003 by Debbie Parker Wayne (Cushing, Texas).

Johnson, Samuel C., Sr., The Consistency and Harmony of Election, Predestination and the Accountability of Man. Waco: Texas Baptist Standard Printing House, 1894.

Mexican War Pension, Series 15. Washington: National Archives.

Riley, Rev. B.F., History of Conecuh County, Alabama. 1881. Reprint, Greenville, South Carolina: Southern Historical Press, 1994.

Samford University, letter. 28 June 1973, to Mrs. Eldon Edge. Photocopy held by Debbie Parker Wayne (Cushing, Texas).

Texas. Angelina County Probate Minutes Index: 1857-1934 (roll number 1035035). Texas County records on microfilm. East Texas Research Center, Stephen F. Austin State University, Nacogdoches, Texas.

Texas. Angelina County Tax Rolls: 1846-1892 (roll 100301), 1893-1907 (roll 100302). Texas County records on microfilm. East Texas Research Center, Stephen F. Austin State University, Nacogdoches, Texas.

Texas. Angelina County. Ryan Chapel Cemetery. Tombstone data.

Texas. Shelby County. 1880 U.S. Federal Census. Micropublication T9, roll 1326. Washington: National Archives.

Thorndale, William and William Dollarhide. Map Guide to the U.S. Federal Censuses, 1790-1920. Baltimore: Genealogical Publishing Co., Inc., 1987.

Wilkins, Frederick. The Highly Irregular Irregulars: Texas Rangers in the Mexican War. Austin, Texas: Eakin Press, 1990.

